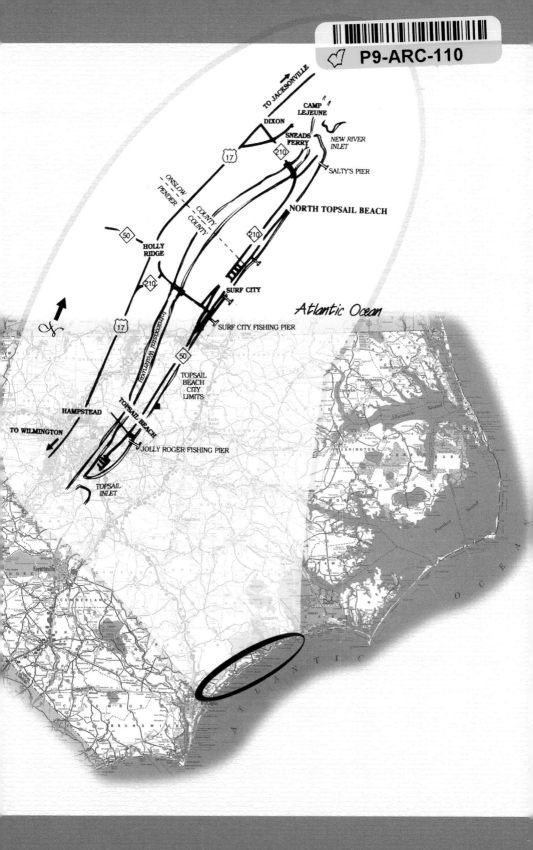

TO JACKSONVILLE

CAMP
LEJEUNE

DIXON

SNEADS
FERRY

NEW RIVER
INLET

17

210

SALTY'S PIER

ONSLOW
PENDER
COUNTY
COUNTY

NORTH TOPSAIL BEACH

50

210

HOLLY
RIDGE

210

SURF CITY

Atlantic Ocean

17

SURF CITY FISHING PIER

50

TOPSAIL
BEACH
CITY
LIMITS

HAMPSTEAD

TOPSAIL BEACH

TO WILMINGTON

JOLLY ROGER FISHING PIER

TOPSAIL
INLET

Intracoastal Waterway

Fayetteville

CUMBERLAND

COLUMBUS

BRUNSWICK

ATLANTIC OCEAN

PERQUIMANS

Albemarle Sound

WASHINGTON

DARE

HYDE

Pamlico Sound

ECHOES
of Topsail
Stories of the Island's Past

David A. Stallman

Also by David A. Stallman

- A History of Camp Davis
- Operation Bumblebee
- TALOS – Smart Sky Warrior
- Holmesville, Ohio – Our Home Town

ECHOES

of Topsail

Stories of the Island's Past

Third Edition

David A. Stallman

ECHOES PRESS

Manufactured in the United States of America

Cataloging in Publication Data
Stallman, David A.
   Echoes of Topsail : stories of the island's
past / David A. Stallman.
       p. cm.
ISBN 0-9708239-2-4
   1. Topsail Island (N.C.)--History. 2. Topsail
Island (N.C.)--Social life and customs. I. Title.
975.627--dc20   96-69943
                                                    CIP

Carlisle Printing
OF WALNUT CREEK LTD

2673 TR 421
Sugarcreek, OH 44681

Dedication

Two people were deeply influential to me in this endeavor. To them, I dedicate this book. Captain Kenneth Andrews and Betty Martin Polzer each affected this work in very different ways. Without them, it never would have happened.

CAPTAIN KENNETH ANDREWS

I grew to know him from a short six month association as he told me about the earlier years of Topsail Island. He was an inspiration to me through his keen recollections and willingness to share them. I could see that Topsail Island history could be recreated, through the people. I hold the memory of our many conversations with real affection.

Captain Kenneth Andrews

Captain Kenneth Andrews presented a deep passion for Topsail Island and a life with the ocean. He was a retired sea captain, who left our world December 9, 1990, at 81 years of age. His last days were in a hospital. He would have wanted to die with his beloved sea.

Thank you, Captain Kenneth Andrews.

BETTY MARTIN POLZER

My first contact with Betty was about 10 years ago when I called her to talk about Topsail History. She asked: *Where are you from?* I responded: *New York.* She said: *No, where are you really from?* It was Ohio. Betty had recognized a fellow Ohioan. I had called her for information about Topsail Island because I was told "the island has no history." Betty, a published writer, could tell me about the island.

We met later and talked about the Historical Society, historic discoveries thus far, and of some people I should see. When I left, Betty said: *Write the book.* I have been researching Topsail history ever since. I never failed to stop by 101 Anderson Boulevard on my many trips to Topsail. Sadly, Betty passed away earlier this year, before the book she inspired would be published.

Betty Martin Polzer

My admiration of such a genuine person cannot be adequately described. Betty's encouragement, advice, and counsel on the quest for Topsail history will always be treasured as an essential ingredient of this work.

Thank you, Betty Martin Polzer.

Photos courtesy of *Topsail Voice*

CONTENTS

The Land- Origin and Evolution
Inlet Migration
Climate
Sea Shells and Sharks' Teeth
Maritime
Sea Life – Fishing
Fishing Piers
Sea Turtles
Storms
Hurricanes
Hurricanes at Topsail Island

PART II

THE ISLAND - ITS STORIES

INTRODUCTION
First Edition

*E*CHOES *of Topsail* is my labor of love to understand the mystique of Topsail Island and document it for those of us intrigued by this special place.

I have invested over seven years in this examination and confidently believe this history accurately represents Topsail Island and its life from its beginnings to the 1990s.

There are several fables that I will have proved to be overstated:

- There was no tunnel from the Assembly Building to the ocean launch pad.

- The Gold Hole was not a flimflam effort where the perpetrators stole away in the night with the treasure.

- Topsail Island was not so named during pirate days.

This account of stories and personal experiences should delight the reader with a picture of Topsail Island origins, disasters, and developments that tested many souls and gave many of us personal joy.

ECHOES of Topsail – Second Edition

This second edition is an update of the Topsail Island history that was published in 1996 as *ECHOES of Topsail* – First Edition. A number of Tops'l folks urged me to do this since Topsail Island has changed substantially in these eight years and has experienced several hurricanes. Hurricanes Bertha and Fran were defining events; a one-two punch in 1996 wreaked such damage that major rebuilding was required. Since then, Topsail Island has been growing by leaps and bounds with new businesses, property development, and enhanced homes. I have attempted to capture the experiences of these recent years, include it and extend the history of Topsail.

This edition includes the original text with some corrections. Later information and stories about the hurricanes, growth of the towns, Karen Beasley Sea Turtle Rescue and Rehabilitation Center, Missiles and More Museum and its expansion, Operation Bumblebee Towers that have been preserved and converted into homes, maritime forest preservation, and more stories about Tops'l people, updates its history.

Topsail Island Timeline

Blockade Running		Gold Hole	Operation Bumblebee	Hurricane Hazel		Assembly Building Purchase	Hurricane Bertha Fran	Hurricane Floyd	
Salt Works		X	X	X		X	X	X	
1800	1900	1930	1940	1950	1960	1990	1995	2000	2004
			X			X	X		X
			Camp Davis WWII Targets			Assembly Building Historic Site	Turtle Hospital Museum TALOS Missile		Museum Expansion

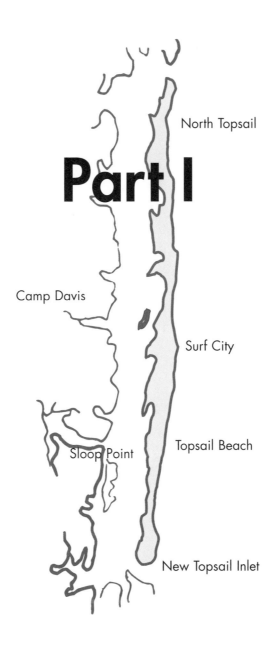

Part I

North Topsail

Camp Davis

Surf City

Sloop Point

Topsail Beach

New Topsail Inlet

PULSE OF AN ISLAND

Approaching the dunes, I could hear the surf. The sun was warm on my back as I climbed the sandy dune speckled with sea oats. It was so quiet. There was a light sea breeze carrying pungent fish smells and hovering sea gulls were talking to each other. I neared the brow of the dune and sounds of surf flooded my awareness. On top, the whole world opened up to the bright sea roaring in my ears, sending wave after wave, rolling seashells onto the shore. Ageless sounds caught my soul, lifting it to a very personal "Ahhhh—this is where I want to be..."

This magic is in Topsail's genes—its history—and it comes from this setting of a quiet place, away from the crowds and a little behind the times. Topsail is a place of raw beauty—an island yet unspoiled. I had dreamed of such a place and now I am here. This sense of *timelessness* brings me back *time after time*. Crossing the swing bridge, I cast all troubles into the causeway, leaving them there, to enjoy the island solitude. Like the loggerhead, we keep coming back to be restored.

Wind and waves relentlessly work the beach. In dynamic equilibrium, unceasing trades among sand, wind, and sea create ever-new shoreline. And if we look, we will find unlimited treasures on Topsail, from the salt marshes and maritimes with creatures who live there, to sea shells and sharks' teeth, some fossilized from ancient times. With all of that, we must heed the wrath of nature's winds that remind us to be thoughtful about the dunes and the fragility of the island.

ITS RHYTHMS

THE LAND — ORIGIN AND EVOLUTION

Topsail Island is a barrier island about 26 miles long, and about 500 to 1500 feet wide, depending on where you look. It is located barely one mile offshore, about 24 miles north of Wilmington, NC off Route 17 at Route 50.

Barrier islands are found up and down the Atlantic coast where the continent is broad with gently sloping, coastal plains. They are the product of wind, wave, and current energy along the ocean shoreline. According to Stan Riggs, Geologist, the barrier islands formed about 18,000 years ago. Today's barrier islands are a geologic feature in motion. They are a product of the wave energy that builds, molds, and maintains them, Riggs says. In response to the continued rise in sea level, the barrier islands are moving inland via wash over and inlet migration.

Ocean Sunrise

Topsail Island is one of a chain of North Carolina barrier islands whose land mass has reshaped but remained essentially the same for recorded history. A barrier island is just that—a pro-

5

tection for the mainland. The island is separated from the mainland by a lagoon that slowly filled with sediment over time. A great salt marsh formed that provides a rich environment for myriad water creatures and birds who thrive there. This salt marsh forms an essential buffer between the sea and the mainland.

Earlier in the island's life, sand was delivered to the seashore by rivers originating from mountains inland. With the rise in sea level, the sand supply simply migrated from the continental shelf and laterally from beach to beach according to energy from winds, waves, and tides. An island can lose a great deal of sand during a storm. Over time, fair-weather waves replenish it. As the sand returns to the beach, the wind takes over and slowly rebuilds the dunes. Thus, dynamic equilibrium restores the land mass, provided man does not interfere.

Waves are constantly moving, shaping, nudging sand toward the mainland. Orrin Pilkey, geologist-author, tells us that the beaches and land volume of the islands essentially stay the same, but must be left unfettered or the dynamic equilibrium that the barrier islands provide is destroyed. Topsail Island has been migrating up and down the coast.

The North Carolina coast is known as "Hurricane Alley." There is no doubt that Hurricanes have served to reshape barrier islands and Topsail is no exception. The most recent devastation that most people recall is Hazel in October 1954.

We have become wiser in giving much attention to the preservation of the dunes. They blunt the sea's constant pounding, and with good prevailing winds and sweeps of sea oats, dunes build and provide protection. In a moment of temporary insanity, early developers bulldozed down the dunes. They wanted a better view of the ocean and found, to their horror, they had destroyed the island's protection from the sea.

There have been concerns, from time to time, about the Southern end of Topsail Island where developers have cut finger channels leaving a 400 foot wide ribbon of land. Some believe that the fingers could make the island vulnerable to over-wash. The Army Corps of Engineers maintain the inlet and periodically have pumped sand over to the beach giving it new life. A groin, proposed in 1989-1990, was turned down by the Coastal Resources Commission. Topsail Beach proposed that the groin, which is a wall of rocks out into the surf perpendicular to the shore, would change the natural flow of sand and reduce beach erosion and re-nourishment costs. Groins have reputedly helped the immediate situation but harmed neighboring areas because of interrupting natural forces. And the inlet continues its march southward.

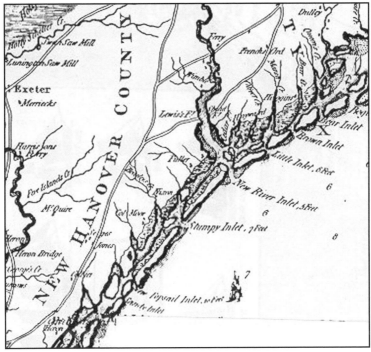

Coastal Map—1775

INLET MIGRATION

Inlets are never still. They move constantly and slowly, pushed by storm and tide. New River Inlet to the north and New Topsail Inlet at the south define Topsail Island. Maps have consistently shown those inlets over time. For a period, Stumpy Inlet was located between Surf City's current location and New River Inlet. It shows on maps as early as 1747. Here is a map showing a major-sized "Stumpy Inlet" in 1775. According to a personal account by Nathaniel Bishop, the Stump Sound Inlet closed due to a storm around 1873.

Aerial View of Southern Tip of Topsail Island - 1978

Both inlets are essential safety valves when hurricane-driven ocean threatens Topsail Island with overwash, and are needed accesses to Topsail Sound. But woe to the navigator who fails to study the treacherous channel before he ventures through it. In a later chapter Captain Andrews, who regularly took fishermen out for deep-sea fishing, told me of his respect for the sea. But he emphasized that the most hazardous part of his day was steering his way out New Topsail Inlet.

The inlets are also an important pathway for millions of fish and other ocean creatures to travel yearly in and out of estuarine habitats. These marshy incubators feed and protect them while they mature before migrating to the ocean. It is estimated that 90 percent of the fish caught by recreational and commercial fishermen spent some time in an estuary.

As a landlubber with roots in Ohio I became obsessed with trying to understand the vagaries of navigating the inlet and sound. I spent many hours in the early 1990's on my cottage porch overlooking Topsail Sound, watching boats traverse the tricky channel. They would refuel at the marina next door and happily take off across the sound, then bog down to a crawl as their props dug into the sandbar. The navigator would jump into knee-deep water to heave the boat free, then motor cautiously up the channel. One morning I woke up to see a 24-foot sailboat sitting high and dry on her keel, impaled on the sandbar awaiting the rising tide that would lift her afloat.

I soon learned to respect the changing tides. I had many joyful experiences sailing my Sunfish and navigating a small Boston Whaler up and down the sound and out through New Topsail Inlet. Having little experience with the sea, I did this with some terror at times, but as the path became more familiar, I could navigate with confidence. Being aware of the tides and understanding the shape of the sound channel, allowed me to enjoy sailing with porpoises and to avoid running aground.

Sound Sunset

Wilson Angley's An Historical Overview of New Topsail Inlet, dated 1984, details the continual movement of New Topsail Inlet. His study indicated that in 1738 a depth of ten feet was recorded, presumably at high water. Such a depth was more than sufficient for the passage of small sloops and schooners. It offered access to the sound for early commerce on the mainland, but was somewhat limited by shallows and shifting channels.

Cartographic evidence indicates that New Topsail Inlet migrated significantly to the north during much of the nineteenth century. A close comparison of the Mouzon Map of 1775 and the Price-Strother Map of 1808 indicates that a northward migration of approximately two miles occurred between these dates. The US Coast Survey Map of 1865 shows that an additional migration northward of approximately two more miles had taken place. Thus, a total movement northward of approximately four miles occurred between the American Revolution and the Civil War. Then, incredibly, the inlet reversed direction and moved southward in the 1900s.

Construction of the Intracoastal Waterway in the 1920s also introduced changes to the natural movement of water and the shallows. Eric Norden's maps show that the width of New Topsail Inlet was about 2550 feet at that time. He also reported that the inlet narrowed to 1250 feet by the mid 1970s. The breadth of the navigable channel within the inlet varied between 239 feet in the late 1950s and 611 feet in the late 1960s. Between 1938 and 1972 the inlet moved some 2680 feet with the maximum movement between 1948 and 1956.

According to A Pictorial Atlas of North Carolina Inlets, a North Carolina Sea Grant publication, authors William J. Cleary and Tara P. Marden characterized New Topsail Inlet as one of the faster migrating inlets along the North Carolina coast. The Atlas also documents an average migration rate of an incredible 30 meters [98ft] southwestward per year over the past decade. It pictures from 1938 to 1996 graphically showing how New Topsail Inlet has traveled.

The inlet photo from an earlier Sea Grant publication shows New Topsail Inlet in 1974 with 1961 and 1966 shorelines indicated. It dramatically shows the movement of the inlet across a thirteen-year period. The Sea Grant publication A Pictorial Atlas of North Carolina Inlets, Second Edition, became available in 2001. It displays aerial photos of New Topsail Inlet from 1938 through 1996. With their permission I have included those photos below. I also include an Army Corp of Engineers photo dated 8-15-2003 in which it is easy to see how far the inlet has moved compared to the 1996 photo.

New Topsail Inlet—1938

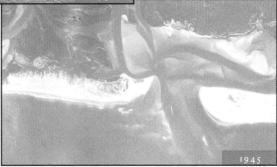

New Topsail Inlet—1945

New Topsail Inlet—1962

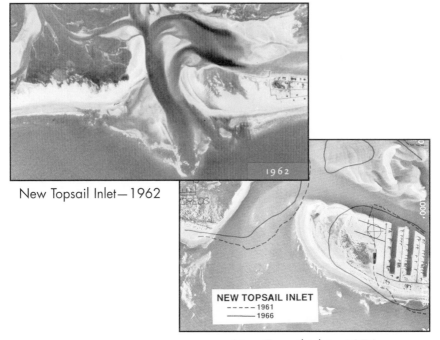

New Topsail Inlet—1974

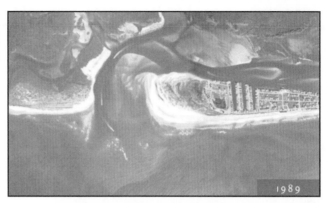

New Topsail
Inlet—1989

New Topsail Inlet—1996

New Topsail
Inlet—2003

New Topsail Inlet
Prediction—2003

In trying to illustrate more tangibly just how Topsail Island is marching to the southwest, I did some calculations. The blockade-runner Phantom was lost September 23, 1863 when it ran aground near New Topsail Inlet. We know, according to archaeological divers in 1975, that the Phantom lay about 200 yards off shore, just south of New Topsail Inlet in 16-18 feet of water. Those 25 years of inlet movement calculate to 2450 feet and would place the Phantom wreck about half way between the inlet and Serenity Point now, assuming the Phantom stayed put. This becomes credible when you consider that the inlet migrated 2041 feet southwest during the years 1971 to 1984. Even so, these figures were staggering to me and I called Mitch Barnes to get an opinion. He has done considerable exploration around the inlet, even looking for the Phantom some years ago. Mitch confirmed that the inlet had indeed moved that far.

Also hard to imagine, in 1946 when Operation Bumblebee was in full swing, the southern tip of Topsail Island was just below where Kip Oppegaard's pier and store are located.

New River Inlet has moved and changed in size less dramatically than New Topsail Inlet. Dredging seems to have moderated its movement. Controlled by the currents of New River that flows into the Atlantic, its width has varied prior to dredging in 1938 from some 217 feet to a maximum width in 1987 at 1254 feet. Over the last 60 years the average width has been 738 feet. New River Inlet has shifted toward the southwest, a net of 1168 feet since 1945. It reversed its course in 1990 – 1992 shifting about 295 feet to the northeast, but since that time resumed moving to the southwest. Between 1945 and 1962 the migration rate was 48 feet per year. With dredging in 1963 the rate was slowed to 13 feet per year and continues to erode the north end of Topsail Island.

Orrin H. Pilkey, Jr., a Duke University Geologist wrote The Beaches are Moving and he states: *Perhaps the most important lesson of the shifting inlets is to remind us that no one barrier island can survive by itself or even maintain its single identity for very long. The islands are only defined by inlets, and inlets by nature make that definition temporary.* Pilkey goes on: *Like any other part of the island that adapts to high energy, an inlet can transform itself quickly. During a storm its channel widens and deepens almost catastrophically. An inlet knee-deep in gentle weather might be twenty feet deep during a storm.*

It follows that sand sharing among the islands is a fact evident in the movement of New Topsail Inlet. The south tip of Topsail Island keeps extending and at the same time Lea Island to the south is losing ground. Lea Island is relatively low and has proved to be unstable. It has diminished in size, and several structures have been lost to erosion. Topsail Voice reported in September 2003, that the state is moving to take over Lea Island and plans to make it a natural preserve.

Topsail Island keeps changing shape because of continual wave activity punctuated by nor'easters and hurricanes. It has become necessary to pull sand from the sound and blow it over to the oceanfront to maintain the beaches and rebuild protective dunes.

Island town officials and geologist/environmentalist folks like Orrin Pilkey will continue to be at odds in protecting Topsail Island and other barrier island land masses. Sometimes we get a little arrogant in the belief that we can control Mother Nature. We have seen that our well-intended attempts to control these natural migrations sometimes do more damage and make matters worse. Hopefully, experience and careful study will result in finding the right balance so that natural resources can be preserved and at the same time people can enjoy them.

References:

An Historical Overview of New Topsail Inlet, Wilson Angley
The Beaches are Moving, Orrin H. Pilkey, Jr.
A Pictorial Atlas of North Carolina Inlets, William J. Cleary and Tara
    P. Marden
US Army Corps of Engineers aerial photographs
Topsail Island, NC: A Case Study in Beach Erosion and Hard Stabilization,
    Abigail Murray

CLIMATE

Topsail's climate is ideal year-round for most outside activities. Its maritime location makes the climate unusually mild for its latitude. All wind directions from the east-northeast through southwest have some moderating effects on temperatures throughout the year making the ocean relatively warm in winter and cool in summer. The daily range in temperatures is moderate compared to a continental type of climate. As a rule, summers are warm and humid, but excessive heat is rare. Sea breezes, arriving early in the afternoon, tend to alleviate the heat. Overhead fans are quite adequate to most of us who would rather not be refrigerated. The ocean also tends to moderate winter cold spells, making snow a rare event. In winter, normal daytime temperatures range from the mid 40s to the mid 50s and in the summer, from the low 80s to 90s. Ocean swimming and surfing is popular from April to October.

SEA SHELLS AND SHARKS' TEETH

Topsail Island has treasures for sea shell collectors. The shores are rich with whelks, sand dollars, olives, and Scotch bonnets, to name a few. The beaches are also prime hunting grounds for fossilized sharks' teeth.

It is estimated that these teeth were deposited some 20,000 years ago. Sharks' teeth as large as five inches in diameter, and more commonly two or three inches, have been found. You can unfailingly find sharks' teeth at Topsail Beach and Surf City if you just pick a spot and focus on small black objects at water's edge.

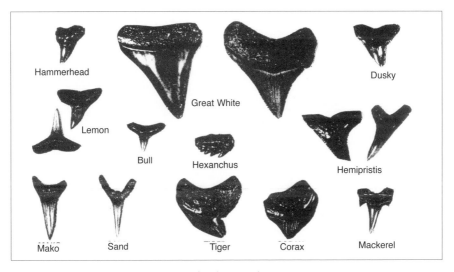

Sharks' Teeth

15

MARITIME

Wildlife abounds on Topsail Island. The Coastal Marine, with its inter-tidal and beach, is where gulls cruise and rummage for sea morsels, crabs burrow in sand for refuge, and darting sanderlings run along water's edge.

The Maritime is a bulwark of support that includes the Dune, with its sea oats, grasses, and yuccas. This system buffers the sea and wind with roots clinging to hold the sand. The next line of defense is Transitional

Clockwise from top: pelican, tricolored heron, white ibis

Shrub of live oak, red cedar, and yaupon. Maritime Forest has larger live oaks, loblolly pine, red cedar, palmetto, and mixed hardwoods. These forests offer a canopy of protection as home to birds and small animals.

L to R: snowy egret, ospreys

Clockwise from top left: common tern, oyster catcher,
black skimmer, willets

There are some 208 varieties of birds identified at Topsail Island, 64 of which are observed year-round. A sampling: tern, herring gull, black skimmer, pelican, blue heron, white ibis, snowy egret, osprey, and sanderlings. Topsail Island is said to be one of the finest bird sanctuaries on the east coast.

An invading bird species has recently been discovered. It is named Eurasian collared-dove, similar in appearance to the ringed turtle-dove, that has established a colony in North Topsail Beach. To bird people, this is a mixed blessing because on one hand it is a new happening in the bird arena, yet this bird is multiplying and it could affect our precious bird population. This species was first discovered in South Florida in the late 1970s and has moved northward. Bird-watchers believe North Topsail Beach is its northernmost location.

We often pass the Maritime Forests as shrubs pruned by sea salt and wind; but on closer exploration, find a whole other world in these groves and twisted vines. The teeming small life sounds nearly like a jungle. And yes, mosquitoes whine and attack intruders. For the most part, developers at Topsail have been respectful of the Maritime Forests, building around trees to minimize cutting these weathered protectors. Some islands have lost their slow-growing Maritimes to developers.

Estuarine Marshes, with their sand and mud flats, sea grass beds and oyster beds, are most vulnerable. They are in constant turmoil from tides and storms and form the delicate interface between sea and land. These wetlands have a vital role in the ongoing life cycle for hidden life in this quiet area. As the tide ebbs and flows, mud flats are revealed and covered again. A mud flat left high and dry by a falling tide seems a barren place, a place where grasses of the marsh can not grow and aquatic plants wither. But on close examination, these tidal flats are teeming with life, such as mud snails, sea lettuce, clams, worms, and shrimp-like creatures.

L to R: Home in Maritime Forest, Maritime Forest at Sound

The salt marsh is one of the most productive natural systems on earth. It is a giant protein factory that supports a wide variety of life. Salty ocean water, enters New Topsail Inlet at high tide, mixes with river and sound water, and at low tide returns to the ocean. This flushing action serves to effect an equilibrium that provides a life-support for oysters, plants, birds, and other creatures. The tidewaters also support microscopic water plants and animals, bacteria, and algae that we do not readily see. Water birds, egrets, blue herons, and stilts find the swamp teeming with tasty sea life.

The extraordinary thing about Topsail's marshes is that they are today much as they were three centuries ago. The one major effect on the marsh is the Intracoastal Waterway that was cut through in the early 1920s. It has tended to level out the tidal and surge effects up and down the coast.

References:

Topsail Island's Real Treasures. Topsail Island Historical Society,
    Betty Polzer.
The Birds of Topsail. Topsail Island Historical Society, Mary Lou Olsen.

Shrimp Boat

SEA LIFE - FISHING

Fishing is a premier activity for young and old on Topsail Island. Deep-sea fishermen can go out to sea on one of several "party boats" for a half or full day of top notch fishing. But the mainstay for Topsail is its fishing piers. Years ago, starting at the north end were Salty's Pier, Ocean City Pier, Scotch Bonnet Pier, Barnacle Bill's Pier, Surf City Pier, Jolly Roger Pier, and Topsail Sound Pier, which is the only one soundside. (The Dolphin Pier used to be active years ago, near Queens' Grant. There are only stumps of pilings remaining.)

Tarpon - 1990

All you need to do is spread the word that "spots are running" and the piers fill up fast. Fishing men, women, and children appear from everywhere and often hunker down for the entire night on the pier.

They can count on a wide spectrum of catches from the pier. Flounder, sheephead, pigfish, croake, angelfish, king, puppydrum, mullet, Spanish, pompano, amberjack, spot, bluefish, and tarpon to name a few. I saw a 109 pound tarpon caught at the Jolly Roger pier a few years ago. A real fighter, it was beached so it wouldn't wrap a piling and break free. Tarpons range from Brazil to Cape Hatteras. The tarpon has armor-like silverside scales and can grow to 250 pounds.

FISHING PIERS

Even if you are not a fisherman it is interesting to see the action at the piers – people cleaning their catch, noisy gulls scavenging the remains, the ever-changing light and surf sounds. Topsail's piers continue to be important landmarks along its shore.

Unfortunately, several piers mentioned above were lost to storms. Hurricane Fran destroyed the Ocean City and Scotch Bonnet piers and damaged the rest. Today the Seaside Pier, [formerly Salty's Pier] in North Topsail Beach, the

Sea View Fishing Pier—2004

Surf City Pier, Surf City's New Pier at Soundside Park, and Jolly Roger Pier in Topsail Beach are all open for ocean fishing. The Soundside Market Pier, [on the sound side] in Topsail Beach, has lost a large section of fishing pier but is still active. The Soundside Market Pier made the national news in 1987 dur-

Sea View Fishing Pier Entrance—2004

ing a July 4th celebration when it collapsed from the weight of the crowd on the pier. They were watching fireworks and a lot of people got wet. Two were injured and Kip Oppegaard, pier owner and mayor at the time, suffered chest pains as he helped in the rescue. He was briefly hospitalized.

The Topsail Off-shore Fishing Club holds a highly popular King Mackerel Tournament every year that brings deep-sea fishermen from far and near. The winner finds the several thousand dollar prize worth going after.

Shrimp is a local delicacy that vacationers enjoy. Often a shrimp trawler will dock to gas up and you can buy fresh shrimp right off the boat. The shrimper will behead your shrimp if you are squeamish about it. Several shrimp trawlers tie up at sound piers, from Topsail Beach up to Surf City. They go out the inlet early each day and are generally back by mid-afternoon, providing catches for the local markets.

Surf City Grill and Pier Entrance—2004

Surf City Pier—2004

New Pier at Soundside Park—2004

Soundside Pier—2004

Jolly Roger Pier—2004

Jolly Roger Pier—2004

SEA TURTLES

Topsail Island people have cared about coastal conservation and have tried to keep its beaches pristine. These uncrowded beaches have been home to Loggerhead and other sea turtles for years. Loggerheads are huge, often more than three feet long and weighing over 300 pounds. Years ago, Loggerhead turtle egg hunting was an activity enjoyed by young and old. I'm told they were a delicacy, but have found no restaurant offering them as a taste treat or cookbook suggestions as such. Now, of course, they are protected because of their endangered status.

There are five species of sea turtles that travel Atlantic waters: Loggerhead, Kemp's Ridley, Green Sea Turtle, Leatherback and Hawksbill. Loggerheads nest all over the world with their major rookeries located on our east coast. They are the major nesters on Topsail Island along with a few Green Sea Turtles. Nesting sites range from North Carolina, south around Florida, and into the Gulf coast. The Office of Protected Resources reports that the Loggerhead population produces about 6200 nests per year from North Carolina to Northeast Florida. Topsail Island typically has about 80 to 100 nests, with a count of 77 nests in 2003. That year nesting began May 13 and the last hatching

Loggerhead Turtle Nest

was November 11.

TURTLE PROJECT AND HOSPITAL

Topsail's Sea Turtle Project has attracted the attention and involvement not only of residents, but also of visitors to the island. Many plan their vacations from across the country just to be part of the project, helping to insure that infant turtles get a chance to survive. It's not unusual to see project members sitting all night long on the beach, waiting for hatching, in order to protect the tiny turtles struggling to the surf. Without their help, an estimated eighty percent of the turtles wouldn't make it to the water. "Turtle watchers" and their families come from as far away as Arizona, Texas, Nevada, New Hampshire, and Washington state.

Loggerhead Turtle Nest

Karen Beasley organized the Turtle Project in the mid 1980s because she saw the need to protect nesting turtles and hatchlings. Karen's enthusiasm was infectious and soon others joined in the effort. I was part of a group she took to a nest where she dug in the sand and described her research. She was collecting information about unhatched eggs that remained after the silver dollar-sized hatchlings had clawed their way out to freedom. Since her untimely death in 1991, Karen's mother, Jean Beasley, has been managing the Turtle Project and continues to devote untold hours to the project and to the nesting program. She has dedicat-

Loggerhead Turtle Tracks

ed herself to teaching anyone who will listen about the plight and dwindling numbers of the sea turtle population, and the need to protect them and their habitat. People also need to be aware of the legal system and the federal laws that apply to their protection. Jean devotes much of her time to the educational part of the project and makes more than forty presentations a year to schools, colleges, civic groups, and visitors to the island.

The Turtle Project takes on the protection of the Loggerhead nests and hatchlings. There are about one hundred volunteers, young and old, who are ever alert to identify turtle nests, stake them off, and start the countdown to when the eggs will "hatch out." As the due date approaches, they sit out with the nests to make sure the baby turtles make it safely back to their home, the sea.

The turtles nest on the twenty-six miles of beach from mid-May through mid-August. Topsail usually has around one hundred nests in a given year. The female turtle comes ashore at night to lay her eggs in the sand. She lays about 120 white, leathery, spherical eggs, covers the nest with sand, and then drags herself back to the sea. The same turtle may return at approximately fourteen-day intervals to lay several nests, but may nest only every two to four years. Topsail Island visitors are urged to avoid disturbing the turtles and nests, and try to protect them from

Turtle Nest Hatching

disturbances. Since turtles are attracted to light, porch lights, flashlights, or even camera flashes can disorient them and cause them to lose their way.

Sea turtle eggs must remain undisturbed in the warm sand for sixty to eighty days, depending on the temperature. When the eggs hatch, the hatchlings remain in the nest for several days to absorb their yolk sacs. Many eggs are eaten by predators, taken by poachers, or lost to erosion before they can hatch. Although female sea turtles lay thousands of eggs each summer, very few hatchlings may survive to adulthood. Hatchlings dig their way out of a nest in a united effort and usually emerge at night. They make their way down the

Loggerhead Hatchling

27

Going for the Sea

beach and enter the surf. Some researchers believe that their crawl to the sea is important to find their proper course in swimming out to sea. The few lucky ones that survive will grow from these tiny creatures to 350-pound Loggerheads and live for about a hundred years.

I personally happened onto a "hatch out" and got to see the sand funnel down as over 100 hatchlings struggled to the surface one evening. They headed out, crawling in lines down to the sea. A "watcher" who had been sitting at the nest for days returned to continue her vigil after leaving for twenty minutes and was dismayed to have missed the whole thing.

There have been rescues of both mother turtle and hatchlings. One large Loggerhead got confused and was found bleeding on the road. Residents and police got her turned around and helped her back to the ocean. In another case, hatchlings got off track because of lights and were going over the dune, away from the ocean. Volunteers and a biology class of children rounded up 113 hatchlings and took them to the ocean.

There is a Topsail Island story about a vacationer who arose early one morning to see strange markings on an otherwise unmarked beach. These deep tracks alarmed her to call the police and request that they come to investigate. She was sure someone had driven a tractor into the ocean. With much relief, she learned that a Loggerhead made the marks the previous night when it nested by her steps.

Turtle Hospital—2004

After some years of protecting nests and hatchlings, the Turtle Project people realized the need to respond to calls about injured turtles. There were virtually no treatment facilities on the east coast at that time. Man's trash and his boats inflict most turtle injuries. In 1995 a small loggerhead washed ashore with a serious skull fracture. He was brought to Jean Beasley who had him treated at the NC State School of Veterinarian Medicine. He needed long term care to survive. Jean named him "Lucky" and set about looking for a place for him to recuperate. Jean and Harold Malpass set up a tub in his backyard and that became the first rehabilitation place, until Lucky was moved to a Florida aquarium for the winter. "Lucky" was first, and from then on turtles have been affectionately named when they are brought in for care.

In 1996 the town of Topsail Beach generously offered to lease a small lot on Banks

Turtle Hospital Tanks—2004

Jean Beasley and Turtle License 0001—2004

Channel for $1 a year to the Turtle Project. The goal was to establish a sanctuary for sick and injured sea turtles in need of medical attention and care. By late 1997 Jean Beasley had organized and built The Karen Beasley Sea Turtle Rescue and Rehabilitation Center. Jean, Executive Director, and her supporters raised the money to build the facility and to purchase all of the equipment. They continue to raise funds to operate the hospital each year. Topsail Island businesses and residents have been very generous in funding this project, which receives no state or federal funding. It is a 501(c) (3) nonprofit organization making all contributions tax deductible. The Rehabilitation Center gained approval for the state to issue NC turtle license plates, which then return a share of the license fee to the project.

The Rescue and Rehabilitation Center is the only

Turtle Release—2004

facility like it on the East coast. Formerly, during the winter months, the turtles were transported to Sea World in Florida. Now they can stay here at Topsail Island year round. The facility has become widely known and is often called upon for advice and turtle emergencies. Injured patients have even been flown to Topsail Island for care. Serious turtle injuries often require a trip to the NC State School of Veterinarian Medicine. Many turtles are saved, but then require months of care at the Center.

The Karen Beasley Sea Turtle Rescue and Rehabilitation Center mission is basically: conservation and protection of all species of marine turtles; rescue, rehabilitation, and release of sea turtles; inform and educate the public about protecting endangered species; provide an experiential learning site for students worldwide.

The Center cared for 19 turtles in 2003, a typical number for the last few years. That same year the caretakers released 20 recovered turtles. Since the opening of the Karen Beasley Sea Turtle Rescue and Rehabilitation Center in 1997, a total of over 130 recovered turtles have been released. This includes the 11 released in June 2004. What an exciting happening! Some 500 people streamed in to watch and help release these creatures back to the sea. There were cheers and tears as turtle caretakers watched their recovered charges leave their care and disappear into the surf. What was unique about this year is that Loggerhead "Chilly" went back to the sea carrying a solar powered tracking device. They hope to learn about "Chilly's" travels in the years to come.

The hospital is staffed entirely with volunteers.

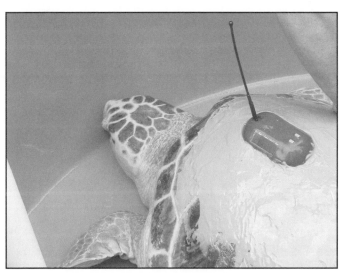

Chilly's Solar Tracking Device—2004

These workers under Ms. Beasley's guidance handle many duties each day, changing hats from feeders and cleaners and medical care givers, to ambassadors and educators, administrators and fund raisers. Twenty or so sea turtles are a challenge to care for considering the special needs of each. They have different personalities, require different diets, different medicines, vitamins and wound care regimes. Workers also need to know the mechanics of redirecting water pipes, monitoring intake and output, temperature and water quality, and they need to be willing to do loads of laundry, laundry, laundry.

The Karen Beasley Sea Turtle Rescue and Rehabilitation Center has a lively internship program. The primary internships are a minimum ten-week commitment. Interns in the full program are provided housing. This became possible thanks to grants from private foundations that enabled them to purchase a lot in Topsail Beach just one block from the Center. Lewis Orr and his family donated a house that was moved to the lot and renovated. This was all completed in early 2003.

The annual hurricane season is a challenge the Rehabilitation Center must face. In 1998 Hurricane Bonnie forced the staff to evacuate seven turtles. Jean recalled: *This was accomplished with a U-Haul truck and a lot of positive thinking. The turtles were all put into smaller evacuation-sized tanks and draped with wet towels to keep them moist. The tanks were stacked in the truck and I drove it off the island to the home where I would be staying during the storm.* She and the turtles waited out the storm. Then after four days they journeyed back to Topsail Island.

The turtle hospital is a very popular place, drawing visitors from every state in the union and from more than 60 other nations. "Turtle Talk" tours that describe the life of sea turtles and how the hospital cares for them draw large crowds. The turtle hospital has from 12,000 to 15,000 visitors each year. It is open for tours during the 12 week summer season, June until Labor Day, 5 days a week - 2 to 4 PM.

The Rehabilitation Center has an overwhelming demand on their resources to accept more turtles. They are currently planning a new site for a much larger facility that can provide for the needs of many more turtles. That new hospital should be ready by 2006 and will be built on the mainland.

The Karen Beasley Sea Turtle Rescue and Rehabilitation Center has a wonderful website that will give you much more information. I urge you to check it out. You can find it at http://www.seaturtlehospital.org.

Credits to:

The Karen Beasley Sea Turtle Rescue and Rehabilitation Center website.
Jean Beasley, Executive Director of the Rehabilitation Center
The Office of Protected Resources website.
Turtle release picture courtesy Ashley Parker – *Topsail Voice*
Turtle Pictures – Ken Taylor, *Wildlife in North Carolina*

STORMS

You don't have to talk long with Topsail residents before they relate some story about a storm. The otherwise serene, laid-back living is punctuated with northeasters, hurricanes, and some of the loudest and most beautiful rainstorms I have ever experienced. Part of the beauty is being able to watch the storm develop, move, and present you with a bright rainbow.

From late winter until early spring, coastal people anticipate the arrival of northeasters with some amount of dread. Northeasters are counter-clockwise rotating low-pressure systems that travel northward along the coast. They often have battering winds, driving rain, and lashing waves that can pick up vast quantities of beach sand.

Northeasters are notorious in North Carolina. Topsail Island had a double-header that wreaked much beach damage. The December 2, 1986 northeaster did more than two million dollars in damage, exclusive of beach erosion. On New Year's Eve a second round battered Topsail Island. This northeaster hit during near record high tides caused by a rare alignment of the earth, sun, and moon. Topsail Beach had the most damage and virtually all of the remaining dunes and beach were taken away. Mayor Kip Oppegaard said: *The dune line is completely gone. This is the worst since hurricane Hazel.* Oppegaard estimated that more than 100 oceanfront houses were damaged in Topsail Beach.

The storms served notice that the ocean will sooner or later claim many beach homes. There were some successes, however. Residents who pushed up sand after the last storm were able to reduce damage to their homes. Emergency personnel were concerned that Topsail Beach people remained in their homes despite warnings. The emergency management coordinator said: *People didn't seem to be greatly concerned about what was coming.*

At the north end, the New River Inlet Road washed out in two places and some 700 feet of sewer line washed away with it. If it were not for man-made dunes pushed up after the December 2 storm, the ocean could have met the sound. Damage was light at the northern-most tip around St. Regis, but some 200 people remaining at New Year's Eve parties were stranded. Onslow County developer F. Roger Page, Jr. was given state approval to rebuild most of the New River Inlet Road replacing roadbed washed away by the storm. The road has since been revised.

Property owners were hopeful for a beach replenishment project approval to restore the beaches and dune protections.

HURRICANES

Hurricanes have been characterized as freight trains of atmospheric energy. Topsail Island is fortunate, having had few direct hits. Still, near misses are not to be scoffed at. Because of the North Carolina coastline shape at Topsail Island, storms seem to pass by to the more vulnerable Outer Banks.

A tropical storm becomes a hurricane when its maximum sustained winds exceed 74 miles per hour. The winds blow in a counterclockwise spiral around a calm center—the eye of the hurricane. These winds spiral at a faster and faster rate as they near the hurricane's center of low pressure. The fastest winds, surrounding the eye, can easily gust to more than 200 mph. These winds are destructive enough, but it is the storm surge that causes the most damage to structures, and the most deaths. The storm surge level can exceed 15 feet, with hurricane waves riding atop

Lewis Orr, Sr. Home after Hazel

it. Beyond that, the force of the water pulling at walls and cottages is overpowering. Water weighs about 1,700 pounds per cubic yard. Throw that weight against a building over and over, and you have a hammer that can demolish almost any structure. Hurricanes can drop six inches of rain in a matter of hours. So hurricane near-misses are to be reckoned with.

Hurricanes At Topsail Island

Hurricane Hazel

Coastwatch Sep./Oct. 1991 reported "The Year of the Hurricanes." They reported on the six hurricanes that struck on or near the coast August 30, 1954 and September 19, 1955. These hurricanes were named: *Carol*, August 26, 1954; *Edna*, September 10, 1954; *Hazel*, October 15, 1954; *Connie*, August 12, 1955; *Diane*, August 17, 1955; and *Ione*, September 19, 1955.

Hurricane Hazel struck the North Carolina coast with a ferocity not seen before or since. To mention her name sends chills up the spines of anyone who was touched by Hazel. In North Carolina she wreaked $100 million in damage [1954 dollars], killed 19 people, and injured 200 others. Hazel struck the North Carolina coast near Shallotte around 10:00 P.M. on October 15, 1954, with estimated sustained winds as high as 150 mph, and measured winds at Wilmington at 82 mph, with gusts to 98 mph.

The following is excerpted from a report written by James D. Stevenson of the National Weather Service in Wilmington:

> Wind-driven tides devastated the immediate oceanfront from the South Carolina line to Cape Lookout. All traces of civilization on that immediate waterfront were practically annihilated. The dune, which in some cases was 20 feet tall, was washed away. So were

Jolly Roger Pier after Hazel (above)
Topsail Beach after Hazel (below)

the houses and cottages that had been built behind the dunes for protection.

Experts have called Hazel a freak, but other folks have labeled her a judgment from a higher power. She was a severe hurricane that jumped ashore in North Carolina on the exact date of the highest tide of the year—the full moon tide of October.

Peter Chenery wrote that Hazel brought tides of 9.6 feet above mean sea level [MSL] to the oceanfront beaches, and 8.5 feet over MSL in the sound. Fifty-four of the sixty houses in Anderson's Topsail Beach development were washed away. Many oceanfront homes built on slabs (as opposed to pilings) atop the dunes north of Topsail Beach were undermined by the combination of high tides and storm waves. The slabs tilted and tipped their houses into the surf. The replacement swing bridge was nearly completed when the hurricane hit, washing out part of the causeway leading to it.

Sears Landing after Hazel 1954

For the entire island, 210 houses, or 65% of the total before the hurricane were lost. A new inlet was cut across the island north of the Pender-Onslow County line, just south of the former Paradise Pier. The new inlet was filled in by the state, but its site was over-washed in 1955 by hurricanes Connie and Diane. Hazel's 9.6 foot tide inundated the entire island and lowered the average level of the beach by two feet. Most of the homes were cottages that were not constructed to withstand hurricane force winds and water.

After Hazel many things changed. New building code requirements called for construction that could withstand winds of 125 miles per hour. Houses were placed on pilings to permit storm floodwaters to pass beneath without harm. Sandbags and snow fences were placed along the previous oceanfront dune line to rebuild the fore dune.

Hurricanes are defining events that force change and as more is learned, safety and protection procedures improve, making structures more durable and people better prepared. Police concerns for safety of residents and security of property have become a real focus for island living.

People's attitudes have also changed over time. Years ago, staunch "island survivors" would ride out the storms. With better education and communication, island folks have become more cognizant of the need to respect storms and the advice of the authorities. Nevertheless, there is a continuing frustration on the part of property owners when they evacuate the island then try to get back to their homes to assess the damage. Property owners understandably want free and total access as soon as possible. However, policing has to be firm and procedures followed precisely to protect vulnerable property from vandalism and looting. Today, instructions are clear and available from all three towns on their respective websites. Basically, if the property owner rides out the storm, he must stay on his property unless escorted elsewhere by police. If the property owner evacuates, he must wait until the police have reopened the island, obtain a permit, and then be escorted to his property. No one is allowed on the island without a permit. The police departments collaborate and have a coordinated plan for managing both evacuation and re-entry. They set up roadblocks and Emergency

Topsail Beach after Hazel (above and middle)
Cottage in Sound (below)

Topsail Island looking north from inlet after Hazel 10/20/54

Operation Centers at the Sears Landing Bridge and the high-level bridge at North Topsail Beach. They also may impose curfews for a time. [See "More Recollections."]

A number of notable hurricanes have affected Topsail Island over the years. Hurricane Hazel in 1954 was the most devastating and seems to be the memorable benchmark of all hurricanes to hit Topsail. The most infamous period in North Carolina's hurricane history was the 1950s when six storms struck over a two-year period. For this North Carolina was dubbed "hurricane alley." Following Hazel there were several decades of relative quiet. Beginning in the 1980s there were several major hurricanes that people at Topsail Island talk about: Diana - 1984, Gloria - 1985, Hugo - 1989 and Bertha - 1996 followed by Fran - 1996, Bonnie - 1998 and then Floyd - 1999. I'm sure others could be mentioned, but these stand out in everyone's mind.

It's interesting to consider overall North Carolina damage costs across four of the major hurricanes. Hazel - October 15, 1954 recorded a property loss for NC at $136 Million. Bertha - July 12, 1996 recorded losses in NC at $1.2 Billion. Fran - September 5, 1996 recoded NC losses of $5.2 Billion. Floyd - September 16, 1999, recorded NC damage at $6 Billion.

Bertha and Fran – 1996

The one-two punch in 1996 was a most difficult season to overcome. Topsail Island had the distinction of being the hardest hit of the barrier islands, with both hurricanes drawing national media attention. The *Wilmington Star-News* published a magazine titled *The Savage Season – Hurricanes Bertha and Fran, summer of 1996* that documented the storms and their impact on the region.

Topsail—Fran—1996

Bertha's thirty-five mile-wide eye made landfall just below Topsail Island near Wrightsville Beach, wreaking damage to the entire island including Topsail Beach, Surf City, and to a greater extent North Topsail Beach. The storm surge was estimated at five to eight feet breaching the dunes and washing out roads. A couple from Ohio had planned to ride out the hurricane in their North Topsail home, then apparently changed their mind and tried to escape in their car. It became

Topsail—Fran—1996

41

Topsail—Fran—1996

swamped in the tides and they waded back to their home in chest-deep water.

Topsail—Fran—1996

Surf City police rescued more than fifty people who had belatedly decided not to stay. A story about a close call was reported in *The Savage Season*, where Police Chief David Jones said: *We went to get a lady that was up at the north end and we got out of the car trying to get to her house, and the roof picked up off her house and just missed the patrol car and us by about 6 feet.* This was the first hurricane since Donna in 1960 to have such a broad impact across the eastern counties of North Carolina. And then, no sooner had the people of Topsail put their property and lives together, they the found themselves awaiting Fran.

As Labor Day approached, another hurricane was being tracked with winds predicted at 115 to 138 MPH and storm surges ranging from eight to twelve feet. When Fran hit with tremendous strength, she was even more potent because Bertha had washed away Topsail's protective dunes, leaving the island even more vulnerable. Nearly all the front-row cottages in Topsail

Beach were destroyed and about half of those in the second row were badly damaged. One intact cottage ended up in the marsh at the south end of Topsail Beach and another at Surf City. The natural environment also took its toll from the over wash and deposit of sand. Beach erosion was serious and every sea turtle nest on the island had been inundated.

North Topsail Beach was devastated with an estimated 90 percent of the structures suffering heavy damage. Reported by *The News & Observer*, the Villa Capriani and St. Regis resorts sustained heavy water damage from waves that topped 14 feet in some areas. The Police and National Guard escorted people to their homes to pick over any belongings, but then they had to go off the island until cleanup permitted reentry. If property owners wanted to stay, they were strictly required to stay on their own property. Unfortunately looting has to be guarded against following such disasters.

During Fran, one Topsail Island resident Georgia Greene died of exposure. In a *Wilmington Star-News* account the following story was documented.

> At 75, the Surf City woman was bedridden and depended on round-the-clock nurses who tended to her needs. She lost her husband in 1993, had no children and had lost touch with most other relatives. She had nobody to ensure her safety. Home care nurses were gone when rescue workers found Ms. Greene Friday on a mattress in the marsh across the street from her demolished mobile home.
>
> Family members don't know why the nurses left her alone. But some say she told people she didn't want to leave. When Hurricane Bertha hit weeks earlier, she stuck it out. During the storm, she called the rescue squad because she thought a tree had fallen on her house, said Surf City Mayor Vance Kee.
>
> Rescue workers believe Ms. Green was out most of the night in the churning waters pushed up by Fran. The same waters destroyed her mobile home, leaving her without shelter for hours in hurricane-force winds and torrential rain. After rescuers dragged weeds that had piled up on top of her, she was rushed to Columbia Cape Fear Hospital. A day later, she was dead.

Another Surf City casualty was the Scotch Bonnet Pier and Restaurant. Fran washed this long-time landmark away. Many hundreds of people came to the restaurant and arcade over the prior 29 years and it was a major loss to residents and tourists alike. In a *Wilmington Star-News* account, Wiley Page who operated the Scotch Bonnet said: *The Scotch Bonnet was more to me than a business. It was a part of life. When it got wiped out it was almost like a death in the family...it'll take a long time to get over the pain of this one.*

Fran devastated Ocean City taking out its motel and damaging the pier, tower and tackle shop building to the point where the Town of North Topsail Beach needed to condemn the pier as unsafe. It was necessary to fence off the structure and stabilize it for future repairs. The loss of the hotel and pier resulted in economic hardship from which the community has not yet fully recovered.

Through all this havoc, the seven observation towers for Operation Bumblebee stood firm, as they have with every storm to hit the island. Evelyn Ottaway's comfortable block home was incorporated into Tower # 3 and withstood storms over the years. But Hurricane Fran completely destroyed her attached home while the tower stood fast.

In the midst of all the devastation, storms often unearth long-lost items. The *Wilmington Star-News* reported this story, "Fran Returns Long-lost Rings."

> Hurricane Fran took away much when it roared through the state that September. For one Belgrade family, it brought back something.
>
> Doug Eastlund of Hampstead was combing the beach in Surf City with his metal detector on an October morning when he found two corroded class rings, likely washed ashore by the storm. One of the rings was from a high school in Sarasota, Florida, and the other was from White Oak High School.
>
> Through White Oak High records, he got the ring returned to Wendy Speight, who had lost it June 1969 as she played in the

Topsail—Fran—Tower 3—1996

water on Topsail Island. Her husband-to-be Mike had given her the 10-karat gold ring, and the loss was particularly distressing because his parents had struggled to save enough so he could purchase the $45 ring.

She had the ring cleaned and sized and wrapped it in a shoebox full of sand and shells. She gave her husband the gift at a church party the Sunday before Christmas. He said: I couldn't believe it. It was a real shock.

As for Mr. Eastlund, he still has one mystery left. He's still searching for the owner of the Florida ring.

Bonnie – 1998

Bonnie, in 1998, was considered much less severe than Fran or Bertha. While not nearly matching Fran's fury, Bonnie washed out a twenty-foot portion of roadbed and floated at least five trailers into the sound from the Rogers Bay Campground in North Topsail Beach. And it forced an evacuation of the turtles. Jean Beasley tells a story about that in the Sea Turtle chapter. Topsail Beach suffered around $1.8 Million in damage, [compared to Fran's $31 Million].

Floyd – 1999

Floyd, September 16, 1999, was a huge mass that lost its force as it approached Topsail Island with measured winds of 80 – 105 MPH. But the breadth and severity of the flooding was reported at a"500-year flood"level. The Hurricane City website reported a rainfall of nearly 20 inches. In Topsail Beach, after property owners were allowed back to secure their properties, notice was given that cars would have to be left at Flake Avenue, in the center of town, and they would have to walk south. Property owners were advised not to stay, but if they opted to remain on the island they were to stay on their own property. Military Police, National Guard and Topsail Beach Police patrolled to prevent unauthorized access and possible looting of private property. North Topsail Beach lost a lot of dunes and large sections of roads were washed out. Properties were damaged, but not to the extent they were during Fran.

Isabel - 2003

In 2003, Hurricane Isabel was bearing down on North Carolina's coast. People were urged to evacuate as this promised to be the largest storm in four years. On Topsail Island many cottages were boarded up and some considered evacuating. At the turtle hospital, Jean Beasley and her staff were preparing the turtle tanks by moving the tanks inside, filling them to the brim and using up every inch of available space in the small hospital. In a Wilmington Star News account, Jean said: We are playing a balancing act, as we always have to be prepared to move them off the island if necessary.

Isabel's winds clocked at 160 mph, then weakened to a sustained wind of 110 mph as she approached about 520 miles south-southeast of Cape Hatteras, missing Topsail Island. But Cape Hatteras and Virginia Beach were severely pounded.

Wilmington, too, was spared the brunt of Isabel. At"The Whiskey"on Front Street, bartenders were dispensing "Isabel Shooters" – four liquors and a dash of cranberry juice - $3. Wrightsville Beach was crowded with beach-goers who were celebrating as Isabel passed them by. It seemed like they were there to shake their fists at the ocean and declare that they weren't afraid of it. Even before Isabel was to hit, many were sunning and walking on the beach as if defying the coming storm.

Topsail Island was spared the fury of Isabel. But when damaging storms hit, recovery and rebuilding closely follows. Despite the level of the damage, it gets cleaned up in several months and in most cases a year later, all looks fairly normal again. It is said that property values that tend to drop after a hurricane are back up again within a year. Rebuilding has created a new face for Topsail Island and new construction using the latest building codes promises a stronger structure for the next hurricane.

References:

North Carolina's Hurricane History, Third Edition, Jay Barnes
"The Savage Season" – *The Wilmington Star-News* - 1996
Aerial views of southern tip of island courtesy J.B. Brame.

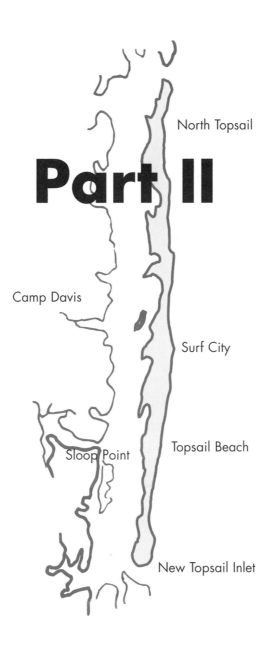

North Topsail

Part II

Camp Davis

Surf City

Sloop Point

Topsail Beach

New Topsail Inlet

THE ISLAND - ITS STORIES

I have struggled mightily to put this story together in a meaningful way, still realizing that it is impossible to capture Topsail's full spirit. Places and events become the setting for *ECHOES of Topsail*. Historic facts and personal accounts weave tales around the following settings, to tell the Topsail story.

New Topsail Inlet -the entry and exit for Topsail Sound and the mainland. This inlet has been the nemesis of many a mariner from Civil War days through today. Pirates and blockade runners sought shelter in the sound via New Topsail Inlet.

Sloop Point Plantation - was built in 1726 and was the focus for stories of salt works during the Civil War and other happenings taking place through the late 1930's.

Stories of growing up on the Sound are told by people who lived on this mainland and were involved in early Topsail Island events.

Gold Hole - a four year dig for Spanish Galleon gold between 1937-1941 on Topsail Island, that became the source of legends and personal experiences.

Military Era - The US Government seized the island in 1941 for military purposes. They needed a place for Camp Davis to do their military maneuvers and antiaircraft firing exercises. After World War II the island became a test site for the US Navy to launch and track rockets in early development of missiles.

PIRATES AND BURIED TREASURE

Blackbeard and his "buried treasure" have caught the imaginations of many a treasure seeker. Topsail Island has been claimed as a possible site of Blackbeard's exploits. A local woman became obsessed with looking for Blackbeard's treasure which she believed was nearby.

Mary Ottaway, housewife, mother, and cook at the Ottaway family's Camp Davis Restaurant for years, has a warm smile and pleasant way about her. She tells a convincing personal story about digging for Blackbeard's treasure and, as incredulous as it seems, you have to believe her.

Mary recalls: *In 1952 my husband, two children, and I lived on Little Kinston Road. It has that name because many people who lived here formerly lived in Kinston. We lived in a small house next door to a property owned by Mr. Rochelle that had a huge tree at the curve in the road.*

In late October 1952, I woke up with an eerie sense of something happening outside. Looking out the window, I saw a bright light, like a huge ball of fire shining down on the big tree next door. It was so brilliant that it glowed all the way down its trunk to the roots. Then it disappeared, like a ghost. I told a few friends about it but nobody would believe me. When it did not reappear, I just let it pass as a dream.

Exactly one year later, in 1953, the light appeared again, lighting up the whole tree and ground around it. This time, I shook my husband awake to see it and the light disappeared as mysteriously as it came. He would not admit seeing it, but I was sure he did. Sometime later, he told someone about the light saying that he had seen it, too. He had denied it at the time because he thought I would be afraid to stay there alone. I was scared of it anyway, and spent some sleepless nights expecting the light to come back.

George Thomas had an old map that showed a sunken ship offshore that was supposed to have been Blackbeard's. I felt sure that this mysterious light at the tree was telling me that Blackbeard had come ashore here. My fantasy of buried treasure could not be stilled. I was absolutely driven to try to dig for treasure at the base of that tree. I convinced my friend Beatrice King of the possibility and we agreed to dig.

When I asked Mr. Rochelle for permission, he looked at me as being a little crazy. He said, "You look determined to do it so go ahead and dig all you want, but I expect to get half of what you find."

We must have looked a little strange, two young women with kids running around, digging a full sized "grave" beside that tree. We knew about an old saying that anytime you dig for treasure, you can't say anything or the dirt will turn to water and the gold will sink. We dug in silence for a couple of hours.

As we were digging, my son Danny was pulling my other son Glen in a wagon to entertain him. By now, we had dug a hole about chest deep and big enough to bury a cow. He yanked the wagon toward the hole and I shouted, "Danny!" and the dirt turned to watery mud. Frantically, we tore at the mud to keep digging but it was just like quicksand and to no use.

Mr. King came out and looked. He said, "You'd just as well stop digging because if there was any, it is gone now." We decided it was hopeless and threw the dirt back into the hole.

We never went back to it, but I have always wondered about it. For sure, I saw the bright light twice, in October and one year later. And the dirt did turn to watery mud before our eyes, defeating us. I guess we were scared enough to stop and even forget about treasure hunting after that happened. So far as I know, the light has not come back to haunt Little Kinston Road.

It is said that Blackbeard sailed his fleet into Topsail Inlet, in the early 1700s. According to a map dated 1747, Topsail Inlet is shown near Cape Lookout. The inlet is shown at Beaufort Harbor in another map dated 1808. From all the research done to try to link Topsail Island to Blackbeard's treasure activity, no proof has been found.

As late as 1822, pirate ships flying the Jolly Roger were still roaming along the coast of the Carolinas. The situation finally became so bad that the United States Congress appropriated $500,000 to arm a naval squadron, charged with the authority to stop, search, and seize all suspicious vessels found in the South Atlantic and Caribbean. By 1830, over 97 pirate vessels had been destroyed and 1711 pirates captured. The majority were hanged. The buccaneers were swept from the southern seas over a century ago. Still, the name of Blackbeard lives on.

BLOCKADE RUNNING AND LOST SHIPS

There are "gray ghosts" lying offshore from Topsail Island. The Confederate blockade runner *Phantom* is one of them, at rest in the deep. Divers' records from 1977 confirm she is still there and earlier divers have removed bars of lead. When the ill-fated *Phantom* ran aground in the War Between the States, it is said that a treasure was lost.

President Abraham Lincoln initiated the blockade of North Carolina's coast in the Spring of 1861. By 1863, the Yankee blockade was acute and focused on the corridor from Beaufort to Southport because the life-line to the Confederacy had to be broken. The Union sought intensely to sever it. A vital artery for supplies and munitions from Bermuda, Halifax, and Nassau, it became a hotbed of activity. Wilmington was the last port to close in the Civil War.

Cotton production was a prime factor in the Confederacy's holding out as long as it did. The world needed cotton, and the South was the only place to find it in abundance. Thus, cotton became the medium of exchange between the Confederates and the Northern states, as well as Europe, and they paid dearly for it. Cotton at Wilmington sold for eight cents a pound, in Europe eighty cents, and in Northern states up to a dollar.

Initially, sailing vessels that normally shipped lumber and other peace-time goods were pressed into service shipping cotton. The Union contingent put a stop to this with their blockade and faster ships. The sailing ships were replaced by small, fast steamers, able to run past the sentry vessels under cover of darkness.

The blockade was formidable and used three separate lines of blockading vessels past which the Confederate steamers had to go. One line was 40 miles at sea, a second, ten miles out, and the third close to shore.

The blockade runners soon evolved a method where they would approach, then sit 40 to 50 miles away from Cape Fear. The runners waited for night cover, then ran full speed for Wilmington, hugging the shoreline for cover.

If they were caught, the crews would burn the precious cargo and escape. The coastal waters from Topsail Island to Shallotte are littered with the remains of these iron-hulled steamers, mute reminders of a wartime era when cotton was king.

It was a 640 mile trip from the Bahamas to the Cape Fear River, often full of adventure. Some voyages had moments of high drama, but the public's perception of the blockade runner, cheating death on every passage, was somewhat exaggerated. For the most part, it was a cat-and-mouse game. The blockade runners were able to set the pace and call the plays. They could select the time, place, and other conditions that, more often than not, included a moonless night and a rising tide. All these factors increased their odds.

Once having bypassed the outside blockade and gaining an inside advantage, blockade runners would utilize the sounds, waterways, and shoreline. With a background of shadowy sand dunes they were practically invisible, even on clear nights.

A trafficker of goods for the Confederacy, the *Phantom* was a prime target of blockade ships. She was a handsome, steel-plated, screw steamer of 500 tons and 170 horsepower, constructed at Liverpool in 1862. The *Phantom* was camouflaged to decrease visibility. The hull and smoke funnels were painted a grayish green to blend in with the sea, sky and the coast-line dunes, to make her invisible even at close range.

Rose O'Neale Greenhow was a bright, beautiful woman who traveled in high company. She was a strong Southern sympathizer and she resided

Blockade Runner

in Washington. Because of her connections, she was aware of Union troop movements and often was able to help the South with information. She became a heroine through her deeds and was imprisoned to quiet her, without success. Later she would travel to Bermuda and on to England aboard the Phantom. Her farewell letter to Jefferson Davis said: *In a few hours I shall be departing, the tide being now favorable. Tonight Captain Porter intends to make the attempt to get out. The Yankees are reported as being unusually vigilant, a double line of blockaders bars the way.* She and her daughter were the only passengers permitted on the *Phantom*. Rose's reputation, the importance of her mission, and the directives that had come down from Richmond gave her priority over others waiting. In the dead of night, the *Phantom*, with all its lights covered, slipped down the Cape Fear River, passed Fort Fisher, and moved into the open Atlantic.

Despite the darkness, ships of the blockading Union fleet sighted the *Phantom* and gave chase, but the faster English vessel soon outdistanced its pursuers. She safely arrived at St. George, Bermuda, and pressed on to England. After a successful mission, Rose returned on the Condor carrying 2,000 pounds in English gold sovereigns. The US blockade fleet was alerted of her being on board and gave chase as they approached Fort Fisher. Stormy seas and a risky attempt to put ashore pitched her overboard and she drowned.

Blockade runners would sometimes anchor in Masonboro, Rich, or Topsail Inlet while waiting for the proper tide. Captain Porter and the *Phantom* enjoyed many successes, but inevitably, she was to have a misadventure that brought her to New Topsail Inlet at the south end of Topsail Island.

The Union cruiser, the *USS Connecticut* discovered the *Phantom* near New Topsail Inlet, as it sped north along the shore trying to escape detection. It overtook and fired on the *Phantom*. Rather than be captured, Captain Porter ran for the shoals and prepared to set fire to her if need be. The Bermuda cargo was valuable government stores consisting of arms, medicines, lead ingots, and sundry merchandise. But there was much more than that on board.

Harry Montgomery, an old salt and crew member, later told his personal story about the *Phantom*, a ship he was particularly fond of. He said: *She would cruise at sixteen knots and could do eighteen if pressed. Not bad for 1863. Phantom, with Captain Porter commanding, was on her third trip, running for Wilmington from Bermuda. There was a mysterious passenger aboard who had stayed close to his cabin most of the four-day trip. He seemed like a Confederate agent returning on a special mission.*

Captain Porter decided the game was up. *Phantom* was cut off and being forced, by the Union ship *Connecticut*, closer to land. The best bet was to get as close to the beach as possible so the cargo could be salvaged, and if not, set afire. Porter grabbed papers and crammed them in a leather dispatch case with other documents. Yankee shells began exploding all around.

Calling Montgomery to his side, Captain Porter gave instructions to secure a line around his dispatch case and lower it to the water's edge. The Confederate agent came to him staggering under the weight of a small, heavy strongbox. Montgomery made the line fast to the box and he lowered both dispatch case and strongbox. If the gunboat caught up with them before they beached, Montgomery was to cut the line and send the valuables to the bottom.

Montgomery tells how he was standing on the starboard quarter, shot and shell whistling past his ears, with his right hand wielding a fire ax and his left grasping that most important line. He said: *The Phantom grounded before she was caught. She hit the shoals head on at eighteen knots. It was one hell of a jolt. The crew soon had fires burning fore and aft. A direct hit from the Connecticut struck one of Phantom's stacks. It exploded and fragments of steel showered everywhere. All three men were knocked to the deck.*

Montgomery looked up in time to see the end of the line snaking over the side. The strongbox and dispatch case went to the bottom like stones. After struggling to shore, the Confederate agent said: *Well, my man, you just let forty-five thousand in gold slip through your bungling fingers.*

To this day, there is no record of such treasure being found, so we can only assume that it is still there. Maybe this story will excite someone about diving for it.

The Journal, Wilmington, NC on October 1, 1863 reported:

> The Confederate States steamer *Phantom*, from Bermuda, was chased ashore near Topsail Inlet by the blockading fleet yesterday morning. She had a valuable cargo of government stores, etc. The crew all made their escape in boats.

Fort Fisher fell January 1865, marking the end of blockade running. Blockade-running captains and merchants who withdrew early from the business amassed fortunes. Those who continued to the end encountered heavy losses. When blockade running collapsed, the Confederacy's days were numbered. The port at Wilmington was one of the last to fall.

There have been a number of lost ships right here at Topsail Island. The Underwater Research Files of Mark Wilde-Ramsing document 17 plus an unidentified Ancient Ship. This ship could be the Spanish Galleon, the aim of the Gold Hole dig in 1938-1941.

Two Brothers	Schooner	02-10-1797	New Topsail Inlet
Adelaide	Schooner	10-21-1862	Inside Topsail Snd.
Unknown I.D.	Schooner	01-21-1863	New Topsail Inlet
Superior	Schooner	11-11-1841	Near Topsail Inlet
Industry	Schooner	02-02-1863	Topsail Beach
Alexander Cooper	Schooner	08-22-1863	Inside Topsail Snd.
Phantom	Screw Steamer	09-23-1863	Near Topsail Inlet
Wild Dayrell	Sidewheel Steamer	01-01-1864	Rich Inlet
Charles E. Elmore	Schooner	04-13-1877	Off Topsail Inlet
W.H. Marshall	Brig	04-25-1878	Near Topsail Inlet

W.J. Potter	Schooner	08-??-1878	Near Sloop Point
Marion Gage	Schooner	07-??-1879	7m S-N. River Inl
Fred B. Rice	Schooner	09-23-1880	Near Sloop Point
Mary Bear	Schooner	09-09-1881	New Topsail Inlet
Mary D. Drew	Schooner	02-03-1882	4m S - N. River Inl
William H. Sumner	Schooner	09-08-1919	Topsail Inlet
Janie	Schooner	09-03-1921	Near Hampstead
Unknown I.D.	Ancient Ship	—	Topsail Beach

Specific accounts tell of four sunken ships nearby. The schooner *Superior* was driven ashore near Topsail Inlet, November 11, 1841.

On October 22, 1862, one week prior to his destruction of the Confederate salt works, Lieutenant William B. Cushing reported the seizure and scuttling of the richly laden schooner *Adelaide* inside New Topsail Inlet.

While in command of the *USS Shokoken*, Lieutenant William B. Cushing reported on August 22, the destruction of the blockade running schooner *Alexander Cooper*, near New Topsail Inlet. At the same time, he reported destruction of nearby salt works.

Blockade runner *Phantom* lies off-shore near New Topsail Inlet. The *Phantom* site was investigated by archaeological divers, in 1975. Some excerpts from this investigation:

> The *Phantom* site is located approximately 200 yards south of the southern extremity of New Topsail Inlet in 16 to 18 feet of water. The *Phantom* site is the remains of a mid-nineteenth century iron hull double screw steamer. Although little of the wreck is exposed, aside from the steam machinery, remote sensing indicates that a considerable amount of additional material lies below the surface.

> It is quite possible that the remains are those of the blockade-runner *Phantom*, which was lost in the area on September 23, 1863. The method of propulsion, twin screw, of the *Phantom* conforms to that found at the wreck site. It is also possible that this was one of the wreck sites that was salvaged at least partially by US Navy divers working for the North Carolina Division of Archives and

History during the early 1960s.

References:

Shipwrecks of the Civil War. Donald G. Shomette.
Civil War Naval Chronology 1861-1865. Naval History Division,
     Navy Dept.
The Blockade Runners. Dave Horner.
Graveyard of the Atlantic. David Stick.
Bill Reaves Collection. New Hanover Public Library.
Rose O'Neale Greenhow and the Blockade Runners. George Johnson, Jr.

SALT: THE ESSENTIAL COMMODITY

I n our time, it is hard to appreciate why salt was so crucial to our ancestors. The very life and economic well-being of Topsail, and its immediate region, once depended upon its availability. Salt was treasured for personal health, preservation of meat and fish, and as a medium for exchange of goods. Today, some 25 million tons of salt are mined in the US. About 75% of it is used commercially in manufacturing or melting snow on highways.

As early as 1663 at Cape Fear River, James Hilton of the Massachusetts Bay Colony reported: *Some of the Indians brought very good salt aboard us and made signs that there was great store thereabouts.* After settlement by the white man, so far as can be determined, there was little local production and all salt was imported from England, France, and Amsterdam until the mid 1700s.

During the 1700-1800s, the export of meat, fish, and crops was essential to the economy and well-being of North Carolina. Such exportation was possible as long as salt was available for their preservation. Poor roads and shipping delays, such as wagons lined up for miles at ferries, caused many long-distance overland trips to the north to take as much as five to six weeks by land. It was much more efficient to ship by sea and waterways increasing trade along the coast. Realizing this, and wanting to cripple the economy during the Revolutionary War, the British attempted to blockade North Carolina ports and waterways.

Salt was as essential to Revolutionary War Armies in the 1700s as gasoline is to armies today. As the Revolutionary War approached, salt shortages were aggravated because of Royal restriction compelling colonists to import exclusively from the British Empire.

At this time, some inland settlers were exchanging as much as 15 bushels of corn for one bushel of salt. Shortage of salt became critical to the settlers. Possibilities of rioting and mob stealing of salt stores became a concern of the North Carolina Government.

As the salt supply ebbed and flowed, policies of export or prohibition of export were enacted. At one point in 1778, salt became scarce enough that mobs broke into stores in Beaufort County several times for a supply.

To help relieve the salt crisis, the North Carolina Council of Safety granted permission during July 1776: *to all known friends to the American Independency to apply for a permit to export any kind of staves in exchange for salt, arms, and ammunition.* The Council reported to Continental Congress: *This permission to export is for express purpose of importing salt and ammunition due to distressed situation of this state.*

The provincial Congress of North Carolina offered a premium of 750 pounds to be given to anyone who shall erect and build proper works for manufacturing common salt within 18 months, to bring focus to coastal salt production.

Salt Kettle

William Brownrigg's publication entitled, "The Art of Making Common Salt" became a well-known handbook which enabled salt makers to get started. It described technical details for setting up a salt work.

Salt was made by two methods on the North Carolina coast. One was by solar evaporation, which necessitated the construction of a series of shallow reservoirs with clay bottoms, often with wooden sides. The sound salt was produced by pumping salt water into the vats and drawing from one reservoir into another until the crystallized salt became of the pure quality needed. The second method was boiling sea water, either by the simple procedure of hanging an iron pot over a wood fire, or by the more sophisticated system of using cast iron rectangular pans

Salt Works

set in a brick furnace. Often the two methods were combined in order for the brine to be fairly concentrated by the time it was put on to boil.

Salt works were fraught with technical problems that needed continued attention to keep the process going. They also needed protection because of anticipated raids by the enemy. In June 1781, the North Carolina House resolved: *That a Company of Light Horse be immediately raised by Voluntary Enlistment consisting of 40 persons for the protection of salt works on Topsail Sound New River.* When the Revolution ended, ships moved freely and salt scarcity ended. It was less expensive to import than to manufacture locally.

Uncertainty of shipping, as the War of 1812 approached, caused another era of salt production. The solar method was brought back into use and some 30,000 bushels of salt were produced annually during the period from 1812 to 1815. After the War of 1812, local production phased out again, because of cheaper imported salt.

SLOOP POINT SALT WORKS

At the beginning of the "War Between the States," salt became scarce again. Salt evaporation plants sprung up once more all along the coast of North Carolina, including one at Sloop Point. Some of them were state owned but most were owned by speculators who made fortunes from them during the wars.

During the Civil War salt demand was high, commanding as much as $70 per bushel in Raleigh to a low of $19 a bushel in Wilmington. Many local land owners cashed in on the bonanza, among them W. D. MacMillan of Sloop Point. It took about 840 gallons of sea water to make a bushel of salt. The system MacMillan used at Sloop Point on New Topsail Inlet, was that of a series of pans. The first pan was the deepest, measuring about 15 inches, and after a certain volume was removed, the water would run-off into the second pan for further evaporation. This process was continued, MacMillan reported, until there remained in the final pan nothing but the clear salt crystals. The pure salt was then bagged and sold for the highest price, which more often than not, was exorbitant.

The process of getting the water from the sea into the pans was as interesting as the actual evaporation process. Slaves, of which there were many, were employed to haul the water from the sea to the pans in buckets. Some plants utilized the windmill to pump the water into the pans.

The local plants managed to operate through to the end of the war. One bumper year was 1864 when a total of 66,100 bushels were produced. By the end of that year, the heyday of salt making was over.

Because salt was such a necessary and costly item, the county regularly made salt allowances to the families of local soldiers. In September 1864, as the effects of the Union blockade had become more severe, the county increased the salt allowance to one peck of salt per month for each member of a soldier's family.

STUMP SOUND SALT WORKS

The most northern salt works, on Stump Sound near the Onslow County line, was operated by Marcus L.F. Redd, Sheriff of Onslow County. He ran an ad in the *Weekly Wilmington Journal*, May 7, 1863:

> The Subscriber is making salt at Stump Sound, Onslow County, which he will sell at his works two dollars per bushel below the Wilmington Market price, or he will trade salt for provisions at the current market rates. Salt is now selling at as low a price as it can possibly be made for, and parties likely to want it would do well to lay in their supply at once. M.L.F. REDD.

In March 1864, when provisions were scarce and transportation difficult, he advertised in the *Wilmington Journal* that he would exchange; *one bushel of salt for one bushel of corn, or other produce in proportion, to be delivered at my place on Stump Sound (Redd's Salt Works).* He probably suspended business shortly thereafter, apparently pressed into military service. In September, two tracts of land were offered for sale; *for any information apply to Lt. Redd, Southerland Battery.*

New Topsail Inlet and New River Inlet were both locations of military engagement, for the express purpose of destroying salt works. The most daring raids on this coast were under the command of Lieutenant William B. Cushing, a zealous and able young officer much admired by his superiors. In October 1862, he was assigned to command the *USS Ellis* at blockade duty off Bogue Inlet. A week later he left his post and carried out a raid inside New Topsail Inlet.

Cushing reported to his superior officer: *I had learned while at Beaufort that trade was carried on at New Topsail Inlet and it was to that point that I was bound. I entered the inlet at full speed, found it not fortified, and saw a large schooner about a mile from the mouth.*

The schooner was the *Adelaide* from Halifax which had arrived the end of August with a cargo of salt and was preparing to depart carrying turpentine, cotton, and tobacco. The *Ellis* took the *Adelaide* in tow, but it soon ran aground and Cushing was forced to burn the prize.

Later in the month Cushing asked for permission to return to New Topsail Inlet, and it was granted. His report: *I again visited New Topsail Inlet on the 29th of October. Three-fourths of a mile from the mouth I discovered a large salt work, and went ashore with an armed party to destroy it. I found that a great deal of labor had been expended on its construction, and think that it could have furnished all Wilmington with salt.*

The next month Cushing raided New River Inlet, 25 miles to the North. One objective was to destroy any salt works he found, and he reported; *when I took possession of the enemy's ground, on the 24th of November, a salt work was destroyed.* His force invaded Jacksonville, stole the Wilmington mail and captured two vessels. On the way out of the Inlet with the two prizes, the *Ellis* went aground. He burned his vessel and escaped in one of his prizes.

SLOOP POINT SALT RAID

In August 1863, Cushing was transferred to the *USS Shokoken* again off this coast. On the 12th he made a reconnaissance of New Topsail Inlet and discovered; *a blockade runner, the Alexander Cooper, at a wharf some six miles up the sound.* On the 22nd, he sent a party to destroy the ship. They said they found; *some extensive salt works nearby. Mr. Cony (in charge of the party) fired the vessel and salt works; these were thoroughly consumed.*

The Wilmington newspaper carried an account of this raid, and warned salt makers that they might expect more of the same:

> It would seem that the blockaders were quite active along shore. We learned that they sent a boat party to a small schooner lying at or in New Topsail Inlet, some twenty miles from here. We are also informed that they destroyed the salt works in that vicinity. The

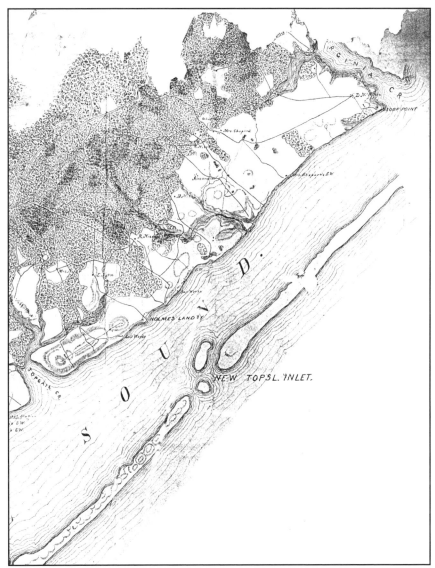

Map of Saltworks along Mainland

salt works belonging to D. MacMillan, Esq. are mentioned posi-
tively, and we presume others may be included, although we have
not been able to obtain particulars. We also learn that the Yankees
there openly avow their determination to destroy all salt works
on the different sounds. We think they will be apt to attempt it, at
any rate. Perhaps this affair at Topsail may mark the inauguration

of this policy.

A. N. Matthis wrote his personal account of the Sloop Point Salt Work raid in the following letter (in his own words) to his wife:

> Topsail Sound August, 23rd 1863 Dear Wife, I drop you a few lines to let you know that I am well & getting a long very well I have got 30 Bu of salt at the Nort East, & will carry 30 Bu more. Tuesday of next week I expect to a lode home by sam. I want you to have me as many sacks made as you can conveniently. Last knight we were a larmed by the Blockad setting fire to that vessel that come in when I was here before the vessel was at slew Point five miles from this place they burnt MacMillans salt works shelters but did not damage his pans. And took three prisoners, burnt three horses to death, they were in the stables. Several others were burnt severely. All quiet to Day. no more news. Your affectionate Husband A.N. Matthis (prop: McRay Bradshaw)

The Civil War Chronology reported the following:

> August 1863 - Boat crew from *USS Shokoken*, Lieutenant Cushing, destroyed schooner *Alexander Cooper* in New Topsail Inlet, North Carolina. "This was," Rear Admiral Lee wrote, "a handsome affair showing skill and gallantry." Ten days before, Cushing had sighted the blockade runner while he was on a reconnaissance of the Inlet. He said: "This schooner, I determined to destroy and as it was so well guarded I concluded to use strategy." The evening of the 22nd, he sent two boats' crews ashore under command of Acting Ensign Joseph S. Cony. The men landed, detailed a dingy, and carried it across a neck of land to the inlet. Thus the assault took place behind the Confederate works with marked success. In addition to burning the *Alexander Cooper*, Cony destroyed extensive salt works in the vicinity and took three prisoners back to the *USS Shokoken*.

Salt works on the Fred Moore place, on Topsail Sound was offered for sale in December, 1863, by W.A. Moore, as well as a flat boat, mules, wagons, and cut wood. He was willing to hire out nine hands to the buyer. The works consisted of ten pans and two boilers, which meant the pans were divided between two furnaces.

W.D. MacMillan ran the plantation at Sloop Point and his descendants lived in the historic home there until 1979. Evidence of salt production still remains to this day, in the form of salt pans. I know of at least one at Poplar Grove Plantation. There is also a highway plaque on Wrightsville Beach road near the Bradley Creek School that tells the location of the State Salt Works during the War Between the States.

References:

Salt That Necessary Article. Isabel M. Williams and Leora H. McEachern, Wilmington 1973.

The North Carolina Historical Review. Volume XXII. R. L. Hilldrup, October 1945.

An Archaeological and Historical Reconnaissance of US Marine Corps Base, Camp Lajeune. Part 2 The Historical Record. Thomas C. Loftfield and Tucker R. Littleton, August 1981.

Civil War Chronology. Courtesy of Phil Stevens, 1861-1865.

Weekly Wilmington Journal. May 7, 1863.

Letter: A. N. Matthis to E. J. Matthis dated August 23, 1863. Courtesy of Historical Society of Topsail Island. Property of McRay Bradshaw.

Wilmington Star Volume 21 Number 47. Larry Johnson, December 4, 1949.

SLOOP POINT

During the colonial period, proprietary grants were issued by the Lords Proprietors, who were responsible for land taxation. These grants reflected ownership of properties and were recorded in government records. Records of the New Topsail Sound region show that John Baptista Ashe owned many acres of land on the mainland that included the "banks" (now Topsail Island.)   They include:

- September 7, 1726 - 1000 acres in Carteret Prec't. on New Topsail Sound, on the west side of Whitehurst Creek. This is Sloop Point.
- November 1, 1726 - 800 acres in Carteret Prec't. being the banks between Stumpy Sound and New Topsail Inlet. Today's Surf City and Topsail Beach.
- November 1, 1726 - 1000 acres in Carteret Prec't. between New River Inlet and Stumpy Inlet. Today's North Topsail Beach and Ashe Island.

The Sloop Point Plantation home was built in 1726 by John Baptista Ashe, the father of North Carolina's first elected governor, Samuel Ashe. Sloop Point also had a harbor and shipyard on the sound, which supported commercial activities of shipbuilding and shipping in sloops. Prior to 1873, when Stumpy Inlet was closed by a storm, access to the ocean was directly through Stumpy.

The plantation house was recognized and recorded in the National Register of Historic Places, January 20, 1972. In 1995, owners James W. and Mae Blake Graves were notified that a wood dating and construction study confirmed that Sloop Point dates from 1726, making it the earliest known surviving structure in the state. Walt and Mae rescued the home from possible demolition 13 years ago and restored it, preserv-

Sloop Point Plantation - 1992

ing this graceful colonial-era home. They had purchased the property from the estate of the late Nellie MacMillan, of the Dougal MacMillan family. This important place begs for a verified and detailed history. Mae Graves fully intends to do so and is eminently qualified. There are some notable features of the house, such as the "air conditioning" shafts that allow a natural flow of air through it; a chimney large enough to fit a doorway entrance through it and serve a fireplace; and the pegged construction said to be of shipbuilding method and strength.

Sloop Point takes its name from sloop building and water transportation of the early settlers. This point was the major mainland harbor between Cape Fear and New River inlets. Prior to the closing of Stumpy Inlet, that inlet was a course from the ocean to Sloop Point Shipyard. A second way was through New Topsail Inlet. This seemed to be the inlet where most skirmishes were recorded during the Civil War. There are still salt pans on the plantation from the heyday of salt manufacturing during the Civil War. Sloop Point was the center of salt-making activity, parties, and of a well-known visitor who traveled the East Coast by canoe in 1874.

BREASTWORKS

The land behind Sloop Point is said to have Civil War earthen works. I found a letter from Thomas Jackson Strayhorn, who was Captain of a Brigade, and camped at Camp Davis, near Wilmington. July 11, 1863, he wrote to his sister, among other things: *I arrived in Camp about an hour ago, having been absent two weeks assisting in the erection of a line of entrenchments near Topsail Sound...* This spurred me to look for them. Richard Sidbury and Gray Justice took me right to five separate groupings of breastworks behind Sloop Point beyond Mullet Creek.

To the hardy explorer the breastworks are fairly easy to find through the woods. The easiest approach is to enter at Grove Point Plantation to Wood Bridge Road. Turn right on Wood Bridge, a sand and dirt road, for less than one mile to a flat wooden bridge. Walk toward the sound and you will see them, overgrown with trees. There are several 10 foot high earthworks of some length there. They must have been used to help defend the Sloop Point Saltworks from land attack.

BANKS PARTIES

The Weekly Star, Wilmington, NC, August 22, 1884 reports:

> TOPSAIL SOUND PICNIC—On the morning of the 7th inst., there assembled on the classic grounds, known as Sloop Point Landing, a large concourse of the natives of this favored section, with a number of visitors from the counties of Sampson, Duplin, Cumberland, Onslow, and your own New Hanover, all admiring the scenery and the substantial schooner *May*, owned and commanded by Capt. L. Standland, which had been tendered to take

the picnickers to the banks...Before we were satisfactorily seated, the Captain gave the command to—well, I don't know exactly what; but down came the jib and fore sail, and before the crowd had recovered from the temporary commotion set up by this necessary adjustment of the sails, the schooner was anchored under the shore at what is know as the "White Hills" on "Topsail Banks" and only a few rods from the ocean...On landing we were joined by a large number who had preceded us in sail boats. On ascending the hill, we were in the midst of a dense and beautiful grove of the native live oak...Large numbers of the finest melons such as only Topsail can produce, were cut and enjoyed, while a rustic table, over a hundred feet long, was constructed; fires kindled and fish and oysters brought from boats in greatest profusion...At the proper time, the company was invited to dinner, the blessing of God invoked in a most solemn manner by that noble specimen of the "old time" Scotch gentleman, the venerable Dougald MacMillan, and all were made welcome...On our return trip late in the day, we had a fine breeze and all was lovely, with music in the air...When Mr. G. E. Shepard, in a very neat and appropriate speech, returned the thanks of the company to the ladies, the managers, the fiddlers, and last but not least, to Capt. Standland, for his kindness in gratuitously taking the company to and from the banks, assuring him that his generosity would long be remembered by the farmers of the community.

SMUGGLING

Sloop Point made the news again in the November 1977, *Wilmington Star*:

> The Coast Guard seized a Bahamian freighter carrying as much as 25 tons of marijuana, allegedly destined for a landing point near Wilmington. In addition to eight crewmen on the ship, nine alleged accomplices were arrested Tuesday night in Wilmington, Topsail Beach, and at the alleged landing site at Sloop Point in Pender County.
>
> Customs Special Agent Jack Dolan said the marijuana—estimated

at 15-25 tons—was the *Sea Crust's* only cargo. It was loaded aboard the ship early in November off the Colombian port of Baranquilla.

The Sea Crust was to serve as a "mother ship," transferring the marijuana to small vessels about 40 miles off Wrightsville Beach. The small craft were to transfer their loads at Sloop Point, north of Topsail Inlet on the Intracoastal Waterway, Dolan said. The Coast Guard had located the ship between 45 and 50 miles off Wrightsville Beach Monday morning and put it under "open surveillance."

Dolan said that Colombian marijuana normally sells for between $350 and $400 a pound on the street. That would make the ship's cargo of an estimated 15 to 25 tons worth between $10.5 million and $16 million.

VOYAGE OF THE PAPER CANOE

This fascinating story tells of Nathaniel Bishop's journey, by canoe, though Topsail Sound in 1874. His book is entitled *VOYAGE OF THE PAPER CANOE: A Geographical Journey of 2500 Miles, From Quebec to the Gulf of Mexico, During the Years 1874-5*. It was written by Nathaniel Bishop in 1878. It is presented excerpted here to capture his experience at Topsail Sound, Stump Sound, and Sloop Point.

> The author left Quebec, Dominion of Canada, July 4, 1874, with a single assistant in a wooden canoe eighteen feet in length, bound for the Gulf of Mexico. It was his intention to follow the natural and artificial connecting watercourses of the continent in the most direct line southward to the gulf coast of Florida, making portages as seldom as possible, to show how few were the interruptions to a continuous water-way for vessels of light draught...Having proceeded about four hundred miles upon his voyage, the author reached Troy on the Hudson River, New York State, where for several years E. Waters & Sons had been perfecting the construction of paper boats.

The advantages in using a boat of only fifty-eight pounds weight, which was both strong and durable, caused the author to change his travel plans midstream, so to speak. He dismissed his assistant, and "paddled his own canoe" about two thousand miles to the end of the journey. Though frequently lost in the labyrinth of creeks and marshes which skirt the southern coast of his country, the author's difficulties were greatly lessened by the use of the valuable and elaborate charts of the United States Coast Survey Bureau.

CHAPTER X - From Cape Hatteras to Cape Fear, North Carolina

...Having bid new friends goodbye at Morehead City on Tuesday January 5th, he rowed down the little sound called Bogue toward Cape Fear.

The watercourses now became more intricate, growing narrower as I rowed southward. The open waters of the sound were left behind, and I entered a labyrinth of creeks and small sheets of water, which form a network in the marshes between the sandy beach-islands and the mainland all the way to Cape Fear River.

The Core Sound sheet of the United States Coast Survey ended at Cape Lookout, there being no charts of the route to Masonboro. I was therefore now traveling upon *local* knowledge, which proves usually a very uncertain guide.

Wild-fowls abound, and the shooting is excellent. The fishermen say flocks of ducks seven miles in length have been seen on the waters of Bogue Sound...The marsh-ponies feed upon the beaches, in a half wild state, with the deer and cattle, cross the marshes and swim the streams from the mainland to the beaches in the spring, and graze there until winter, when they collect in little herds, and instinctively return to the piney woods of the uplands.

...Emerging from the marshes, my course led me away from New River Inlet, across open sheets of water to the mainland, where

Dr. Ward's cotton plantation occupied a large and cultivated area in the wilderness. It was nearly two miles from his estate down to the inlet. The intervening flats among the island marshes of New River were covered with natural beds of oysters, upon which the canoe scraped as I crossed to the narrow entrance of Stump Sound. Upon rounding a point of land I found, snugly ensconced in a grove, the cot of an oysterman, Captain Risley Lewis, who, after informing me that his was the last habitation to be found in that vicinity, pressed me to be his guest.

The next day proved one of trial to patience and muscle. The narrow watercourses, which like a spider's web penetrate the marshes with numerous small sheets of water, made traveling a most difficult task. At times I was lost, again my canoe was lodged upon oyster-beds in the shallow ponds of water, the mud bottoms of which would not bear my weight if I attempted to get overboard to lighten the little craft.

...In twelve miles of tortuous windings there appeared but one sign of human life—a little cabin on a ridge of upland among the fringe of marshes. It was cheering to a lonely canoeist to see this house, and the clearing around it with the season's crop of corn in stacks dotting the field. All this region is called Stump Sound; but that sheet of water is a well-defined, narrow, lake-like water-course. Stump Inlet having closed up eighteen months before my visit, the sound and its tributaries received tidal water from New Topsail Inlet.

It was a cold and rainy evening when I sought shelter in an old boat-house, at a landing on Topsail Sound, soon after leaving Stump Sound. While preparing for the night's camp, the son of the proprietor of the plantation discovered the, to him, unheard-of spectacle of a paper boat upon the gravely strand. Filled with curiosity and delight, he dragged me, paddle in hand, through an avenue of trees to a hill upon which a large house was located. This was the boy's home. Leaving me on the broad steps of the veranda, he rushed into the hall, shouting to the family, "Here's a sailor who has come from the north in a PAPER boat."

Sloop Point circa 1880

This piece of intelligence roused the good people to merriment. "Impossible!" "A boat made of paper!" "Nonsense!"

The boy, however, would not be put down. "But it *is* made of paper, I tell you; for I pinched it and stuck my nails into it," he replied earnestly.

"You are crazy, my boy," some one responded; "a paper boat never could go through these sounds, the coon oysters would cut it in pieces. Now tell us, is the sailor made of paper, like his boat?"

"Indeed, mother, what I tell you is true; and, O, I forgot, here's the sailor on the steps, where I left him." In an instant the whole family was out upon the veranda. Seeing my embarrassment, they tried like well-bred people to check their merriment, while I explained to them the way in which the boy had captured me, and proposed at once returning to my camp. To this, however, they would not listen; and the charming wife of the planter extended her hand to me, as she said, "No, sir, you will not go back to the wet landing to camp. This is our home, and though marauding armies during the late war have taken from us our wealth, you must share with us the little we have left." This lady, with her two daughters who inherited her beauty and grace of manner, did all in their power to make me comfortable.

Sunday was the coldest day of the season; but the family, whose hospitality I enjoyed, rode seven miles through the woods...to the little church in a heavy pine forest. The next day proved stormy, and the driving sleet froze upon the trees and bound their limbs and boughs together with an icy veneer. My host, Mr. MacMillan, kindly urged me to tarry. During my stay with him I ascertained that he devoted his attention to raising ground-peas, or peanuts. Along the coast of this part of North Carolina this nut is the chief product, and is raised in immense quantities.

...Wednesday opened with partially clearing weather, and the icy covering of the trees yielded to the softening influences of a southern wind. The family went to the landing to see me off, and the kind ladies stowed many delicacies, made with their own hands, in the bow of the boat. After rowing a half-mile, I took a lingering look at the shore, where those who four days ago were strangers, now waved an adieu as friends. They had been stript of their wealth, though the kind old planter had never raised his hand against the government of his fathers. This family, like thousands of people in the south, had suffered for the rash deeds of others. While the political views of this gentleman differed from those of the stranger from Massachusetts, it formed no barrier to their social intercourse, and did not make him forget to exhibit the warm feelings of hospitality which so largely influence the Southerner. I went to him, as a traveler in search of truth, upon an honest errand. Under such circumstances a Northerner does not require a letter of introduction to nine out of ten of the citizens of the fifteen ex-slave states, which cover an area of eight hundred and eighty thousand square miles, and where fourteen millions of people desire to be permitted to enjoy the same privileges as the Constitution of the United States guarantees to all the states north of Mason and Dixon's line.

From Sloop Landing, on my new friends' plantation, to New Topsail Inlet I had a brisk row of five miles. Vessels drawing eight feet of water can reach this landing from the open sea upon a full tide. The sea was rolling in at this ocean door as my canoe crossed it to the next marsh thoroughfare, which connected it with Old Topsail Inlet, where the same monotonous surroundings of sand-hills and marshes are to be found.

The next tidal opening was Rich Inlet, which had a strong ebb running through it to the sea. From it, I threaded the thoroughfares up to the mainland, reaching at dusk the "Emma Nickson Plantation."

I then traveled south to Cape Fear and on to complete the 2500 mile journey.

To an unknown wanderer among the creeks, rivers, and sounds of the coast, the courteous treatment of the Southern people was most gratifying.

References:

History of Pender County, North Carolina. Mattie Bloodworth.

Weekly Star article, files of Bill Reaves Collection, New Hanover Public Library.

Wilmington Star article, files of Bill Reaves Collection, New Hanover Public Library Discussions with Mae and Walt Graves.

VOYAGE OF THE PAPER CANOE: A Geographical Journey of 2500 Miles, From Quebec to the Gulf of Mexico—During the Years 1874-5. Nathaniel Bishop, 1878.

GROWING UP
ON THE SOUND

RICHARD SIDBURY

Richard Sidbury lives at Watts Landing and lived around the Sloop Point area all his life. He worked on the Gold Hole from its beginning in 1937, until abandoned in 1941.

Richard was recalling the early days. He tells his stories in a slow drawl that pulls you in. He said: *The island did not amount to anything except for grazing. We used to put hogs over at the beach. They would feed on the island oak acorns. We would also take corn over to them and they would know where to collect for the feeding. Some farmers would drive their cows over to the beach at low tide to winter there and graze. When the Intracoastal Waterway came in, it caused some changes. It was not practical to swim cows over to the beach but we would still haul hogs over there in our boats. The waterway has changed the water level and also has allowed large boats to speed up the channel that is causing erosion and other changes to the sound.*

My mother was blind but she taught me well. We learned conservation as a habit. While we were poor, we were not hungry or ill-clothed. With conservation a habit, I believe the side effect is respect. Another lesson of life learned was to "practice patience." My cousin, Kenneth Andrews, was a good practicer of that—he could wait.

He recalls a special teacher, Catherine King: *She was a good teacher and a real disciplinarian. Man, you didn't get away with anything. I did not mind her pulling my ears, but she would pick me up and drop me. Looking back, it was a forming experience and I learned a lot.*

They always had a huge cast iron pot somewhere. This pot was important because it had many uses. They would boil water in it for washing clothes, cooking oysters, and have hot water for hog killing time. He said: *We would cut fat pieces of meat and boil them down into cracklin' bread and biscuits. For entertainment we had a battery powered Sears Roebuck radio.*

They did a lot of mullet fishing. They would get about 10 people together with a seine that had cork floats at the top and lead weighting the bottom. Fish travel southward and after a lookout lets the group know of a school of mullet, the group would fan out with the seine and trap them in large numbers. The catch would be sold and the proceeds shared. He said: *Another way we used to fish is to watch for where porpoises were blowing, because the trout would run ashore to the coves. You could station yourself at the coves and net or gig them. We've gotten some record catches that way.*

We used to gig for flounder all night. Today they have bright lights on their boat powered by battery. We would use "fat" wood, or wood that would burn easily and brightly for light. The wood sticks would be in a basket and we would use a torch for striking. Just when you needed the light, the glow would dim or go out.

He grinned and said: *To be a genuine "Sloop Pointer," you have to be able to stand up in a Jon boat in a stiff wind, hold the boat in place by holding a paddle under your arm. Then you roll a cigarette and light it using wet matches.*

On my uncle's farm, Claude Wilson found a sea chest in a field while plowing. He ran to get my uncle and they dug it up. It was surrounded with some kind of preservative but they only found old papers in it. Local folklore has claimed that something more was probably found and the family won't reveal it. But this has been debunked, except for locals who claim that he lived pretty well without working after that.

About 1941, after the Gold Hole, I helped build the pontoon bridge at Sears Landing. This bridge took two men to operate, and was the first means to get vehicles over to the island under their own power. I was Bridge Tender for a year or so. We always had a pot of oysters, potatoes, and such going on the stove.

When they had the antiaircraft firing range, during WWII, they had me and a friend take targets offshore about a mile or two out in the ocean. It was about eight feet square and the shape of a tent. We would put six by six inch timber across the gunwale of the boat, load the target, and take it out in the ocean. They told us to dump the target and get out of there fast. Once, we did it and the motor quit. We could not get it started right away and were shaking at the thought of dodging antiaircraft shells.

KENNETH ANDREWS

Kenneth Andrews lived most of his life around Sloop Point. His daddy had a small country store in the early 1920s. He would sell to farmers on credit until after the crop harvest, then the farmers would repay it. He went out of business after a few years. Mr. MacMillan had sold or traded off land to William Nunon Atkinson to settle debts. Kenneth's father married Atkinson's daughter acquiring some of the land. He then bought two shares of land for peanut farming.

Kenneth had a faraway look in his eyes as he leaned back in his chair and recalled his earlier life: *I was born October 1908 and raised on my father's farm that adjoined the MacMillan Plantation at Sloop Point. The farm produced peanuts, corn, and cotton. I worked on the farm as I grew up but living on the sound gave me a chance to earn extra money fishing commercially. This was useful in future years as a means of making a living between other jobs.* He left school before graduating to join the Coast Guard. He worked several jobs then on the WPA building roads for $1.35 a day during the depression. This does not sound like much but you could buy a week's groceries for $2.00. Beer was 11 cents.

He chuckled, leaning forward: *I remember when I was about 18, my cousin and I were gigging flounder all night and the fog closed in. Our "fat sticks," used for light, would not burn because of the rain and we got totally lost. The boat was pounding with the surf and we just knew we had drifted to New Topsail Inlet, which was further north then.*

Shivering and scared that we would drown, we hung on all night until daylight broke. We heard our rooster crowing and could not believe we had spent the night a stone's throw from home.

In the mid-20s a three masted schooner from South America anchored 12 miles out in international water. There was liquor on board and it was brought by small boats into New Topsail Inlet to the mainland near Watts landing. It was reputed to be an Al Capone operation, with trucks, guns, and all, waiting for the booze. Kenneth said: *I know one truck went to New Jersey.*

He remembered that Catherine King's father built a fish camp on Topsail Island in the early 30s. Dr. Porter had a log house just below the Gulf Lodge. There was a prison camp built near there on King's property, during the late 30s too. Trustees would stay there and they would fish for mullet for North Carolina prisons.

Kenneth's sister Lena Mae tells a 1930s story about Miss Nellie MacMillan. Nellie, known as a cantankerous "old maid," farmed the Sloop Point plantation and always wore overalls. Lena Mae said: *Once MacMillan's cow got out and Kenneth corralled it. He took great pleasure in first milking Miss Nellie's cow, then returning it to the MacMillan's. Kenneth was always serious about his work as Sea Captain, but he knew how to have a good time at home. He and his bachelor cousins were often into hard drinking, laughing, and telling stories.*

Kenneth's eyes twinkled as he said: *You know, in those days there was no entertainment or money. But we still knew how to have fun. People would gather on the first Saturday in May, for a "Banks Party," on the island. Anyone was invited and they would have a big barrel of lemonade, huge piles of oysters, and a roast with a giant fire.*

And there were great times at Sloop Point too. Miss Nellie MacMillan and sister Joanna were the owners of the Sloop Point Plantation. They used to have dances there on the front porch of the plantation house in the 20s and 30s. They used a mouth harp and violin for dance music.

The Wilmington News, May 4, 1936 reported a community affair near Sloop Point:

A Community Sing, diversified with some regular old-time fiddling and square dancing, will mark the opening night program of Music Week at the Isaac Bear school auditorium tonight at 8:15 o'clock. ...Tonight, fifteen minutes of the program is devoted to the Clam Diggers of Topsail, who will render a group of tunes that originated prior to the 1860s. They will be played by J.W. and J.N. Sidbury, D.B. Howard and J. S. King...

Wilmington News, May 5, 1936:

A howling success is the only way to describe the Community Night program at Isaac Bear auditorium last night. The self-styled Clam Diggers from Topsail were very graciously received with their old tunes. Many in the audience felt they were again greeting a very old and true friend in "Pop" Sidbury. When the Clam Diggers were joined by the square dancers, the crowd simply went wild, and dance after dance was called for and all were forthcoming...

Kenneth recounted a historic dig for treasure on Topsail Island: *From 1937-1941, I worked on the Gold Hole on the island. Bill Walker, nephew of Jimmy Walker and former mayor of New York, and several other men came over to Sears Landing and asked for someone to take them over to the beach.*

Bill had some kind of map that showed a Spanish Galleon had sunk where there was an inlet. Abraham Spice, Ivey Lewis, and I took them over to the Bland property, now owned by Ms. Mayrand. After having a look, they went back to New York, returning in a week or two to start the project. They hired us and we set up wood frames to screen sand and started digging with shovels and wheelbarrows. Ivey Lewis and I each had a boat and motor used to transport people and supplies to the site from Moore Landing.

He was married by now and lived with his wife on their land near Sloop Point. He worked the Gold Hole for four years until 1941 when the project ended because of WWII. He mused: *It was a blue day when they bombed Pearl Harbor. As the war kept on, it had us all scared. We could not use lights at night. German submarines were sinking ships daily. The Coast Guard patrolled the shore day and night. A tanker was torpedoed, about 40 miles out, and I saw it light up the whole sky. I located the sunk tanker while out on a charter job years later, and made a sonar print of it.*

KATHERINE TROTH

Katherine Hall Troth was born in 1913 to a poor farming family on the mainland. She is an energetic, tall, white-haired lady who has a keen memory of the past. She spent many years teaching school in the Topsail area. Kenneth Andrews was her cousin as well as Richard Sidbury and Lena Mae Brock. Her grandfather is Nunon Atkinson.

Katherine's father worked hard trying to raise peanuts on the land next to MacMillans at Sloop Point. It was hard plowing and he worked alongside of Ms. Nellie (MacMillan), who also plowed her land in overalls. The land was at the end of Virginia Creek. Katherine often went with her daddy all the way from present RT 210 to the farm, taking the road around the swamplands to a log bridge on a mule and cart. It was quite a journey as she recalls it: *Mother would pack a lunch of beans, potatoes, dumplings, ham, and peaches, which they would eat for their lunch, while working in the peanut fields. The land at the end of Virginia Creek also had orchards of peaches, pears, and apples.*

We were poor farmers but we knew how to have fun. There was a yearly "Banks" party where families from Vista—Sloop Point—Watts Landing, and surrounding communities would go to the Banks with baskets of food. These parties took place in the 1920s and were on the first Saturday of May. Families would head for their landings and boats on foot or mule and cart.

The boats were homemade and they moved them with a long pole-paddle. Daddy pushed and guided the boat to get us where we wanted to go. The first stop was a spring of the freshest, sweetest water near Gabe's Point. Then we headed for the oyster beds. Daddy knew where to find them and at low tide, oyster rocks were showing. They could pick up all the oysters they would need, and if not there, more were close by. Sears Landing had the biggest oysters. They would load the oysters in another boat with others and would long pole across the sound to White Hills, near where the Seafood World once was.

At the marshy point, they would land boats and men would start looking for wood to lay oysters on, in stacks about one foot high. This stacking was strung out 20 to 30 feet and dead marsh grass laid across the oysters. They would light the marsh grass, feeding it more when needed, and the oysters would roast. Mothers would spread tablecloths on more marsh grass and by the time the oysters were done, they had laid out cornbread, biscuits, cracklin' bread, chicken, smoked ham, and oysters. Desserts of cake, cup cakes, and pie of all descriptions such as sweet potato pie and lemon pie completed the feast.

She said: *After we ate until we could bust, we climbed to the top of White Hills and rolled down the hill to the channel. Had to be careful at high tide, or we might roll into the water. Then moms and dads would take us through the woods-oaks and pear pods (cactus), to the big dunes full of sea oats to the beach. We all carried big paper bags to pick up shells.*

Shells on the beach were nothing like today. They were at least six inches deep and everywhere. We couldn't walk there easily. Big conches and shells mounded all over. We would go wading in the surf with Daddy holding our hand. Then he carried us back tired, a happy day at the beach. We would have to sadly leave so there was time to get back before dark. There was a mule and cart ride home after getting back to Sloop Point.

The Banks parties lasted until the government began taking over the island, in the early 1940s. She said: *The families began gathering over on the mainland, across from White Hills at Moore's Landing, where Nunon Atkinson's children inherited acres of land around the sound. The picnics were a gathering of brothers, sisters, and their families (ten of them). They also included neighbors and friends, everyone bringing baskets of food. They moved the picnics to July 4th, which also gave us the best watermelons from Daddy's patch. It was so great to get to see all of your cousins at one time and play and catch crabs from the pier.*

IVEY LEWIS

The Lewis Family has been in the boat business since 1936, right here in the Topsail area. Ivey Lewis, Sr. bought some 1,500 feet of waterfront land near Sloop Point and the family has operated from there as commercial fishermen and boat builders. Ivey fished for mullet before and during the second World War: *We used to tote 'em across the beach in bags* and salt 'em. Back then, mullet brought from one half cent to two cents a pound. They would truck their catch to Wilmington and sell it in barrels to a man named Sam Bear in an old market on the Cape Fear River.

He said: *My Daddy said that 60 years ago New Topsail Inlet was up about the Breezeway. We built Seafood World about 25 years ago and ran it for 15 years. Called it Lewis Brothers. My Grandfather used to turn cattle and hogs loose on the beach. Nobody was there, and I would go over to feed the hogs.*

I understand there was whiskey brought in through New Topsail Inlet to trucks. There was some jealousy and competition because they made booze here. There are some wrecks out there, and we have snagged some nets on them. They used small sailing boats in the old days to ship turpentine, resin, tobacco, and peanuts. They had a shallow draft and we could not get but small flat-bottom boats in, south of here.

They had found some breastworks north of Sloop Point Road. He said that the main road ran through where the little bridge is on Mill Creek. That old road was one the mailman with a pony would travel bringing mail from the train.

He remembered Nellie MacMillan: *She was an old maid and headstrong. Always had to have her own way. Daddy wanted his money from the peanut crop. She wanted to store it until after the first of the year. They got into a fight with pitchforks. It scared everyone—just could not reason with her.*

Fishing was much better than farming. In those days you could work hard plowing dawn to dusk for 50 cents, being paid 25 cents cash and 25 cents in crops. You could earn $15 a day fishing.

He said: *Kenneth Andrews and I were always good friends. We worked together first on the Gold Hole and later as co-captains on a party boat five years or so.*

GULF COTTAGE

Here are some recollections about the early days at Topsail Island, excerpted from D.S. Johnson's autobiography. During the early Depression years, he and his brothers and two cousins, enjoyed trips to the beach "Gulf Cottage" for a week of fishing and duck hunting. His cousin Robert was one of several Gulf dealers who built a cottage on the sound side, in the 30s. His recollections:

> There were only two other cottages on the island at that time. The only access was by boat and it would remain that way for 10 more years.
>
> The trip would start by meeting at Herbert King's Landing, loading groceries and supplies for the week. We would leave our cars at the landing. Robert's boat, with an outboard motor, would tow the supply boat with a couple of passengers. We would go about a mile and half north on the Inland Waterway, turn east at Nixon's Creek, go about another mile to the sound. The cottage was about another half-mile southeast across the sound.
>
> We brought in a gasoline motor generator for a little light at supper time. We would cut the motor off as soon as we could after supper in order not to attract mosquitoes and sand flies. Otherwise it was dark. We kept supplies in an ice box with a 200 pound block of ice. Used sparingly, it would last a week. Water came from a pump on the back porch, and it had the sulfur flavor typical of shallow wells.
>
> Beds were homemade bunks made of two by four scantlings. The only favorable thing you could say was that the beds were about a foot and half off the floor for air, and owing to a delightful breeze, were reasonable for sleeping. In a couple of years, we graduated to army cots.
>
> We caught our own shrimp for bait, using a small shrimp seine. Beheading the shrimp was a real chore. Occasionally we would catch a few large enough to eat, a real delicacy.
>
> Robert would tow us out to a fishing hole. He was familiar with the Sound and its creeks. When we were placed, he would head for another fishing hole. Fish were plentiful and we could catch all we needed for supper all week. We found ourselves in the middle of a school of trout once, and pulled them in until we had a boatload.

Another time Robert saw several sharks out a couple of hundred yards from the cottage. He baited a large shark hook and tied it to a long hemp cable. He took the baited hook by boat to the area where he had seen them and fastened the other end to a boat on the beach. Some time later, the cable tightened and we helped him pull it in. This was an eight foot shark we beached, and after a council we decided that a decaying shark nearby was not what we wanted. We tugged him back and released him deciding not to bait any more shark hooks.

Clams were in abundance in the sound. The Johnson brothers were the clam team. We would go to the mouth of a creek as low tide approached and rake the bottoms. Soon as the rake struck something solid, we knew it was a clam. Robert was a good cook and made great clam chowder.

We always had a radio so we would not be caught in a hurricane. During WWII, the radio reported a hurricane, and when the sound became unusually rough we decided to head for the mainland. Three of us headed for King's Landing, nearly capsizing several times. From King's Landing we drove the car to the pontoon bridge and asked permission to cross and rescue the rest of their party. We made it.

Later, we made some improvements on the Gulf Cottage. An early incarnation of solar energy, we used a 55-gallon drum up on the roof, where it had constant exposure to the sun, and connected it with the water pump. It gave us a very satisfactory shower arrangement. A large screened back porch made our stays free from mosquitoes.

Because of death and old age, the group began to break up and we had our last fishing party about 1970. In the mid-70s, the property was sold.

THE GOLD HOLE

The Carolina Exploration Company came to Topsail Island to search for a fortune in gold from 1937 to 1941. The search took place on Bland property, now owned by the Mayrands, just south of the current Topsail Beach - Surf City town line. It was known as the "Gold Hole" and their search ended when WWII began. It was headed by Bill Walker (nephew of Jimmy Walker, former Mayor of New York), with the assistance of Julian Jacobs, Harry Gunning, and Mildred Stone—all from New York—Eddy Ives from Hartford, Connecticut, and consultation of Simon Lake, inventor of the submarine.

Old historic records document:

> In February 1750, a Spanish Flota of five vessels heavily loaded with treasure and the private cargoes of the captain-generals of

Gold Hold Landing

the fleet, cleared from Veracruz following the usual defined route across the Gulf of Mexico. Beating against the trade winds, it was four weeks before the ships dropped their hooks in the Havana harbor.

It is not known why the fleet delayed their departure until hurricane season, but it was late July before the galleons unfurled canvas and headed homeward. Sailing northward the ships passed through the Florida Channel, past the Bahama Banks seeking favorable westerly winds to carry them East to Spain.

In the meantime, the wind freshened to gale force and the vessels running before it were scattered and blown far off their course. About August 17, 1750, somewhere between Cape Fear and Cape Lookout, the shrieking wind and mountainous seas overtook the helpless galleons. It is said that the *El Salvadore* was the first ship of the Flota to strike, and probably went ashore broad-side to the sea at New Topsail Inlet and was stove to pieces.

She was loaded with 240,000 pieces of eight regular, besides what is on private account. Nearly all the hapless crew were swept into the raging surf where they drowned. Only four were saved. As early as 1752 this vessel was covered with seven or eight feet of sand.

This probably accounts for the failure of the treasure hunters of a later era to discover it.

It was 1939. A giant "A" frame with pulley and rope towered over the hole. One man jerked the winch device that was pulling up the "clamshell" bucket, carrying something up from the depths. Sand is piled all around and just over the mound of sand, the sound is sparkling in the sunlight. The workers wonder what is in the bucket. Is this what they have been driving themselves for these three years?

Kenneth Andrews tried to contain himself. He was slim, sinewy, tall and energetic. His impulse was to be the first to touch it. He thought: *I've been digging in this hellhole for three years. Fought storms, stinging sand, breaking*

A-frame

my back throwing sand through the screens, wondering if the treasure was just a pipe dream. What if there is nothing down there after all? If we do get rich beyond our dreams, what will we do with it? Is this what we want? I'll just lie back and let whatever happens, happen.

With that, he backed off and sat on a dune 30 feet distant and daydreamed back three years to when he first met Bill. New Yorker Bill Walker, was out of place at Sears Landing. Not prepared for the sand, he was dressed in a business suit and dress shoes.

Walker said: *Do you know anything about that island?*
Andrews answered: *Just a worthless piece of sand. We graze cattle and pigs there for the winter. They grub for nuts and grass. We take corn to them several times a week and that's all they need.*

Could you get a boat and take me over? Walker asked.

Sure, but what do you want to do that fer?

Look at this map. I know that a Spanish Galleon sank there at an old inlet. We have studied the maps and it looks like this spot is where it went down. Blands

Beginning stage by hand

gave us permission to dig. They even said we could use their cabin. There's no inlet there now, Andrews stated.

Walker: *I know — that's why I need you or someone who really knows the island and can help locate it. If we find it, there is treasure beyond dreams and you could share in it.* His voice was low and sure. He pointed to his map, then surrounded a chest of gold with his arms.

Andrews' heart was pounding. *I'll get a couple of guys and we can go this morning. I couldn't believe that they hired Ivy Lewis, Abraham Spicer and me right on the spot. In two weeks, we had built wood framed screens and started digging with shovels and wheelbarrows...*

The clanging of the bucket jolted him back to the present. The bucket was open and it looked like another piece of wood, but it was not part of a chest or ship. He thought: *Will we have to give it up after all this?*

At that time, local newspapers watched and reported on the project. The *Wilmington Star* dated June 6, 1938 reported: *SYNDICATE SEEKS GOLD IN WRECKAGE OF SUNKEN VESSEL — SHAFT IS BEING DUG.*

> Since last Thursday, the feverish hunt for the treasure has been underway. Under the direction of four engineers, workmen have

been sinking a shaft into the center of the island near the inlet, over the spot where records and science show an ancient merchant ship, loaded with gold when she sank, now lies...Sunday they were 22 feet beneath the level of the sand dune into which they are sinking their shaft. Calculations indicated there was but ten feet of sand and water between them and their expected treasure...Meanwhile, an option on the property, it is reported, has been secured, so no one could stop the work which had been carried on very secretively.

...Preliminary digging brought the treasure hunters to the water line. Now a huge cofferdam, with lock-steel sheet piling, 45 feet long, has been sunk over the ship. The quicksand is being removed, but simple drilling indicates that the goal is 40 feet below the water line and that means months more of work. Nevertheless, Jacobs and his crew are not discouraged. Every step downward has seemed to confirm the accuracy of the treasure-finder. Pressure pumps have boiled up sand from the depths and have brought up bits of rotten wood which Jacobs says were obviously hand-tooled. How did it get there? On top of the site salvagers cleared off stumps of pine trees estimated to be 150 years old. Allowing any reasonable time for the ship to become "sanded up", the wreck

Shoring up walls

must be between 300 and 400 years old.

...The treasure hunt is being conducted on one of the loneliest of North Carolina's strands. The only way to get there is to hire a boat and search the place out. The top of the excavating machine's derrick can be faintly discerned from the mainland. There is a crew of local workmen laboring in a little grove of windblown live oak and yaupon—a desolate but picturesque spot which would gladden the heart of a gold-bug devotee except for the raucous evidence of civilization's methods of treasure hunting.

Gold Hole Shaft

Personal interviews with Richard Sidbury (Watts Landing), and Kenneth Andrews (Sloop Point), corroborate closely with newspaper accounts.

Sidbury said: *In the morning, I'd go about a mile to Moore Landing. I would take my boat over to Sloop Point and pick up four or five people and be at the island by 7:00 A.M. It was* **hard work**. *Every thing we did took hard labor. Any heavy timbers were brought over by barge or small boat. Throwing sand through a screen 10 hours a day in all kinds of weather was backbreaking. I remember manning the pumps all night long then working all day at times. Being below*

Richard Sidbury in boat (on left)

sea level made water in the hole a real problem. We brought supplies of all kinds over from the mainland in our boat. I would also bring seven 55 gallon drums of gas at a time, until the boat started to crack.

We had an awful accident at the Gold Hole, with Oscar Jarman getting caught and wrapping up in the ropes. He was winding up in it and hollering until we could get the engine stopped. We cut ropes with axes saving him but he was left with a withered arm.

But we were glad for the work, since they paid us $2.50 per day. Saturday at 12:00 was payday. We worked 10 hours a day for 55 hours a week at 27 cents per hour. This gave us the astounding sum of $14.85 less 15 cents for Social Security. This was the most money I had made in my 22 year life! The work was hard but compared to what you could earn working harder on a long row of cotton, this was a good life.

They fed us well too, often bringing steaks. It was probably the first steak I ever saw. Most often, they would have roasted oysters. Take a five gallon can with the top out of it, fill it with oysters, and put it on the fire. There's nothing better. Walker even promised a share of the findings. They were well organized and managed things right.

Mr. Jacobs was in charge and was easygoing. He and Walker would come and go leaving me to caretake while they were gone. I had an old radio and stayed there alone. They let me use their Packard, a big car with two spare tires. Walker called it a hearse. When they were here, some stayed at the Bland Cabin and at the Slocum Tourist Home on Market Street in Wilmington. It seemed they would run out of money, go back North, then return in a few weeks.

When hand digging was no longer practical, they brought in well drilling folks from Scranton, Pennsylvania to work a more advanced operation. A dragline was used to be more efficient. The sides kept falling in and they shored up the sides with steel for about a 20 by 20 foot hole about 20 feet deep. By the end of the project, the hole was about four feet square down to an overall depth of about 40 feet.

A year later, the *Wilmington Star* reported on May 21, 1939: *TOPSAIL TREASURE HUNTERS HOPE TO SOLVE MYSTERY 300 YEARS OLD.*

"I may not get it, but it's there," said Julian S. Jacobs firmly. By "it" he meant an ancient ship, still 25 feet away from the top of the muck his crew is steadily reducing with a steam bucket. And in that ship, which mysteriously piled up on a wilderness reef perhaps 400 years ago, is gold and silver.

How much? If Jacobs knows, he won't say. But there is a clue to this, too. The Carolina Exploration Company of which

Richard Sidbury - 1995

Gold Sensing Device

Jacobs, a mining engineer from New York, is president, has been going after that ship for a year. Excavation work alone has cost between $15,000 and $20,000, according to local contractors. Jacobs thinks his find—if and when he makes it—is going to return a handsome dividend on that investment. This including a percentage of all treasure for Dr. William H. Walker, brother of former Mayor James J. Walker, of New York, who owns rights to the scientific instrument responsible for locating the booty.

Gold Hole 1990

In the first place, Jacobs became interested in the scientific metal locator in connection with prospecting. His company operates several mines in North Carolina, and apparently his faith in the invention is based upon the success in that field. For the fun of it, as he says, Jacobs came to the Carolina banks to try out his instrument, hoping merely to pick up some interesting old chest. At Topsail Beach, a lonely strand a few miles off the North Carolina coast, north of Wrightsville Beach, he got a response that excited the crew of "chest" hunters. Down there somewhere, buried in the shifting sand, was a large mass of gold, silver and iron, according to the behavior of the "diviner," which operates on some unrevealed principle of radioactivity of elements.

This island of blinding white sand, wind-twisted trees and huge sand dunes was uninhabited. This special instrument, used between two men, would locate gold and silver. They tested it by looking for Jacob's gold watch, which he had buried, and found it with ease. Using their map and the instrument like a 'divining rod,' they marked the shape of a treasure ship on the ground, so they would know where to dig. It was reported that the detector was so persistent in its signals, that Jacobs hastily made an arrangement with Harvey Jones, owner of one of the properties. In exchange for excavating rights, Jacobs gave Jones an undisclosed amount of stock in a tin mine which Jacobs was operating near Gastonia.

Andrews recalled: *The Gold Hole work was discouraging and downright boring at times. We left the project several times to try other nearby ventures. They dug steel shafts on the Catherine King property and Harvey Jones' property. The Jones shaft was a 32 inch cylinder 110 feet down to bed rock.*

Sidbury said: *We used a drive bucket to take out the sand and two pumps kept the water out. When we hit rock and broke it up, they would lower someone small down the hole to get it. I only went once. We had to stop two times on the way up. Kenneth Andrews went down once and got the bends so bad that he was in the hospital for two weeks.*

There is a pond at Route 17 and 210. Claim was that during the Civil War, the Confederates threw a chest of gold in the pond, so the Yankees couldn't get it. We pumped out the pond, built a ramp out the middle and drilled down. There was not much confidence that anything would be found so the attempt did not go any further.

When the Gold Hole was abandoned in 1941, we had to admit defeat. While we were on the project, our belief got ever stronger the longer we dug. The pieces of wood that excited us since they looked man-made, kept us going, but we never found a Spanish Galleon or a chest of gold.

The *Pender Chronicle* surmised in 1965:

> It is said that one evening the local men were laid off. The next morning the entire expedition was gone. Did they find treasure and take it away in the night? It adds romance to the story to think of them stealthily hauling chests of gold across the sound in the dead of night—but no one seems to know for sure.

The Gold Hole still exists, but over the years there have been attempts to fill it in with refrigerators, cement blocks, and such. It is located on Mayrand family property just south of the Topsail Beach town line.

References:

Newspaper accounts were unearthed by Bill Reaves and are in the Bill Reaves Collection, New Hanover Public Library.

CAMP DAVIS

Camp Davis brought upheaval to the quiet town of Holly Ridge. It was established to prepare troops for war. Later it became a separation center and finally a base for the early development of missiles for our nation's space program.

In 1941, the tiny town of Holly Ridge, North Carolina was staggering with feverish activity as Camp Davis was created. This stampede of growth made Holly Ridge "Boomtown" for several years then it was deserted as suddenly as it started.

CAMP DAVIS — Birth to Death

Camp Davis was erected within five months. The contract was let December 10, 1940, and the first cadre arrived in April 1941. Incredibly, a Holly Ridge population of 28 people exploded into gold rush-like growth in 1940. The peak of 110,000 people was reached in 1943 and a

Main Gate

107

census revealed 486 people in 1980.

The War Department commandeered 46,683 acres of land for this reservation over the years 1941 through 1948. This comprised 119 tracts of land, owned by local residents, including Topsail Island, then known as Sears Landing or the "sand spit." Topsail Island was leased for a target range and for beach recreation. (See Map and List of Property Owners 1943—Appendix.)

Camp Davis became "home" to various military units. Coast Artillery Antiaircraft Regiments were the dominant force moving thousands of recruits through basic training and antiaircraft weaponry. Officer Candidate Schools trained hundreds of officers for troop leadership.

The first Barrage Balloon Training Center was formed at Camp Davis. This camp had the distinction of being the only post having three principle elements, antiaircraft, seacoast defense, and barrage balloon, under one command. One year later the Barrage Balloon Training Center transferred.

Antiaircraft training continued at a fevered pitch from April 1941, through September 1944 when the operation was closed and transferred to another base. After the war, the Camp Davis command was assumed by the Marine Corps for training of marines, and for several months as a separation center.

Camp Davis sprang to life again when the navy took charge June 1, 1946. It became the base for "Operation Bumblebee," a secret guided missile testing program for the US Navy. They operated a scaled-down version of the camp since they only had 500 to house.

The Navy Bureau of Ordnance and John Hopkins University Applied Physics Laboratory had undertaken another building "binge" including camera towers, roads, buildings, and a revised pontoon bridge for a missile test facility on Topsail Island. On this 26 mile beach test range, some 200 experimental rockets were fired from 1947 to 1948.

Through these tests, the ramjet engine was proved to be a success.

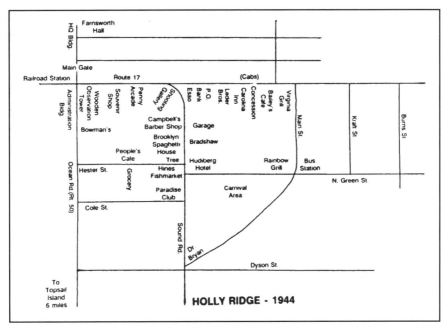

Holly Ridge Street Map

Modern jet aircraft engines have built upon this original design. The Navy Bureau of Ordnance then closed down activities in 1948 parceling out the rocketry programs to Inyokern, White Sands, and Cape Canaveral. Camp Davis was declared surplus and was dismantled to salvage and to be sold. The leased land was to be returned to the original landowners, some of which included some buildings.

Thus ended Camp Davis, which over time has decayed to what you see today, excepting the spark that keeps the memories alive. The Camp Davis Restaurant carries on as a harbor for various memorabilia including pictures and old camp newspapers among other things. A steady trickle of visiting former "Davisites" stop in at the restaurant to see what remains and to reminisce about the Camp Davis heyday. One such visitor from Pennsylvania was leafing through old yellowed AA Barrage papers and discovered a picture of a 90mm gun. He blurted out: *I used to sit right there and fire the 90.* Then he asked to take the paper out to the car to show his wife. This is typical of those who will not forget their time here.

Camp Davis aerial view

CONSTRUCTION

A reporter describes Camp Davis under construction in the State Vol. VIII, No. 53 dated May 31, 1941:

> If you haven't been down in the southeastern part of the state

during the last few months, you can't even begin to imagine the changes that are taking place. It is a truly amazing sight. It's the most stupendous thing that has ever happened in that section. Millions of dollars are being turned loose every week. Thousands of men have been given employment.

Gone completely are the traditional calm and easygoing way of living. The slow-moving tempo of villages and towns is a mad rush that seems to have everybody within its grasp. Cars and trucks fill the highways. New houses are going up everywhere. Around practically every filling station is a huddle of trailers and tents where people have taken up temporary quarters. Land sales are almost a daily occurrence and it seems as though every third

Camp Davis aerial oblique view

man you meet is in the real estate business.

Holly Ridge, prior to last December was just a store or two, a couple of filling stations and a half dozen homes. Then came the announcement that a huge new antiaircraft base was to be located there. That was last December, just a little more than five months ago. It would take you that long to build almost any kind of a house, but imagine putting up 978 buildings in that period of time!

That's what has happened at Camp Davis. Among the buildings are barracks, mess halls, recreation buildings, theaters, post exchanges, hospital, post office, telephone building, laundry, bakery, cold storage plant, warehouses and a number of others. There are 32 miles of paved streets. The camp itself is over four miles long and about a mile wide.

When news of the project was public, a grand rush began in the direction of Holly Ridge. Men came from great distances, seeking work. Any number of them camped in tents, waiting to be put on the payroll. Then, when they finally succeeded, they traveled back and forth daily from their homes. Large numbers made the trip in trucks in which benches were placed on each side and a canvas cover installed overhead. Stoves were put in during the cold weather so the occupants could keep warm. On trips home after the men had received their weekly pay, those same trucks were the scenes of some of the most exciting crap games you can imagine.

Your first glimpse of Camp Davis will bring forth a gasp of amazement. You'd been reading about it in the papers but when you actually see it you discover that you had absolutely no conception of the magnitude of the project.

HOLLY RIDGE, *Wilmington News*, Dec. 10, 1940—Sam Ragan

There was not much to see—two stores, a little railroad station, and seven houses in which live the town's seven families and the

Maintenance Building - Camp Davis - 1990

entire population of 28. But in about three months the vanguard of the 20,000 men that will make up the army's antiaircraft training base will move in. A city that is beyond imagination will be under way. It was just like sitting on the scene of a gold rush that will start tomorrow and knowing that it will happen and wondering just what it will be like. You have to stretch your imagination mighty hard to see a large city growing up out of the straggly pines. But to one person, at least, it's real enough.

That man is C.C. Hines, the village postmaster, operator of a general store, adviser and unofficial mayor of this town of a half-century age. I found that Mr. Hines knew more about the Holly Ridge army camp than anyone else. He's been the scout and guide for all survey parties in the area. It took a long time for him to accept that the little village he has doctored along for years is going to be a city.

"It's hard to realize, though," he said. "It's something you read about—you know like what used to happen out west."

Mr. Hines and the rest of the natives who gathered about the iron stove in his store are taking it rather calmly. "It's no use to get het up over things," one of them said, "but we'll be ready for it when it

Boomtown - 1990

comes." Like the proverbial dead pig in the sunshine, Holly Ridge is happy about it all. It knows that a boom town is to be theirs and they are just sitting around waiting for it to arrive.

It is two miles from Holly Ridge to Morris' Landing, located on the inland waterway, and just south of the landing is where the army plans to erect its firing base. The firing proper will be out over the water.

Postmaster Hines says a lot of people have stopped at his store and asked: "How in the world do you people make a living here? I'll tell 'em, he says, that if we can get a little bread we can get plenty of oysters nearby. Within a mile and a half are a half dozen oyster roasts."

Mr. Hines is already consulting contractors about building a large new building that will house his store, post office, a barber shop, a cafe, and a theater with living quarters over the top. He will be ready when the first soldiers arrive.

The first arrivals should be coming in by December 20. Tents will be erected at first and permanent buildings are to follow.

MAJOR GENERAL DAVIS

The camp was named for Major General Richmond Pearson Davis, who was born at Statesville, North Carolina, in 1866. He was a member of the 1887 class at West Point. During WWI he commanded the 151st Field Artillery Brigade in France, and later was Chief of Artillery for the Ninth Corps. For his services in this command he was awarded the Distinguished Service Medal. After the war he served for a time as commanding officer of the Coast Artillery Training Center at Fort Monroe, Virginia, and later was assigned to posts in the Philippines and Hawaii. He was promoted to Major General in 1927.

FIRST TROOPS

In April 1941, the first cadres arrived at Camp Davis. Seasoned soldiers from posts throughout the United States were sent here to assist in administration and training. Brigadier General James B. Crawford was in command. The first selectees came from Camp Grant, Illinois, in early May, and were assigned to the 93rd Coast Artillery, a new antiaircraft regiment, first to be activated at Camp Davis.

The influx of troops continued into the summer months until the 93rd, 94th, 95th, 96th, 99th, and 100th antiaircraft regiments reached full strength. The 99th and 100th Coast Artillery consised of black soldiers. The six regiments all originated at Camp Davis. In May, the 54th Coast Artillery, only black 155mm G.P.F. (tractor-drawn) regiment in the army was transferred to Camp Davis from Camp Wallace, Texas, where it had been activated in February 1941.

BARRAGE BALLOON TRAINING

Before organization of the new regiments was well under way, the War Department announced that a Barrage Balloon Training Center and School, first of its kind in the army, would be established at Camp Davis. The War

Barrage Balloon - 1942

Department's announcement was the first indication that the army has decided to adopt the use of barrage balloons as a defense weapon against airplanes.

The balloons, according to the undersecretary, have proven their value in the defense of London and other English cities. Their 15,000 foot lightweight cables force bombing planes to altitudes where it is impossible to score direct hits. They have also proven useful, the undersecretary said, in combating dive-bombers.

FIRING POINTS

The camp is unique in that its antiaircraft firing points are not on the main reservation. One is on the historic site of Fort Fisher, 50 miles south of the camp proper. The second antiaircraft firing point is at Sears Landing, a narrow strip of land between the inland waterway and the ocean, four and a half miles east of Camp Davis.

This latter point was completed after two months of arduous clear-ing, digging, dredging, and building. It was necessary to build a road through the woods from the camp to Sears Landing. To facilitate traf-fic through the inland waterway, a retractable 75 foot steel barge was installed between mainland and landing. Only 22 buildings were con-structed in the area since Sears Landing is but a short distance from, and easily accessible to Camp Davis. Troops might be called upon to camp overnight occasionally at Sears Landing.

The 90mm gun was the heaviest and largest antiaircraft artillery gun in use by the Coast Artillery. The "90" could fire at 18 rounds per minute and be loaded by hand or mechanically. Operating with a crew of 15 men, the gun was mobile beyond belief. An experienced crew could be ready for action in 13 minutes. The length of the gun was about sixteen feet and fired a projectile weighing 23 pounds. It was probably one of the best guns in WWII used against Germany and used in North Africa, Guadacanal, and other fronts. Richard Sidbury of Watts Landing recalls: *When they had the antiaircraft firing range, they had me and a friend take targets offshore about a mile or two out in the ocean. We were told to dump the target and get out of there fast. Once, we did it and the motor quit. I panicked*

Tents at Sears Landing

117

and kept yanking on the starter. Finally it caught and we got out of there. We were sure we'd be dodging antiaircraft shells.

On March 20, 1943, the 559th AAA Auto Weapons Battalion gained its birthright with a nucleus of twenty officers and one hundred and eight enlisted men with Major Samuel H. Back commanding.

A day in the history of the 559th was recorded that will bring back memories to any service personnel who endured inspection of high ranking officers.

May 30, 1943 will not soon be forgotten by the members of this battalion. Advance warning had informed us that Lieutenant General Ben Lear was to inspect Camp Davis and Fort Fisher. Major Back had been told his battalion would be inspected by the General on the anti-mechanized firing range. C Battery was selected by the Major to be on the range with the other batteries waiting behind to come on the line when C completed firing. Lt.

Anti-aircraft guns at beach - 1942-43

Ricketts, commanding C Battery, was on the platform of the range with Major Back. His officers and men were ready and waiting for the General, who was expected at 1100. At 1030 one of the 40 mm guns shot and cut the cable of a ground target. The range was temporarily out of action. At 1100, three shiny military cars were seen approaching. The first and shiniest flew a red flag with three stars, behind it came the next shiniest flying a red flag with two stars. Then came a smaller, but still shiny car with a red flag and a solitary star. In the cars were General Lear, Major General Green, General Townsend, Camp Davis Commander and General Milburn. The assembly of high ranking officers, stars glittering, proceeded to the tower. Upon hearing the range was temporarily out of action, the constellation, led by General Lear, proceeded to D Battery.

Firing at the beach - 1942-43

The Lieutenant General was dressed in his famous uniform of campaign hat, black boots and frown. He queried Lt. Oritt, Commander of D Battery and asked a chief of section a few questions. He then returned to the tower. Lt. Ricketts reported to him. The General asked Ricketts a few more questions and was answered immediately, much to the General's satisfaction. "You seem to know your job, Lieutenant," was the General's comment.

The Target was finally fixed and C Battery commenced firing. The General watched with interest, made a few comments to General Green on the condition of the range and then came down from the platform. The General and his party then climbed into their respective cars and drove off, flags waving. A spontaneous sigh of relief arose from all members of the 559th. The inspection had gone well, after all.

TARGET TOWING OVER TOPSAIL ISLAND — WWII

At the Camp Davis site, there are still in evidence two gigantic airstrips back in the trees. These runways span at least 100 yards wide and eight tenths of a mile long. The airstrips were used for training pilots and ferrying supplies and personnel in and out of Camp Davis. They also trafficked airplanes towing targets for antiaircraft gunnery practice.

Robert Clifton and four other male pilots reported to Camp Davis replacing some old timers who had been out of school up to two years. They went through the gamut starting with the L-4 type planes dubbed "Junior Birdmen." Later, the WASPs would live by the same rules until they had proved proficiency.

Camp Davis was remote, hot, humid, and full of mosquitoes. It was not the most sought out assignment. For Clifton, it was pure luck. He said: *I was 65 miles from home (Faison, NC) and could regularly take a plane home over the weekend. Colonel Stevens brought some men from Mitchell AFB to do some duck hunting at North Topsail. One of my more unusual assignments was to fly an L-4 Cub between RT 17 and the waterway. If there were no ducks near the duck blinds they had set up, I was to go where the ducks were and scare them over the blinds.*

WOMAN AIRFORCE SERVICE PILOTS [WASPs]

The Army Air Forces in 1941 took the first steps toward the use of women pilots. Earlier, American women pilots could only serve as civil flying instructors or as test and ferry pilots for light aircraft manufacturers. The Army Air Forces Ferrying Command asked Miss Jacqueline Cochran to join its staff in order to analyze the problems involved in

WASP Aviatrix

broadening the use of women pilots.

By 1943, The Woman Airforce Service Pilots [WASPs] became a vital part of the WWII antiaircraft training effort here at Camp Davis and Topsail Island. Male pilots viewed the new "darlings of flight," as invading their domain, yet the scarcity of pilots for combat depended on the WASPs to do important non-combat pilot chores. In the past, women had been trained to ferry airplanes from post to post, but had now been reassigned to one of the most crucial assignments in the Air Force.

Thirty top female pilots selected to participate, were in their first briefing July 1943, in Washington, DC. Jacqueline Cochran new Director of Women Pilots, was talking about this top secret mission that would fly planes faster than women had ever piloted.

Jacqueline Cochran hailed from Pensacola, Florida. She learned to fly in 1932, earning her private pilot's license after three weeks training. By 1937, she had flown in a number of international races, set some 18 records, and won the women's division of the Bendix event and third place against a field of men pilots. A year later she won the coast-to-coast dash setting a new women's transcontinental record of 10 hours, 7

121

minutes, 10 seconds. Later she became the first woman to fly a bomber across the Atlantic, to fly a jet across the same ocean, and to break the sound barrier.

General Arnold saw the young attractive women go past his office. *You did say they could fly Major*, he remarked—skeptically. *Towing targets for green air gunners and ground artillery is not the safest flying job around, but it's one of the most war-essential duties. If this experiment works, I'll have more pilots for combat missions.*

With the enlargement of the pilot program to include other operations, an experiment was set up at Camp Davis. Its purpose was to determine capabilities and limitations of women as tow target pilots. It was eventually to release male pilots from all kinds of flying except combat, gunnery, and formation. There were about 100 planes at this field. Pilots had to be proficient in instrument flying, radio, radio telephone, oxygen equipment at high altitude, and first aid. The WASP organization was to be taken into the army as part of the Air Corp and commissioned immediately as Lieutenants. Qualifications were set at age 18 $\frac{1}{2}$ and 35 hours flying time. Average age was 25 years.

WASP training

122

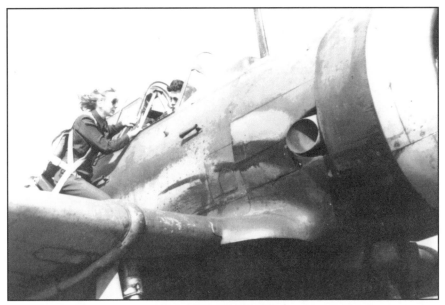

Last minute instruction

Their training kept them flying an average of 15 hours per week, sometimes as much as 25 hours. There was minimal time for recreation. The WASPs moved up to heavier craft with more experience; L-4, L-5, A-24, then B-34 tow target. The tow target was a cloth sleeve about 20 feet long towed behind the ship, on a cable about 2400 feet from target to plane.

For those first 30 or so WASPs, in an army base of 100,000 men, there was much ogling and male attention. On the other hand, some of the male pilots appeared threatened. There were even some claims of sabotage to make the WASPs look bad, but they showed their stuff as aviators. Some men rationalized the situation by claiming that the Air Force could not risk men pilots for target towing, so women pilots were assigned to it. The women, of course claimed that the men didn't have the guts. Since this was a new era for women, they were eager to prove themselves and became willing learners and risk-takers.

For the most part, the women were remembered as pretty aggressive and tough. One recalled, after the funeral of a fellow pilot, that a WASP said: *If anything happens to me, put a fifth of bourbon on the casket and have a party.*

Ruth Florey was a WASP stationed at Camp Davis in 1943. She flew the L-4, L-5, A-24, A-25, and the B-34. She flew strafing, tracking, and tow target. At night, they flew out to sea and came in for radar. She had the tail section of her A-24 shot up on a towing mission. The man in the back reeling target for her yelled over the intercom: *Get the hell out of here.*

Ruth said: *I had a few choice words about what they were using for brains and was heard on the radio. The General agreed with me, but had to ground me a few days. Our Air Force had no Officer's Club at Camp Davis and we were not very welcome at the Antiaircraft Officer's Club, so we would fly to other bases for dinner and dancing. It was all an experience only the young could do.*

The WASPs had to prove their proficiency by doing the same things as the male pilots. They did some night flying with instruments for searchlight training. The lights were so bright the pilot could read a newspaper. The mission was to be a target for searchlights to follow, and sometimes for the 90mm guns to fire at.

Not many people realize it, but from 1942 to 1944 the Army Air Force

Target Towing Pilots

Antiaircraft Searchlight

trained 1,074 WASPs, who earned wings, and were to gain military status. At the same time, the public never knew the WASPs even existed. WASPs were flying every kind of plane the Army Air Forces owned in 1942, 1943, and 1944. They flew 60 million miles in various aircraft, from small primary trainers up to the B-29 Super Fortress.

Women who fly have had a long tradition. In 1929, the Ninety-Nines became a female flying organization with 99 licensed pilots as charter members. Amelia Earhart was the first president. Sixty-five years later, the 99s still flourish with some 6,400 members internationally. The central mission of the 99s is to combat the entrenched prejudices that still confront each female who wants to fly. These pioneers have worn such labels as "Sweethearts of the Air," "Flying Flappers," "Petticoat Pilots," participating in events like "Powder Puff Derbies."

When asked why they had gotten hooked on flying, most have said "freedom." Aviatrix Amelia Earhart turned down marriage proposals a half dozen times but when she finally accepted, she wrote this touching letter to her future husband:

> You must know again my reluctance to marry, my feeling that I shatter thereby chances in work which means so much to me... Please let us not interfere with the other's work or play, nor let the world see our private joys or disagreements. In this connection I may have to keep some place where I can go to be myself now and then, for I cannot guarantee to endure at all times the confinement of even an attractive cage... I must exact a cruel promise, and that is you will let me go in a year if we find no happiness together...

SPORTS AND RECREATION

Athletics play an important part in the morale program. Among the selectees in training were former football, basketball, baseball, and boxing stars. An athletic officer was in charge of arranging sports events.

One of the first sports to receive attention was boxing, and some of the finest amateur boxers in the country participated in weekly shows. With the ocean so near, it was a simple matter for the men to enjoy surf bathing. Motor convoys took hundreds of soldiers to the beaches each weekend during the summer months. Indoor sports events were staged in the field house.

Camp Davis

JOE LOUIS HERE

Camp Davis, *AA Barrage News*, Jan. 22, 1944

Boxing, always a strong attraction for antiaircraft soldiers stationed here, broke all existing attendance records Wednesday night. Fully 5,000 Farnsworth Hall fans jammed every bleacher and ringside seat. They occupied all available floor space, and actually clutched overhanging rafters to witness an all-star ring show brought to them by world's heavyweight champion Sgt. Joe Louis and his cross-country exhibition company. Sears Landing, with all due apologies, gained a worthy rival, in this night firing session at Farnsworth Hall. Except that leather-throwing supplanted steel for the occasion.

Martha E. Vann recalls:

During WWII, the big GI bus was an important part of the home front scene. Each of the olive drab cumbersome vehicles seemed to have a personality of its own, and its moods no doubt were influenced by the type of transportation it provided.

I recall particularly the GI busses that ran between Wilmington and Camp Davis during those busy years of the early 40s. With gasoline rationed and use of passenger cars cut drastically, many of the military personnel and civilian employees who lived in Wilmington depended on GI bus transportation.

USO junior hostesses were bussed from Wilmington, Camp Davis, Camp Lejeune, and Bluethenthal Field during the war years. Many a romance blossomed at bus-side late in the evening after a Service Club dance. The hostesses would bid goodnight to their heroes after plans had been made for future dates; then they would board the bus and gaily sing their way back into town. The wheels of the bus seemed to roll in happy harmony with the feminine chorus of wartime songs such as "I've Got Sixpence," "Lily Marlene," and "Goodnight, Sweetheart."

AA GUNS CEASE FIRE AT DAVIS - TRAINING CENTER CLOSES SEPT. 30

Camp Davis, *AA Barrage News*, Sept. 2, 1944

The deafening roar of the nineties—the sharp, staccato bark of the fifties will be heard no more at Camp Davis after September 30 when the Antiaircraft Artillery Training Center complies with orders received from the War Department to suspend operations. Thus will end a great chapter in the training of thousands of antiaircraft artillery troops for overseas action.

Gen. Schuyler in announcing the cessation of AAATC operations declared the troops from Camp Davis "marked a definite chapter in US antiaircraft history. This was our army's first AA Training Center. Here it was that modern AA training methods and procedures were first conceived and successfully applied then later adopted by other training establishments throughout the country."

CAMP DAVIS AS MISSILE TEST BASE

Naval Ordnance Test Facility—June 1, 1946—January, 1948

A construction project in which resourceful salvage overcame shortages of materials completed recently at Camp Davis, Holly Ridge, NC. The Navy's Bureau of Yards and Docks for the Navy's Bureau of Ordnance was in charge. The two-phase contract called for the construction of the East Coast Test Range along the Atlantic Ocean Beach, near Camp Davis, and construction of housing facilities in the camp itself. Salvage work was accomplished at both locations.

Camp Davis, a former training base for army, and later, marine personnel, was chosen as the site because of the availability of facilities. These facilities could be converted easily and they found the nature of the range useful. It was also accessible to APL and the Bureau of Ordnance. The only new construction has been that required to house the instruments for the testing program.

Hospital quarters are being converted into family apartments and existing dormitory facilities will be utilized for housing civilian and military personnel. Surplus government-owned materials from other war activities are being used widely in conversion work. Barracks which will not be needed have been turned over to the Federal Housing Administration.

Kellex is currently employing 400 men and women in construction and operation activities.

LOCAL RECOLLECTIONS

Herman G. Alberti, mayor and former Holly Ridge postmaster for 25 years, said that German prisoners were housed at the rear of the camp, which stretched two miles of both sides of town. Alberti's girlfriend, Loney, who later became his wife, worked as a telephone operator next door to the post office.

Mrs. Alberti said: *Local families benefited from the construction by crowding together in their homes to make room for boarders. Bulldozers and construction work almost turned the town into a mammoth pig pen. The camp was so wet and muddy that soldiers would carry the women workers in their arms to the buildings where they were employed.*

The town's concentration of men and money drew bootleggers and prostitutes, according to reports. In *A New Geography*, Sharpe said a construction worker was shot in the Bucket of Blood Cafe one night, staggered to Mayor L.E. Colburn's house and died in his yard.

"Business was so good that merchants were forced to lock their

People's Cafe

doors and allow only a few customers in at a time because of the lack of space. A crate of eggs in a cafe might last 30 minutes," Sharpe wrote.

Charles Jones and Stanley E. Smith, Sr. recall:

Our Dad, Pop Jones, owned and ran the People's Cafe. It started as a small hardware that sold carpenter tools to workers looking for a carpentry job as Camp Davis was being built. They were hurting for carpenters and all you had to have was a hammer, square and saw to get a job. Later, according to need, he changed it to a cafe restaurant. Food became hard to get so he then changed it to a beer joint. He had three young girls working there. All the shops and joints tried to have good-looking young girls to attract GIs to their place.

We were about 11-13 years old at the time and worked in the joint selling beer. We sold more beer in those years than one could drink in a lifetime, often 100 cases a night. Warren Campbell owned and ran the barbershop. He would often stay open till 11:00 at night and we would carry beer over to those waiting.

MPs would hang out at Dad's place. As kids we were king. We were accepted and allowed almost anywhere without a pass. We could play at Farnsworth Hall and buy candy at the Service Club. Candy was hard to come by in those days. We could buy big Hershey bars for 10 cents.

As kids, we used to play with wooden ammunition boxes using them as forts. Sometimes we could find shells, even grenades, in the boxes. A wonder that someone wasn't hurt.

C. C. Hines was postmaster. He also ran a gas station. A fellow had raffle tickets he traded for gas. Later, the ticket won and the car was delivered to the gas station. Hines wanted the car out of there and eventually called the police to have them tow it away. Their investigation found it belonged to Hines, to his surprise.

Topsail became more accessible when Route 50 was paved. It was known formerly as an old dirt road through Swamp Hollow back of Camp Davis. Story has it that mosquitoes at Swamp Hollow were so bad that they would say: "Shall we eat him here or take him back with us? No, the big ones might take him away from us."

During the old "cost plus 10 percent profit" construction days at Camp Davis, when some got greedy, there were reports of kegs of nails buried. I even heard of a reported case of a bulldozer digging its own grave and being subsequently buried.

At the oak tree (corner of Hester & Sound Roads), they would bring in boiled shrimp from Tar Landing and sell them for 15 cents a quart. GIs would bring them into the cafe to eat with beer. They would also sell oysters, watermelon, and such at the tree. (It is still there today.) The "in" thing to do was to go to Tar Landing and eat oysters. You could have all you could eat for $2.00. A 50 cent tip would please the women opening oysters.

The Main Gate shack at Camp Davis (near the current stoplight) had a high ledge where confiscated bottles of booze were collected. If the GI denied having a bottle, the common practice of holding one in his sock was thwarted by breaking it with a night stick to the leg.

At Holly Ridge city limits, left of the 27th Street Gate, and across the street, was Sloppy Joes, run by Joe Popkins. The Pines was a joint north on Route 17. They had slot machines and were closed down several times because of prostitution. Ruined by its reputation, it later burned. No subsequent business has been able to survive.

John D. Larkins ran the Carolina Inn. He was a self-styled pool shark and claimed he could take anybody until Wimpy Lassiter took him. He was good, but Wimpy—of international billiard fame—put him in his place.

Ringling Brothers Barnum and Bailey Circus came on the train and off-loaded at the railroad station. Betty Grable came to entertain at Farnsworth Hall. Kay Kiser came too, with his famous "Ischabibble" who always had outrageous jokes.

At the end of Camp Davis' time, an enterprise came in and built the Paradise Night Club. Opening night, they had local politicians, and Betty McGuire and her all-girl orchestra with sound systems, baby grand piano, and all. About a week or two after opening, it flopped and later became a movie house. The last movie I recall was "Alexander's Ragtime Band," with Don Amechi and Alice Faye.

Camp Davis Restaurant circa 1990

In late 1944, as Camp Davis was phasing out, Pop Jones and Pop Halpin (from AA Barrage) were pictured at the old Oak Tree. They were looking down on a mock grave with broken bottles and a sign, "Here Lies Boomtown."

Darrel and Mary Ottaway have lived in Holly Ridge all their lives, following other generations. When Camp Davis was built, Darrel was 13 years old. Darrel's father helped some of the construction crews. Later he was a civilian worker, working in the boiler rooms firing boilers. Darrel's father bought a small country store on Highway 17, just as ration stamps became the standard.

Darrel remembered: *Every member of a family got a certain amount of stamps. I remember that the red stamps were for meat. Grocery stores, laundromats, and all other businesses came about. They did not have grocery stores before the war. Almost everything we ate we grew on our farms.*

During the war everything was rationed. You had food stamps, specially for canned goods, canned meats, and gasoline—all the hard-to-get items. We used the stamps in our store. They also had stamps for sugar and for shoes, too. Clothing during this period was not rationed unless it was made of leather. All leather goods were in short supply and carefully rationed.

People moved in to capitalize on the economic benefits of Camp Davis,

132

then moved on when the military left. The natives mainly wanted to survive through it and more or less keep the same old pace going.

During the period of 1940 through 1944, Holly Ridge went through many alterations. In 1940 the area went from about 30 people to about 100,000 soldiers and civilians— it really had to change.

The community of Holly Ridge kept its name during and after the war. Holly Ridge was so-named because local people would gather holly from the woods and ship it up north by train, thus "Holly Ridge."

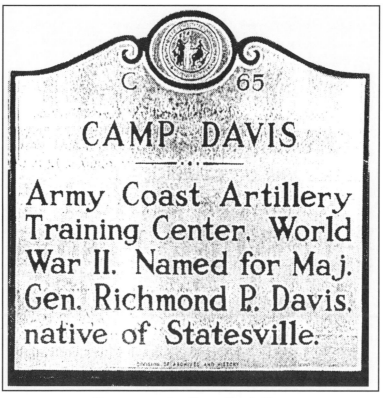

C 65

CAMP DAVIS

Army Coast Artillery Training Center, World War II. Named for Maj. Gen. Richmond P. Davis, native of Statesville.

DIVISION OF ARCHIVES AND HISTORY

Commemorative Camp Davis Sign

Holly Ridge as a whole did not seem to mind the invasion of Camp Davis. The soldiers were friendly. We liked it, because it was exciting, said Darrel. *And in the process, Holly Ridge families were not forgotten. One time they invited the entire little community to come eat. After the troops were fed, we walked through the chow line. I thought those pinto beans were something else! Being kids, the PX would sell us candy. There was a shortage of candy everywhere else. Otherwise, civilians could not shop on the base.*

Mary remembered: *It was a little scary when we saw soldiers crawling on the ground in the woods in back of their house where they trained. Everyday life changed very little for the area farmers as life during a war does not just stand still. Dirigibles would be floating over us as we worked in the fields. I was scared they were going to pop and fall.* The dirigible transported many different items for training, such as explosives.

When Camp Davis moved in, local families were not moved out. The small train depot was moved and a larger one was built. Most of the building materials came in by rail.

When the military abandoned Camp Davis, most leased property was returned to original owners. Buildings were auctioned and salvage companies purchased many of the buildings. Some of the two story barracks sold for about $60. The salvage companies would chop them up and ship them all over the country. Sometimes they would get seven houses out of one building.

A few WWII structures are still in use today. The old fire station and a few barracks are now apartments. A bacon plant was built around the Camp Davis cold storage plant. The largest building still in use is the warehouse used by the Holly Ridge Builder Supply. The Camp Davis Restaurant is a building that was once part of the administration building. At the front entrance are two brick columns that once stood at the main entrance of Camp Davis on Highway 50. The restaurant has welcomed people who served at Camp Davis with many artifacts and pictures. Former soldiers are pleased when they can find pictures and old newspaper clippings about Camp Davis. They hosted at least five reunions there. Holly Ridge hosted a three-day 50th Anniversary celebration April 27, 1990. Troops, bands and many former Camp Davis GIs attended. North Carolina Department of Cultural Resources presented a Commemorative Camp Davis sign.

References:

A History of Camp Davis. David A. Stallman, 1990.

Public Relations Office; H.Q. Camp Davis, 6 October 1943.

Letter-Ruth Flore-January 19, 1991. Compliments of R. V. Richards [TBOLT].

New York Times Magazine. May 7, 1995.

Silver Wings Santiago Blue. Janet Dailey, 1984.

Interview, Robert Clifton. 1993.

Interview, Richard Sidbury. 1992.

Defense Environmental Restoration Project Real Estate Information For Camp Davis Military Reservation, NC. March 27, 1989 (includes War Dept. Corp of Engineers drawing dated December 21, 1943).

Camp Davis Book - Officer Candidate School. Courtesy of Herman Alberti, 1942.

The State Vol. VIII No. 53. May 31, 1941.

The Wilmington News. Excerpts Courtesy New Hanover County Public Library.

The AA Barrage - *Camp Davis Military News.* Excerpts Courtesy Glen Ottaway.

Camp Davis Project - US Dept. of Navy Press Release. May 14, 1947.

The News - Applied Physics Laboratory. March 1947, Johns Hopkins University.

Historical Tour - Topsail Beach. October 10, 1989.

Military Announcement to All Hands. US Dept. of Navy, January, 1948.

Coastal Courier Vol. 4 No. 37 dated September 21, 1943.

Wilmington Star News. July 15, 1984.

Men Didn't Have to Prove They Could Fly, But Women Did. Smithsonian Magazine. August, 1994. David Roberts.

OPERATION BUMBLEBEE
1946 - 1948

"That's it! It will be 'OPERATION BUMBLEBEE'." Merle Tuve had just spotted this aphorism hanging on the office wall of Capt. Carroll L. Tyler:

> **THE BUMBLEBEE CANNOT FLY**
> According to recognized
> aerotechnical tests, the
> bumblebee cannot fly
> because of the shape and
> weight of his body in
> relation to the total wing area.
> **BUT, the bumblebee
> doesn't know this, so he
> goes ahead and flies anyway.**

Well aware that this new undertaking to develop a supersonic guided missile for the Navy would face impossible challenges, Dr. Merle Tuve named the project "Bumblebee."

RAMJET ENGINE

"The Ramjet is the basis for all our jet aircraft. If you consider our dependency on jet transportation, Topsail Island's contribution to today's technology and ability to travel globally is significant."

[Lt. Commander Tad Stanwick]

The Ramjet engine was proved here on Topsail Island. This development is as significant to jet travel as the first-flight, venerated at Kitty

Hawk, is to propeller flight.

GUIDED MISSILES

"Another triumph was the successful missile-borne radar beam riding tests. This was an early proving of feasibility of control and guiding of missile flight."

[Lt. Commander Tad Stanwick]

"This project gave the Navy enough knowledge and know-how to put the Terrier, Tartar, and Talos missile systems aboard US Warships with the capability of destroying enemy airplanes at a range far beyond that of naval guns."

[Lt. Bruce L. Goodwin]

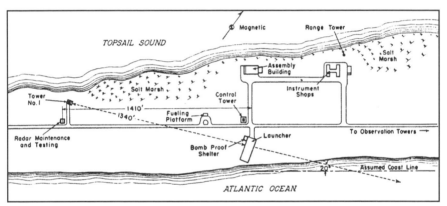

Map of Topsail Island - Missile Launch Site

The concrete structures in our midst have stood the test of time and ravages of storms. They have fueled the imagination of Topsail people and, over time, some of the secrets were revealed, but they were still shrouded in mystery. Discovery of declassified military documents and pictures in the Johns Hopkins University Applied Physics Laboratory (JHU/APL) Archives finally gave us military proof of Topsail Island's missile heritage.

The Topsail Island Historical Society was determined to preserve these historical structures. They applied for historic recognition, and though that designation is generally reserved for older structures, the Assembly

Aerial oblique of Firing Point

Building was acknowledged as the only remaining intact structure of its kind. In 1993, the Topsail Island Historical Society received recogni-

View of Firing Point

tion for the Assembly Building, Control Tower, and Tower Number 2 (Queen's Grant) as a group, in the National Register of Historic Places. Tower Number 2 was included as it most accurately represents a tower in its original state.

The Topsail Beach Economic Development Council officially signed the purchase agreements in 1994 for the Assembly Building. It is their aim to restore the building as a historical site and provide Topsail Island with a community center that can serve many purposes.

This historical recall includes personal accounts, official Navy and JHU / APL descriptions of the project and actual pictures. Every attempt was made to ensure accuracy of the information. It is hoped that the reader will find this as exciting as I did in the discovery.

The personal accounts by Tad Stanwick, Bruce Goodwin, Jim Heathcott, Harold Dail, and Bill McKinsey were invaluable, and I thank them.

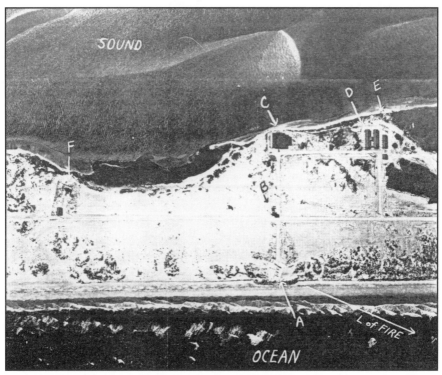

Aerial photo of Firing Point

Philip K. Albert, Sr. of JHU/APL Archives was instrumental in the breakthrough discovery of pictures and documents, and I owe him sincere thanks. Other Navy and National Archivists also provided information and direction to sources.

ROCKET PROGRAM - BIRTH TO DEATH

On the heels of WWII, Topsail Island (known as the sand spit) was seized by the US Government for use as a secret missile test site. Johns Hopkins Applied Physics Lab (JHU/APL) was committed to the long-range role of defense support for the Navy. Their aim was to develop a supersonic missile that could swiftly reach out ten or twenty miles to hit and destroy an air threat. They needed more range than possible at former sites in New Jersey and Delaware.

The project was one of the earliest developments of the nation's missile program. It was managed by the Navy Bureau of Ordnance and guided by the Johns Hopkins University Applied Physics Laboratory. Topsail Island was ideal for such a secret project because of the few residents and limited access via a pontoon bridge.

An existing Camp Davis at Holly Ridge was reworked as a base for 500 personnel. Water and electricity were "piped in" from Camp Davis. Eight observation towers were built along what they called this "sand spit" to house timing instruments and cameras to record performance data. All stops were pulled out and the range, incredibly, was built in one year. This missile test range was to be a permanent installation and claimed to be one of the best equipped fields in the country.

The Assembly Building was a hardened structure constructed for assembly of the rockets. It was carefully designed with copper grounding and lightning rods at corners of the building to prevent explosion. Some 200 experimental rockets, three to thirteen inches in diameter and ranging from three to thirteen feet in length, were fired in the 1946-1948 period and were dubbed "Flying Stovepipe." It was here through these tests, the ramjet engine proved to be a success. Modern jet aircraft have built upon this original design.

In 1948 it was decided that more range was needed and the weather was not stable enough for the precise instrumentation required. The program was transferred to test sites at Inyokern, White Sands, and Cape Canaveral. The land and buildings were turned over to the land owners and salvageable equipment to local town and county governments.

MISSILE SITE

The missile site was principally made up of an Assembly Building, Control Tower, Launching Platform, Bombproof Room, and eight Photographic Towers. They are all basically intact except for several of the Photographic Towers.

There were also other support type buildings such as Mess Hall, Sleeping Quarters, and Repair Shop which were located at the present Breezeway Motel site.

Assembly Building circa 1990

ASSEMBLY BUILDING: This building was used for missile storage and assembly. It is a hardened structure with reinforced walls, built on four feet of concrete secured by 20 foot pilings. Ground-straps on doors were to minimize risk of spark and explosion. It also had a lightning rod at each corner of the building for protection, of which three remain. (See architectural drawings in Appendix.)

Control Tower

FIRING POINT CONTROL TOWER: The Control Tower sits on a line between the Assembly Building and the Launching Platform. Originally the tower had a control and observation deck from which the launchings were controlled. There was two-way communication between the control tower and the Photographic Towers.

LAUNCHING PLATFORM: The platform was a 75 x 100 x 1 foot concrete slab and now serves as part of the Jolly Roger Motel patio.

BOMBPROOF ROOM: The bombproof room was built of 14 inch reinforced concrete walls with a four inch by three foot window slit for rocket scientists and technicians to observe rocket firings up close. Access to the room was through a heavy steel sliding door at the street side. It now is in use as part of the Jolly Roger Motel basement.

PHOTOGRAPHIC TOWERS: The towers were precisely located with distances scientifically derived. They were rigidly constructed of reinforced concrete and built on pilings driven to a minimum of 20 feet and 15 tons bearing. To preclude distortion of tower frameworks due to temperature changes, the sides of the towers were protected with plywood shields. Triangulation of photo equipment from the towers would record the flights over 10-20 miles at speeds of 1,500 mph, so accuracy of the data was paramount.

PERSONAL ACCOUNTS

MR. IRVINE B. IRVING

In a *Fayetteville Times* interview, 1978, Mr. Irvine B. Irving, staff member of Johns Hopkins Laboratory recalled: *We first went down to Topsail in the summer of 1945 to look around and survey the site. At the time, APL was a prime contractor with the navy in the development of a ramjet propulsion system for supersonic missiles. We moved on the island in March 1946, and lived in the old army barracks while the firing and tracking systems were being constructed. As I remember the Kellex Corporation and several other contractors were involved and navy and civilian personnel numbered as high as 200 at times. The first test missiles were launched around October or November 1946, and from then until the project was moved west in early 1948, we fired some 200 experimental rockets.*

Missiles ranged in size from three to 13 inches in diameter and from three to 13 feet in length, and were fired along a range that ran some 20 miles in a northeastward direction.

According to Irving, the testing program produced vital information on guidance systems, aerodynamics, solid propellants, booster configurations, and similar scientific data, all extremely important to the still fledgling missile project.

Off-shore Range Patrol Boat

Everything went smoothly, he said. *There were a few storms, but no serious accidents, and our work resulted in development of the Terrier and the Talos which were the first supersonic missiles utilized by the Navy.*

Nicknamed the "flying stovepipe," the six inch diameter ramjet was fashioned from the tailpipe of a Navy Thunderbolt airplane. It was powered by a mixture of propylene oxide and the oxygen of the atmosphere scooped into the front end of the open pipe, compressed in the chamber by the speed of the vehicle, and ignited.

Much of this experimental development occurred on Topsail in 1946-47 as the Navy refined its "flying stovepipe," and kept well ahead of the Army which did not successfully test fire a similar missile (Corporal E) until May 1947.

TAD STANWICK
LT. COMMANDER

Mr. Stanwick owns a house on Topsail Island. He was at the forefront of Operation Bumblebee and remained the naval officer in charge for the duration of the project. He shares his perspective and recollections.

First they sent two carloads of Navy and Johns Hopkins officials down to approve the site. March 10, 1942 was the date of establishment of the contract between the University and the Office of Scientific Research and Development. Lt. Commander Tad Stanwick, Officer In Charge of Naval Ordnance Development Unit, APL/JHU, was placed in charge at Camp Davis. Stanwick was to work with APL for five years.

Tad Stanwick, Lt. Commander

The Bureau of Ordnance had the facility built, and was remarkably able to put such priority and resources on the project to complete the facilities in about one year. (According to documented building schedules, the towers and Assembly Building were on a three month building plan.) They brought in water and electricity from Camp Davis. Stanwick had towers and roads built and obtained fire trucks, etc. He said: *The towers were precisely located at documented longitude and latitudes with distance between towers scientifically derived. Photo theodolite cameras which would do telemetering of rocket firings were installed. Data accuracy was paramount to the success of the project.*

The pontoon bridge had to be rebuilt. The original one was an atrocity on which you could load one or two trucks, turn winches on until it arrived across the channel, and drive off. The Corps of Engineers built a more permanent bridge.

Some 580 APL, Navy, and Marine people were assigned to the

Tower Tracking Camera

Inland Waterway Patrol Boat

"Bumblebee" project. Navy radar technicians and scientists were all under Stanwick's security responsibility. *We had two patrol boats operating in the sound and a 65 footer in the ocean based at New River Inlet. Their prime responsibility was to monitor fishing boats. They would let fishing boats work, but would warn them of firings. Of course, suspicious activity considered a threat to project security would be reckoned with too.*

The sand spit (Topsail Island) site was fully intended to be a permanent installation. The government had obtained 99 year leases where needed and seized the land. The project moved from Fort Myers, Delaware, because of the need for more space. Stanwick said: *The mission was to get the ramjet up to supersonic speeds and demonstrate that it developed thrust. Booster development was being proven here and the island's long shore line provided 26 miles for the range. The ramjet engine was proved practical here. Up to then, the ramjet would light and burn but they couldn't prove the theory. With their instrumentation they proved the ramjet could develop and maintain thrust.*

The ramjet is the basis for all our supersonic jet aircraft. If you consider our dependency on jet transportation, Topsail Island's contribution to today's technology and ability to travel globally is significant.

Another triumph was the successful missile-borne radar beam-riding tests. This was an early proving of feasibility of control and guiding of missile flight.

Stanwick continued: *The Research and Development was done in Silver Spring, MD. APL would test components. Solid rockets as boosters came from Cumberland, MD. All parts were shipped here, assemble, and fired. There were*

Fueling ramjet rocket

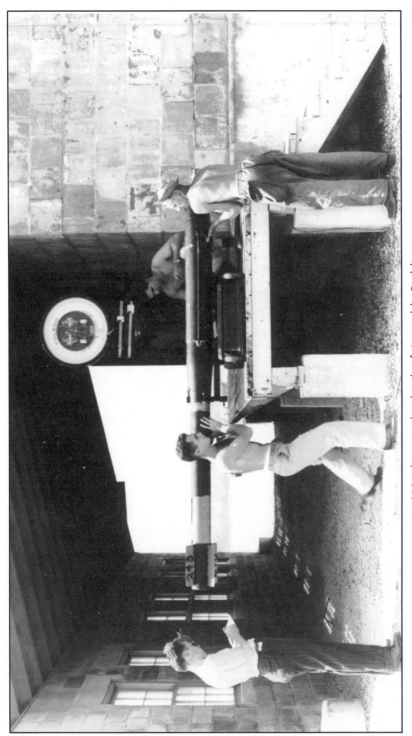

Weighing rocket back of Assembly Building

two stage rockets. Solid rockets would boost it off the launch platform and the ramjet would take off away from it at supersonic speed. It is hard to estimate the number of firings. It would take about two to three days to get one rocket ready for firing and dummies were fired to test equipment.

Scientists proved to be difficult at times. They liked to get in there and play with it, tweak, or try different things. Just wouldn't let it go. They did accomplish much however. One interesting fact is that early on in dealing with electronic suppliers such as Capehard Farnsworth measurement standards became a problem. They were working with beam-riding missile receivers for the missiles and all had to work to precise measurements. Tad Stanwick established the microsecond measurement standard in support of the technical work. *The electronic technology has just exploded since then. You simply can't keep up with it.*

Ramjet Two Stage Launcher

It was pretty desolate at that time, particularly at the north end. Commander Stanwick said: *I would often take an inspection trip in a jeep from the north end to the south end of the island. It was deserted at the north end—scary—not a soul there. With the secret equipment used on this project nobody was allowed on the island without special security.*

Rocket and launchers

Launchers at launch pad

A lot of resources had gone into making this a permanent installation. It was discovered that the weather was not conducive to good instrumentation and the range length was proving inadequate. There were other areas available that would prove to be better suited. Stewart, Florida (Cape Canaveral/Kennedy), Inyokern, California, and White Sands, New Mexico, all got pieces of the project when it was dismantled.

The site facilities were left intact and turned over to the navy yards and docks to dispose of by selling or giving to bona fide town, county, or state government agencies. The only thing sold was piping and supplies. All else, such as electricity and water systems went to the respective towns/counties. Stanwick said: *Mayor Elvie White of Wilmington begged them not to remove the facilities. Many people wanted to dig up pipe for salvage. A lot of stuff went to the City of Wilmington, fire trucks went to Holly Ridge and Hampstead, bulldozers and road scrapers went to state roads people.*

MR. BRUCE GOODWIN - LT. KELLEX GUARD

Mr. Bruce Goodwin, a retired Lieutenant of the Kellex Guard Force shared his recollections: *The first time I visited Camp Davis was in April 1946. The firing point, concrete towers, and assembly building were under construction. A year later, I was employed by Kellex as Lieutenant in their guard force. The missile range was already in operation.*

Kellex was the prime contractor and was responsible for construction work and for overall security. They even had two patrol boats operating in the sound and a 65 footer in the ocean to monitor fishing boats and keep the project secure from access by water.

Crates of missile parts shipped from the JHU/APL location at Silver Springs, MD by railroad under guard. Kellex Corp. would dispatch technical and guard personnel to transport the missile parts form Wilmington to Topsail. The concrete towers had two-way communication with the control tower at the firing point. Their job was to photograph the missile as it roared down-range and check it out by telemetry. The firing point control tower was located between the assembly building and the launching platform. It had a control and

Bruce Goodwin, Lt. Guard Force

observation deck on top from which the launchings were controlled.

On a firing day, the solid propellant powder was loaded into the missile. It was trundled to the launching platform on a rubber-tired dolly to minimize risk of explosion. The launches were ramps made of wood and a steel half-casing about 15 feet long set up at an angle. Once the missile was in the launcher, it would go through a series of checkouts. If the checkout was not successful, the missile would be carefully returned to the assembly building for the night and extra security precautions were in effect. Sometimes it took several days to launch one.

The first stage solid fuel rockets would boost the rocket off the launch platform and the ramjet would take off away from it at supersonic speed. These launches were scary affairs. Being this new, we weren't sure what would happen sometimes. Rockets went awry and did crazy things at times, so safety was paramount.

Rocket at Assembly Building (above)
Rocket Launcher (below)

Once Bruce was in charge of security near launch control tower. As he took up his post, the range officer bellowed at him through a bullhorn to move out of the area. He was chagrined that he was treated in such an undignified way, after all, this was his post. As he vacated post, a maverick rocket crashed and exploded right where he had been standing. The safest place to observe from was the bombproof room. He said: *Accidents were few, though, considering the high explosives used. I guess we were cautious because we were scared of it.*

It should be pointed out that this project gave the Navy enough knowledge and know-how to put the Terrier, Tartar, and Talos missile systems aboard US warships with the capability of destroying enemy airplanes at a range far beyond that of naval guns.

Rocket at final checkout

Blast-off

Bill McKenzie—Harold Dail—Jim Heathcott

JIM HEATHCOTT - HAROLD DAIL - BILL McKINSEY

In 1994, I had the rare opportunity to talk with three men who were technical personnel working on the Operation Bumblebee project in 1947. Jim Heathcott of Gainsville, Florida, is an outgoing person with a reputation for doing some unusual things. *We were "jack-of-all-trades" on this project. Each of us had technical jobs to do but we often found ourselves doing other supportive things because there was no one else to do them. I maintained cameras in the towers that tracked the rockets from blast-off to splashdown. Blast-offs were a thrill. I saw that rocket in the museum that was found on the beach. There should be more out there because several rockets broke up at launch.*

Many people ask about the secret tunnel. He said: *I have had so many ask about that. There is a true story I would like to tell. The "secret tunnel" was a steel conduit about 10 inches in diameter that ran from the control tower to the launch ramp. This conduit was crammed full of control cables. I happen to know this because an engineer was in serious trouble in that he needed to thread a new cable through that conduit. I proposed an unorthodox method of a #3 tomato can with a fishing line knotted to it. They then blew that can and line through the "tunnel" with compressed air and it emerged at the launch ramp end, making me a hero. That is the story of the secret tunnel. You heard it first, from me.*

Harold Dail hails from Kinston, NC. He worked at Island Beach on this project before coming to Topsail. The firing range was limited there and his manager was looking all over the US for a better test site. Harold said: *You should look at Camp Davis. The NC coastline dips inland making it somewhat protected and I believe we would have the space the project needs. They looked at it and moved the project here. My job was to track the firings with cameras at #1 station behind the launching ramp. We measured elevation, speed, and distances. This data collection was a first for this type of project. The towers were built to stay. The Assembly Building has a three foot deep concrete floor. What makes it unique are the copper grids imbedded in the*

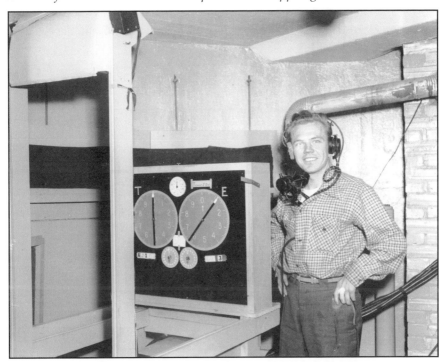

Bombproof Room at Launch Pad - Harold Dail

floor to prevent spark and explosion. We had to wear special shoes around the explosives. I remember one launching where we fired a small rocket using five five inch booster rockets to get it started. We fired it at 70 degrees, almost vertical. It took off so fast we lost it and never saw it splash down.

Our wives stayed at apartments in Camp Davis. They went to Wilmington to buy groceries and other supplies. There was a small grocery store in Holly Ridge but it did not go much beyond basics of bread and milk.

When Bill McKinsie came in from Texas to be part of the team, he started a long career in rocketry. Even after the project moved, he stayed with it for many years. He followed this early experimental work to Inyokern, then through successive years to more sophisticated launchers and guidance systems. Bill recalls: *I was originally from Nashville, Tennessee. My job was to operate radar tracking and guidance equipment. We were launching two types of rockets; the flying stovepipe, with a ramjet engine, and a solid rocket with early guidance systems. We would track the rocket at launch, then try to get the guidance system to respond. These beam-riding missiles were not very reliable. They were the predecessor to the beam-riders in the Gulf War that were accurate enough to shoot down other missiles. Early development happened here.*

Pontoon Bridge—Sears Landing

DOCUMENTS

I. Navy Survey Report - April 26, 1946

PONTOON BRIDGE

The Sears Landing bridge was critical to the functioning of this project. While it served a purpose of security by making access difficult, it was woefully inadequate for Bumblebee. The following is from Navy report enitled, "Survey of Camp Davis, NC for use as an East Coast Guided Missile Site."

> Existing 90 foot barge, equipped with winch and cable arrange-
> ment for opening-closing and approach lift will be abandoned,
> since this portion of the bridge is in very poor condition.
>
> A new barge, operating on the present fixed pivot swing principle,
> is to be constructed of 54 units of the navy's five by seven foot
> pontoon barge equipment. Swinging power will be provided by
> a navy "Sea Mule" outboard power unit with another as standby.
> Barge approach runs are to be counterbalanced, elevated, and low-
> ered, manually. Present cables strung across the channel, which
> must be dropped to clear all waterway traffic will be eliminated.
> The repaired bridge will be maintained in closed position.

[This bridge remained in use until 1955 when the swing bridge was opened.]

II. Navy Department Bureau of Ordnance - May 3, 1946

In a Navy Department Bureau of Ordnance document, the proposed Camp Davis, NC East Coast Guided Missiles Test Range (Project No. Ord 659) was described.

> The Secretary of the Navy approved retention of leases on the
> Camp Davis, North Carolina site for this bureau's use in connec-
> tion with the development of guided missiles.

Initial experimental instrumentation of prototype work was first flight tested at Island Beach, New Jersey, and is continuing on an interim basis at Fort Miles, Delaware. This bureau was first advised of the impending need for an east coast guided missile test range on 8 October 1945 by the Applied Physics Laboratory, Johns Hopkins University. An intensive investigation of all available government or civilian facilities on this coast was made, the result of this survey being the selection of Camp Davis, North Carolina, as the only site with potentially adequate facilities.

For proper functioning of the subject contractor-operated establishment, it will be necessary to furnish complete range instrumentation, together with modification of existing facilities and installations at Camp Davis. This will include provision for housing and subsisting 250 personnel. It is estimated that the following breakdown of the proposed installation will fulfill existing requirements for operation of the east coast guided missiles test range. The following descriptions were among the requirements:

- Explosion proof assembly shop. 60' x 80' explosion proof building with reinforced concrete deck supported on piles. Walls of building for 5' of height to be of reinforced concrete. Next 10' of height, walls to be of concrete block. Steel beam truss supported roof made of corrugated transite. Monorail and chain hoist to run 80' length of building. There is to be a 25' section partitioned off at one end as explosion proof room. Building to be air conditioned and heat controlled for 70 degrees constant temperature. Four steel doors, 2 double, 2 single. All electrical fixtures explosion proof. A 10' platform is to be along one 60' side and one 80' side of building, outside, with a 20' wide shed overhead.

- One bomb-proof shelter 10' x 10' x 10' reinforced concrete 1 ' thick by launching ramp.

- Nine stable platform foundations for instrument mountings. Pile formation supporting a 30 ft. square platform of reinforced concrete beams with reinforced concrete between the beams. On top of this platform, a 15 ft. square structure, 35 ft. high of reinforced concrete beams with concrete blocks between beams. There are to be a total of four decks for placement of instruments; 10 ft. between all decks. Top deck to be open, with 5 ft. high rail of concrete blocks, surrounding.

- One stable platform foundation for mounting launching ramp. A reinforced concrete platform 300' x 50' x (approx) 1 '.

Warehouse Building—Surf City

III. Navy Press Release - January 1948

NAVAL ORDNANCE TEST FACILITY

A construction project in which resourceful salvage measures overcame extreme shortages of materials was finished recently at Camp Davis, Holly Ridge, NC by the Navy's Bureau of Yards and Dock for the Navy's Bureau of Ordnance.

The two-phase contract called for the construction of the east coast test range along the Atlantic Ocean beach, near Camp Davis, and construction of housing facilities in the camp itself. Salvage work was accomplished at both locations.

Camp Davis was originally constructed by the US Army, starting in 1940 and reached an eventual capacity of approximately 70,000. After the war the army turned the camp over to the US Marine Corps, which used the camp for training and also for several months as a separation center. The Navy assumed possession 1 June 1946. Since the present Navy plans call for a complement of four to five hundred persons, only a small portion of the central area of the camp will be used. Outside the central area, some 700 camp buildings of army standard design "semi-permanent" frame construction, have been declared surplus. These have been transferred to the FPHA which has dismantled many of the former barracks and mess halls and shipped them to the Cleveland and Washington areas for re-erection and conversion to GI housing at college campuses.

Among the structures being continued in use by the Navy are: Administration Building, Central Steam Plant, Telephone Exchange, Family Quarters, Community Center (former Officers' Club), Gymnasium, Bachelor Officers' Quarters, Barracks and Mess for enlisted personnel, Dispensary, Hospital Wards which have been converted into Residential Apartments, and Guest House and various Shops and Warehouses.

The range facilities were constructed on a sand-spit beach along the Atlantic Ocean, approximately 20 miles long and a quarter to half mile in width, and located five miles from the main camp. The range facilities comprise a Launching Platform, located at the south end of the beach with adjacent shops and services, and eight observation towers dispersed along the length of the beach.

Communications for the range required the construction of 10 miles of road over the sand dunes and 20 miles of transmission pole line carrying a 7.2 kva power circuit, six synchronization circuits, and 24 communication circuits. A four inch water line was also constructed to carry service from existing mains at the center of the beach to the facilities at the south end.

Of the range facilities constructed, five were existing frame structures that were dismantled in camp and re-erected at the new site. These were a garage, 26 by 79 feet; a spare parts storage shed, 26 by 46 feet; a welding shop 26 feet square; and two instrument repair shops, 25 by 110 feet each.

An unusual design feature encountered in this project was the requirement for extreme rigidity and stability on the part of the observation towers. These 30 foot high towers serve as platforms for instruments which photograph and locate by angular measurement the positions in space of missiles ten to 20 miles away traveling at speeds of 1,500 mph. To insure accuracy in results, it is essential that these instruments be fixed and not subject to movement due to tower vibration or sway. To obtain this stability, the towers were constructed of reinforced concrete and were placed on the centers of 30 by 30 foot concrete slabs supported on creosoted piles driven to a minimum depth of 20 feet and 15 tons bearing. To preclude the possibility of distortion of tower frameworks due to temperature changes, the sides of the towers were projected with plywood shields to prevent undue increases in temperature due to direct sunlight on the frame.

Construction work was performed by George and Lynch, General Contractors, of Wilmington, Delaware. Plans and specifications for the project were prepared by the Kellex Corporation, a firm of civilian contractors associated with the Applied Physics Laboratory of Johns Hopkins University and under whose technical direction Kellex is also operating the range for the Bureau of Ordnance.

IV. Johns Hopkins University Applied Physics Laboratory - 1946

JHU/APL documents explained that a theodolite system at Naval Ordnance Test Facility, Holly Ridge, was established primarily to obtain velocity and acceleration measurements for supersonic guided missiles.

Basically, each cine-theodolite was "zeroed" on another tower about a mile away with each tower "zeroed" on the next. In that way they could be synchronized and accurately record telemetered data. They tracked the flights using dual 16mm cameras. It was designed for Mach numbers to 5, maximum altitudes of 60,000 feet and ranges up to 80,000 yards. Their measurements were from tower 1 to 5 miles down range.

Basic facilities in the technical area consist of eight reinforced concrete, stable platforms or towers and three radar observation platforms located along a 20 mile broken "base line." There are also a concrete launching apron with bomb-proof shelter, a control tower and a number of secondary instrument emplacements. All significant points have been surveyed by the Coast and Geodetic Survey.

Technical support facilities include an explosion-protected rocket assembly building, assembly building for inert components, photographic laboratory, optical instrument and camera shop, electronics shop, radar testing building, welding shop, machine shop, and stockroom tool crib.

V. Navy Bureau of Ordnance - 1947

A September 19, 1947 document provides proposed modifications to make the facility larger and more capable. These modifications included construction of an additional assembly building, enlarging of the launching platform, and other modifications. Before any further work was done, the project was moved to Inyokern.

A November 6, 1947 document lists a Plan for Implementing the Deactivation of Camp Davis. "The last missile firing will be November 15 after which no further Bumblebee activity will be planned." It also covered disposition of equipment, water and sewer plants and security. May 1, 1948 was set as target date for ending the contract.

VI. Johns Hopkins University Applied Physics Laboratory - June 1994

In the *APL News*, Johns Hopkins announced that Bumblebee

research would be featured at the new Topsail Island Museum. The Applied Physics Laboratory Archives would provide Bumblebee artifacts, including missile mock-ups and films showing Camp Davis activities and rocket test flights.

The "Autumn With Topsail" event, September 17-18, 1994 showcased the "Operation Bumblebee" artifacts. They have prominent places in the Topsail Island Historical Society Museum. Connie Finney and Phil Albert of JHU/APL agreed that the museum would be their "East Coast Archive Site" for these artifacts.

We thank Johns Hopkins University Applied Physics Laboratory for their generosity. The videos of launchings and the rocket displays make the program real for museum visitors.

ROCKET RESCUED FROM THE SEA

After a storm and some beach erosion, a rocket was visible at ocean edge. Frank, Julia, Haynes and Neill Sherron found it about one fourth mile north of the Jolly Roger Pier, in front of the property of Norman Chambliss, Jr. It was during the Fourth of July weekend, July 1994, and the four foot tube with broken fins on one end was corroded and encrusted with marine growth. It weighed about 100 pounds, and it was feared that there may be explosives inside.

The police called in an explosives team from Camp Lejeune to inspect the device, but it proved to be harmless. The military team estimated that the rocket was probably of early post World War II vintage. On further examination, and comparison to pictures from Johns Hopkins APL, it was confirmed to be a booster rocket from the Operation Bumblebee Rocket Program, of 1946-1948.

On checking with the Underwater Archeological Lab at Fort Fisher, Eric Peterson, Town Manager, was advised to get it back underwater to preserve it. Eric saw to it that a large aquarium was brought in. The rocket remains on display at the Topsail Island Missiles and More Museum.

PICTURES	CREDITS
Control Tower & Assembly Building	5/57-J.B. Brame
Ramjet Rockets	Historical Society
Patrol Boat Inland Waterway	Historical Society
Off-Shore Range Patrol Boat	Historical Society
All Others	JHU/APL*

*JHU/APL - Johns Hopkins University Applied Physics Laboratory

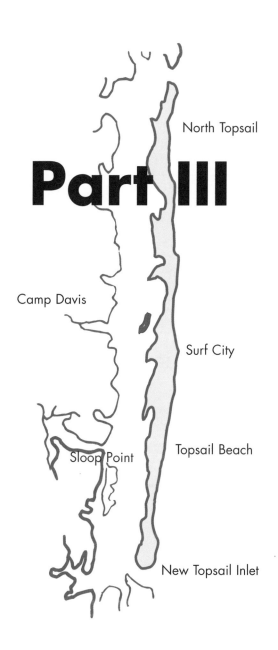

Part III

North Topsail

Camp Davis

Surf City

Topsail Beach

Sloop Point

New Topsail Inlet

TOPSAIL ISLAND COMMUNITIES

Topsail Island includes several communities. Its population is about 3,000 year-round residents but swells to 30,000 vacationers during the summer.

SURF CITY, at island center, is where most of us enter Topsail Island. We cross the swing bridge, built in 1955, one of the few that remain along the east coast. Surf City, a hub of island activities, accommodates a variety of life styles from trailers to elegant homes. Surf City was incorporated March 1949, with David Lucas named the first mayor, and Gerald C. Mercer and Al Ward serving as original commissioners. Al Ward doubled as public works director. He would also serve later as mayor. Two of the long list of mayors, Douglas Medlin and Joe Paliotti, served three separate terms each. The current mayor is Vance V. Kee.

NORTH TOPSAIL BEACH is the newest community, incorporated in January 1990. It includes the former North Topsail Shores, Ocean City, Del Mar Beach, and West Onslow Beach. Rodney Knowles was the first mayor. The first commissioners were Nathan McDaniels, William Keister, Charlotte Tippett, Weldon Hall, and Leland Newsome. The current mayor is Marty Bostic.

The north end of Topsail Island has developed as high-rises with swimming pools, resort condominiums, and a convention center have been built. Some controversy erupted in the late 1980s as wash overs isolated residents necessitating re-routing of the road and considerable dune building to protect it from the sea. It is now one of the fastest growing areas of the island.

TOPSAIL BEACH, to the south, is a quiet cottage and family community with uncluttered, quiet beaches. Topsail Beach incorporated in 1963 with Lewis P. Orr, Sr. the first mayor. Both Lewis P. Orr, Sr. and Michael A. Boryk served two separate terms. The current mayor is Milton R. Oppegaard. The original commissioners were Dewey D. Justice, Herbert Williams, J.A. Godwin, Forest McCullen, and Tom Humphrey.

Over the years, the individual communities have been independent in their town affairs. There have been attempts to combine functions, such as police departments, but each have thought it best to be independent. The roots seem to be in early life on the island where everyone found it imperative to be self-sufficient. In recent years, however, there has been a growing trend to cooperate at an island level. For example, the Assembly Building started as a Topsail Beach endeavor and is now defined as the Topsail Island Community Center.

In a newspaper recap of 1990, a number of activities island-wide were identified. This was the year that marked the crumble of invisible walls in an effort to unite the three Topsail Island communities: North Topsail Beach, Surf City, and Topsail Beach. Where divisions once separated Topsail Beach and Surf City, the past year proved that new boards, new goals, and new attitudes would join the neighboring towns in several cooperative efforts. Town boards came to a mutual decision to meet with each other on a routine basis for the purpose of discussing issues of relative importance.

Joint ventures included hurricane evacuation plans, the planned development of a new recycling center to be centrally located in Surf City, and most recent discussion of Topsail Beach possibly tying into the Surf City sewer system. With the coming of 1990, Surf City and Topsail Beach welcomed and aided their new neighbor North Topsail Beach.

The early Topsail Communities have many stories that are told by their people. Each community will be discussed through the eyes of the people. The reader will find that North Topsail Beach, Surf City, and Topsail Beach each are unique, even though they share the same island.

SURF CITY

EDGAR L. YOW, ATTORNEY AND ENTREPRENEUR

Edgar L. Yow, attorney, was probably the most important individual to Topsail Island's coming into its own identity and giving birth to its early development in the late 1940s.

Edgar impressed you on first meeting as a sincere, principled, and capable man. To associate with him would confirm this. His six feet three inch frame, bright blue eyes, and white hair were striking and his manner projected a purposeful way of dealing with problems and causing change.

Ed was an attorney who had a vision of the potential of Topsail Island. He bought land over the years, some of which the US Government

Thomas Tackle Shop - Surf City

leased during the war for gunnery practice, and later for their use as a missile test site. In 1948, he took aggressive steps to get the government to release the area back to the landowners so the island could be developed.

Edgar was a self-made man who had to drop out of school at age 16 when his father suddenly died to work and keep the family together. His family lived on a farm in Chatham County, near the middle of North Carolina. The eldest of six brothers and one sister, Ed tried to maintain the farm but finally left to work at various jobs around the country. One job even took him on a merchant ship around South America. He sent money home for the family.

In the late 1920s, he settled in Wilmington and started a mattress manufacturing firm which later burned. He then went into furniture rebuilding and upholstering. Ed studied at night, determined to become a lawyer. He passed his bar exam in the early 30s and started practicing law.

His father's dream was to live on the east coast and Ed eventually brought the rest of the family east to this region.

In the early 40s, Edgar was mayor of Wilmington and he worked tirelessly to ensure the safety of the town. The threat of German U boats nearby caused great concern and he worked with high level officers at Camp Davis to remain informed and keep them apprised of Wilmington needs. He was the kind of person that the military would take into their confidence. This background would serve to prepare Edgar for what he needed to do for Topsail Island.

There was a severe shortage of

Edgar Yow circa 1960

Pier at Surf City

building materials right after the war and Ed could see the opportunity to buy Camp Davis and sell the buildings and piping for salvage. Many of the buildings were re-used on Topsail Island. He formed "Land Associates Inc.," and it became the acting agency to effect disposition of salvageable buildings and support facilities. Land Associates also took on the responsibility to ensure that the island would have a water supply and electricity. This turned out to be enormously difficult.

Picture what needed to happen. Camp Davis would be dismantled and island property turned back to owners, along with military buildings that remained. Edgar Yow would help the military solve the dismantling problem by forming Land Associates, Inc. It became the acting agency to dispose of salvageable materials and buildings. This also included setting up the waterworks for what would become Surf City.

Ed introduced Mr. Al Ward to the island. Mr. A.H. Ward established his real estate company and became the original developer of the island. When Edgar drew up the Surf City Charter of Incorporation, Mr. Yow named David Lucas the first mayor, Al Ward as public works commissioner, and Gerald Mercer as treasurer. No one knew of their appointments until they read it in the newspaper.

Edgar had the foresight to believe in the need for blacks to own property on the beach. This was not a popular belief at that time because racial discrimination was still in practice. He engaged Mr. Wade Chestnut to head Ocean City Developers. Mr. Chestnut renovated the tower to be a restaurant and tackle shop. He then passionately engaged in fostering black ownership to the present day Ocean City.

ISLAND WITHOUT A NAME

Ed should be credited with the official naming of Topsail Island. There is no evidence on maps or correspondence prior to 1947 to this island being so-named. Maps back to 1774 name New Topsail Inlet and Topsail Sound, so the folklore of Pirates hiding behind the island and merchant ships watching for the topsails is a plausible explanation for Topsail Sound being so-named. Until 1947 the island was named: The Banks, Ashe Island, Sand Spit, Sears Landing, and sometimes, Long Island.

Edgar held meetings in a narrow room at the front of the waterworks building (current Surf City Fire Department). This room was torn down in 1971 and was replaced by the wooden structure. In Ed's files, there is a yellow legal-sized sheet of paper, in his handwriting, from one of those meetings. It states, "I think it is agreed that the island should be known as Topsail Island..." And from that day forward, this historic gem has been know as Topsail Island. Ms. Peggy Lewis, formerly Ed's secretary, verified his handwritten note.

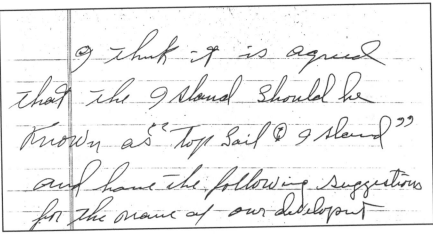

Ed's Handwritten Note

Our beloved island owes much to Edgar L. Yow. Because of Ed's insight and initiative, the island was able to shed its military yoke, and now we can claim our history as a recognized island. Edgar named Topsail Island and even suggested names for many of the island's streets which remain to this day.

Edgar L. Yow served the Topsail Island communities for many years right up to his last days. He died in 1983 and was buried on Memorial Day. This seemed most fitting because he was a patriotic man who thought a lot of his country.

ARLENE YOW RECALLS EARLY DAYS

Arlene Yow resides in Surf City and shares some recollections of her early days on the island with her husband.

Arlene is an active lady who has a firm and sure voice and clear recollections. She sits impatiently and gets up to show me pictures, such as the beautiful painting of the mansion that her husband Edgar built near Tar Landing. She paces around talking about her involvement in the early Topsail Island days recalling Ed's many contributions to the turnover of the land from military control. She clearly was a partner to his efforts, putting herself forward to work with him during a time when living conditions were primitive and undoubtedly helped assure many of his political successes.

Ed had started his practice of law in the early 1930s. He was buying land in the 30s and had a keen eye for opportunities to buy over the years. He was clearly ahead of his time. He built the first house on the ocean about 1943. There was no electricity or inside plumbing.

Back when Ed and I first came to the island, only old fishing shacks existed. There was a fish camp and lodge owned by George Rountree. People would come down from Sloop Point in small boats.

Ed owned property all over the island. Most holdings were around Surf City and north. He also owned some property south, with some in proximity to Harvey Jones' "Queens Grant." Ed and his brother Cicero also owned the tower there.

Yow Apartment - WWII Barracks - Surf City

I have a vivid recollection of living in our apartment in the old barracks (near the Officer's Club). A man from the government came to the apartment and insisted that he had to find a place to stay on the island. After much insistence, I consented to have him stay the night in the guest room hoping Ed would arrive soon. I simply didn't know what else to do because there was no place to refer him and he did have government credentials. I told him that my husband would be home soon and maybe he could help him.

When Ed came home, the government man said, "I'm looking for Ed Yow. Could you help me find him." After the introductions, he said, "Your wife must be the smartest woman in the world." He was from Washington, DC and stayed for three days. A big car came filled with men and toured all day long. I fixed meals for them all. He stayed several days longer. His purpose in being here was to determine if they must move the "Bumblebee" project because it had overshot the range. Ed had written letters to the military insisting that they must move the project because of the hazards to people living in the area.

When the Navy was disbanding, Arlene asked the Major why the road was so close to the ocean and so crooked. He replied: *I was sitting on the jeep which was laying a string behind to mark the path for the road. We were all miserably black with mosquitoes and I allowed everyone to drink to help them through it. I saw the crooked line and told them just get us to the end. Where the string lay was how the road went.*

The Navy had an Officers' Club at the Barnacle Bill location. This was on Yow land and it came to him at the return of land from the military in 1948. They had a nice restaurant and oyster roasts there. Bill Lindstrum from Michigan ran it for them and it closed when he went home around 1953. Hurricane Hazel took the Officers' Club in 1954.

Arlene said: *There were also barracks left by the military beside the Officers' Club. Ed and I stayed there in an apartment. We also rented rooms to two captains and two lieutenants from Camp Lejeune for two years.*

Ed was lawyer for many service people which resulted in good relationships with the military. We also entertained high level service officers and I cooked a lot of dinners for them. Ed had a lot of family support too, that included a distant relative Lieutenant Commander Robert Darden in Washington, DC. He helped to make the right contacts there so Ed could get the attention and power to get the swing bridge in.

In 1948 when the pontoon bridge was opened to public traffic, the Yow, Ward, and Lucas families were the first to cross. The pontoon bridge was built in the early 40s and was a scary thing to negotiate. Ed won the attention of senators in Washington and Raleigh officials to get the current swing bridge built in 1956. Arlene says: *No one can realize what it took to get attention to this problem. It also was a front runner for the high-level bridge at the upper end of the island.*

Sand Piper circa 1990

She paused for a moment and said: *You just cannot imagine what it is like after a hurricane has passed. Hazel blew everything loose into the sound. Sheets, quilts, mattresses, and clothes adorned the trees. Just devastation everywhere, with everyone searching for losses and grieving for each other.*

The Mermaid Lounge has had considerable reputation and press. An earlier version was built in 1949. It was an old wooden building on the ocean—a beer joint. It burned down in 1951 and Ed built a concrete block building that was very nice. Dr. Hunter Heath dubbed it the "Mermaid Lounge." Hurricane Hazel cleaned it off in 1954 and it was rebuilt with the remains of an old house and relocated to its current site.

Willy Largen, a sergeant at Camp Lejeune ran it for a time, then Mrs. Kathryn Williams, a refined and well-liked lady, ran it for years. She retired at 90 years of age. I believe Willy Largen was probably the one who dug up the stories about ghosts and all.

There are so many people here on Topsail Island, that we have known over the years and I still have close ties with them. I had my house built here in Surf City and decided this is where I will stay.

AL WARD

Al Ward has headed the Ward Realty business for 47 years. He is the original developer of Topsail Island, opening his business as the Standard Realty and Construction Company. He has offices at Surf City and in Wilmington.

Al appears to be in his early 70s, always on the move with the activities of real estate. He is short, a little stocky, has gleaming white hair, a ruddy complexion, and warm, friendly face. He loves to talk and rambles in his conversation about his favorite topic—Topsail Island.

He said: *Ed Yow, a lawyer, had a love for Topsail Island. He bought property as early as the 30s and devoted much time and energy to Topsail Island's benefit. It was Ed who suggested that I come and consider buying property.*

We'd come out to the island before there was electricity with a half gallon of

Al Ward - Ward Realty - 1994

kerosene with a potato on the spout and a 10 cent block of ice in a pasteboard box. Of course some of the ice would be melted but you could get a good sized block of ice for 10 cents then. Our kerosene cookstove had two burners and I never was successful at getting the whole wick to burn all the way around so we had a lot of smoked eggs, bacon, and grits. Hot for the cook, too. We would then cross the pontoon bridge which moved up and down with the tides—a devastation to mufflers, which were often ripped loose getting on and off the bridge.

That pontoon bridge was very dependable. You could depend on it being either stuck open or stuck closed. If stuck open, we would borrow a skiff and float across. The pontoon bridge was the only access for us and served fairly well from when we first came here. We would have to get a pass from Camp Davis and then hope we could get across.

In 1954, Hurricane Hazel took out the bridge and after the storm passed it was found ripped loose from its moorings and sitting high and dry, like Noah's Ark. Tugs had to pull it back in place. The present bridge was under construction at that time.

DUKW - used when pontoon bridge was out

The Marine Corps at Camp Lejeuene was a big help during emergencies. For example, they furnished transportation to the island via DUKW, "Duck," to make sure kids could get to school and that other island needs were met.

There were housing shortages from time to time, like during the Korean situation. Marines were called back to the service and were looking for a place for their families. We tried to help them the best we could. I had a small office that I used which used to be a radio shack. We fixed it up for a marine, his wife, and son.

In the early 40s, Topsail Island was an antiaircraft training range. Planes would tow a sleeve and they would fire at it. Installations were spotted behind dunes up and down the coast. The US Government commandeered most of the land but where the owners could be found they leased it.

There is a remnant of the antiaircraft target practice days on the beach, just south of the Surf City tower beside the public access. It is a three-sided concrete 'privy' about six feet high lying on a jaunty angle. This was used as a bullet-proof place for the referee to keep score of antiaircraft hits. There is also a second one covered by a dune nearby.

The island was used in early days for cattle grazing driving them across at low tide and leaving them here for months at a time. A heavy Nor'easter in 1899 sent cattle bounding back to the mainland and a lot were caught in the marsh and drowned. Later, the Intracoastal Waterway was cut through so the cattle grazing was no longer practical.

Earl Bell, a farmer, had a lot of property here. We helped him subdivide it. J.K. Warren Jr. also sold a lot of property to developers on the north (east) end. The Jeffreys family owned one and one half miles on each side of the high-level bridge, which is now developing. The Sidbury family and Batts family also owned a lot of Topsail Island land.

The first houses had gasoline generators. Septic tanks varied since there were no rules or pre-cast tanks. You would dig a hole in the ground, pour a concrete bottom then lay cement block sides, baffles, and a poured concrete top. If you dug the hole on a dry day, chances are you end up with a hole three times the size needed as sand sides fell in.

You could drive a pipe 12 or 15 feet to drinking water. If you went deeper, you would get into salt water again, on the ocean side. On the sound side, it had a sulfur taste and good water was more difficult to find.

The Wards developed some 18 subdivisions over time. Delmar was an early subdivision with lots at $1,000, 10% down, balance in five years at 6% interest. Those waterfront lots were more difficult to sell under those terms than to sell at $100,000 today. He is justly proud of his development "Channelbend." which nestles among island oaks just south of Surf City "S" curve. In all, they have built about 600 to 700 homes over the 42 years. Of course, they are all built on pilings now, which will ensure a better survival rate.

We have rented cottages for years accumulating tenants that come back year after year. We have one, May Davis from Massachusetts, who is here for her 30th consecutive year.

We owned the fishing pier at the north end of the island, and leased it to Bill McKee, for several years. My two sons and I then managed it and the restaurant in the early 80s. It is the longest pier at 850 feet in length.

Al was in the Coast Guard Reserve. Reserves were busy because of submarine activity here during the war. Private boats were commandeered by mine patrol one night a week. Buildings were blacked out. They had horse patrols and kept huge stables 60 foot square for the horse patrol units. An incident during WWII, that defies explanation, happened at Fort Fisher. A Nazi submarine surfaced and shot up the water tower.

When the island was opened to the public in 1949, there was a small notice in the paper and throngs of people came to the island. It seemed that they thought it was a scavenger hunt because a lot of the buildings were ransacked. Officials closed the bridge to the general public, and would allow only those who had business on the island to pass. They would make everyone get a pass and take their stuff out of the car.

Many trips to Washington were made to get power over to the island. There had been power for the "Bumble Bee" project and the poles were left but salvage people took down the wires. Also deep wells at Camp Davis were piped to Topsail Island, but salvage people had dug up the pipes.

After Surf City was incorporated, it was still *dark*. Al furnished the first street lights. These were simply galvanized pipe with a gooseneck with green shade. REA put them together and installed them. He said: *I was mayor when Hurricane Hazel hit us. I had just completed a new shopping center 30 days before she hit and took it away. I'd pick up the phone and the tears would come right out of the receiver. We had bought a railroad car of surplus roofing material several months prior to Hazel. It did many roof jobs. Roofs had to be replaced everywhere and it got so hectic we couldn't keep track of it. Some roofs never did get paid for.*

Al often found himself at hard labor before storm threats. Once he was working to protect eight of their concrete block houses in Delmar. Al bulldozed all night long, piling sand to the eaves of the houses. He said: *I was blessed with a working companion, my wife, who helped me without questioning. She kept the car headlights on my bulldozing all night, moving the car as needed. (The storm never materialized so I had an un-piling job to do later.)*

Al also put tremendous efforts into dragging small trees, branches, and other debris to the oceanside in order to trap sand as it blows and develop new sand dunes as soon as possible. Hazel flattened the dunes and Al knew the dune protection had to be rebuilt.

I asked Al: "With all you suffered through, and many others like you, what kept bringing you back to rebuild?" Al said: *I believe it was a combination of tenacity and stupidity, although, in all fairness, sometimes there simply weren't a lot of choices for us. I have always had a home here and continue to have a home on the island. Something about it gets you and keeps you coming back.*

In the older days, things didn't move so fast. We had a lot of mountains to climb but we had time between problems to wipe the sweat our of our eyes and get a clear view of what was around the corner. Today on the speedway of progress, it seems a blur as to where we are going.

During the Civil War there were salt works near here. Salt got so dear during the war that the meat curers would sometimes scrape the boards in the smokehouses to get salt. Another interesting fact—salt treated pilings weigh twice the weight of untreated ones and would last longer.

DIANE GEARY

Diane grew up on Topsail Island. She and her family are "salt of the earth" folks that participated in the early days of Surf City. She, like her parents, is humble about her involvement, so most of the information is from others such as Arlene Yow.

Arlene Yow said: *Roland and Sally Batts were two of the finest people I have known. They lived in an old firehouse left by the military and had a grocery store and Post Office at the large doors. Sally Batts always had a pot going; she cooked and gave it out to anyone. They would go to Holly Ridge to get the mail and bring it to give it out until a formal post office was in place. It was all voluntary. In 1954 when Hazel hit, they took the mail to Holly Ridge for safety.*

They tried to do their part to help military folks who lived on the island. Sally would often keep their children so the parents could have free time to enjoy themselves. They were such wonderful people who would do anything to help. It didn't matter what the situation, they simply would take care of it.

Later, they built a cafe and grocery and official post office across the street from the firehouse. (The old wooden firehouse building was just torn down a couple of years ago. Diane Geary says the big doors always leaked water. Hazel blew some water under the door but there was no substantial damage.)

Diane recalled: *Fortunately for them, nothing was lost when Hurricane Hazel devastated the island.* Her parents set up "headquarters" in the building at today's Ship's Wheel to help out. She said: *We went to school via bus and military amphibian "DUKW." It was used to transport people back and forth to the mainland until the pontoon bridge could be rebuilt after Hazel. The*

Military Fire House - Geary Grocery - 1990

"DUKW" would be waiting for the kids to come from school then would take them across to the island. The next day, it would be waiting for the next trip.

There used to be a great amusement park at Surf City. They had a go-cart track at the causeway near the current Mayrand Real Estate office. For three years there was a carnival with a roller coaster and ferris wheel near the current waterslide. The man who ran it was sent to prison for tax evasion and the carnival folded.

In 1960, Diane's father Roland Batts was in charge of the Governor's visit to the Pender County Fair. She remembers a stern rebuke when she wasn't where she was supposed to be for an introduction to the governor. Roland used to work at Camp Lejeune in the Provost Marshall's Office as Special Deputy. He kept up his connections and was often politically involved.

Roland was mayor of Surf City from 1957 to 1964 when he died. His wife Sally finished out his term, appointed as mayor.

In recent years, Diane and her husband owned and operated the Ship's Wheel, clothing and souvenir shop in Surf City, selling the business in 1987. She also served as president of the Topsail Historical Society for several years and continues to be involved in community matters.

SEVERAL ADDITIONAL SURF CITY ITEMS:

Herring's Bait and Tackle Shop

Peggy Bailey grew up on Topsail, went away for 17 years, and returned in 1974 to run the Herring Bait and Tackle Shop when her father died. Edgar Herring came to Topsail after Hurricane Hazel in 1954. He started in construction then got into the bait, tackle, and reel repair business. His was the only reel repair shop on the island.

Herring's store was first located at the Surf City Marina in 1962 then he built the current location in 1968. His expertise in reel repair was a sought after skill when we made reels that last for years. In 2004, the Herrings remodeled to become "Herring's Outside Sports."

Surf City Pier

On May 13, 1954, a freak storm took the pier down. It was replaced by a steel pier which was thought to be permanent. The steel wouldn't last because of the salt ocean and was replaced over time. Hubbard Barwick built the pier and R. L. Church managed it.

CHARLES H. JONES

Charles is a life-long resident of the Topsail area who grew up on Topsail Island. Charlie has a vivid memory and is quite a story teller. He has many tales about Camp Davis and Topsail Island. In fact, if you ask him some questions, he is likely to tell you more than you wanted to hear.

His very first recollection is of his father, "Pop" Harold Jones, running his Peoples' Cafe at Camp Davis. His father had to be flexible as well as ingenious. The "Cafe" started out as a small hardware store that sold carpenter tools to workers looking for jobs when Camp Davis was being built. Later, according to need, he changed it to a cafe restaurant.

There were two pontoon bridges before the current swing bridge across the intracoastal waterway. The Army Corps of Engineers built the first pontoon bridge. It had two outboard motors that would pull it to one side for the passage of boats. The second bridge was a semi-rigid one with a large center section floating on metal rectangular drums. There was a ramp at each end that raised and lowered with the tides (a real muffler eater). Powered by diesels, cables would swing the bridge to the south so boats could go through. The bridge would hold two cars and had a blacktop-like surface. As the steepness of the ramps raised and lowered with the tide, cars with low-hanging exhaust pipes often lost them. He recalls: *There was a time when a school bus got hung up and had to wait for a higher tide.*

And there is a story that Governor Scott's brother lived on Topsail Island and he came to visit at extremely low tide. The tailpipe of his Cadillac was torn off and within a week or two, the announcement was made that there would be a swing bridge built, eliminating the pontoon bridge.

In October 1954, Hurricane Hazel ripped its way through the island. Evacuation was tenuous since the only way out was through this bridge. The bridge held two cars and one would go quickly forward so the second one could come on and balance it so the first one could drive off. Since the height of the bridge was according to the height of the tide, it was a scary experience for many to negotiate, even under normal circumstances.

Charles continued: *Earl Batts, Walter, and James Hall were bridge tenders. They would put oysters and sweet potatoes on top of the pot belly stove in the tender's shack. Seemed like anyone could stop in and help themselves to them. Everyone was willing to share what they had. When activity was low, they could take a gasoline lantern and pick up eight to ten flounder within 300 feet of the tender's shack.*

The first tackle shop was built at the Sears Landing location and was called Thomas' Store and Tackle Shop. Howard O. Batts, Sr. built the building around 1946-48. George Thomas, Sr. ran it for a couple of years, then he left the area returning in 1955. They used to have big oyster roasts there in the early days.

At the northern end of the island, the Jeffreys had a fishing and hunting camp. They had deer and lots of snakes. It was located about two miles from the current high level bridge. They raised mustard plants and greens of all types for salads. They farmed between Surf City and New River Inlet. Before the beach was opened and the military was still in charge, there was a story about a GI who was swimming off shore, floating around. He saw a fin and thought he was about to be attacked by a shark. As he thrashed around the water in a panic, the porpoise nudged him to shore.

Charles said: *I remember seeing pieces of remote control planes washing up on shore for years. The planes were used as drones for antiaircraft target practice. I remember dances at Barnacle Bills' (current name). It had formerly been an officer's club during the second World War.*

My father was quite a character. Nobody could get the better of him in a conversation. He liked "corralling" someone in a discussion. Pop built a pavilion across from the Sandpiper in 1948-49 and ran it until 1967. It was called Ocean View Pavilion. They had dances on Saturday nights, a jukebox, games, and a bathhouse.

Pop rode out all the hurricanes except Hazel. During storms, my father would rig up the jukebox and outside speakers and you could hear the strains of "This Old House" over and over. We would have a pot of stew going, eat and listen to

Surf City - Toward Sears Landing circa 1960s

"This Old House" and, on one occasion watched the Surf City pier go to pieces. "Ain't gonna need this house no longer, ain't gonna need this house no more; ain't got time to fix the ceiling, ain't got time to fix the floor. Ain't got time to fix the window or to fix the window pane, ain't gonna need this house no longer, I' getting ready to meet the same."

SEARS LANDING

The Sears Landing Pontoon Bridge was in use for auto traffic since WWII days. In 1955, after construction was interrupted by Hurricane Hazel in October 1954, a new swing-span bridge was opened.

The Pender Chronicle reported November 1955:

> The new Surf City Bridge over the inland waterway, which connects the mainland with Topsail Island was opened to the public on Saturday, November 5th. It is really a very handsome bridge and around 200 or more guests attended. The $432,000 Swing-span type bridge was under construction for the past two years.

> In the early days New Topsail Inlet was one of the deep water ports in North Carolina. Many sailing vessels landed at Sloop

Point to take on and discharge cargoes, etc., all of which came in through New Topsail Inlet.

It is the longest stretch of coast line in North Carolina, entirely

Surf City Swing Bridge—2004

Surf City Swing Bridge—2004

surrounded by water where boating, fishing, and crabbing can be carried on with other recreational activities, this close to the mainland.

The bridge requires a bridge tender to operate it, 24 hours a day. I'm told that earlier, the pontoon bridge stayed open for boat traffic until auto traffic needed it closed. Now, the swing-bridge remains closed for passage of auto traffic and opened for boat traffic as needed.

Lottie Glover was interviewed in the 1980s and described her job: *You cannot plan to crochet and read, you have to be alert all the time. Duties include greasing the giant cogwheel that rotates the bridge and keeping a log of weather conditions and of all the vessels that pass.*

The bridge house, the nucleus of the drawbridge operation, is a small two-story building perched on the side of the bridge. The lower floor contains the guts of the operation, the intricate electrical gear that supplies power to move the bridge and a back-up generator in case the electricity fails. The control room is dominated by a control board and a worn, comfortable easy chair mounted on a small rotating platform.

It takes about four minutes to close all the gates and open the bridge. Ships too tall to pass under the closed bridge are required to radio the bridge operator while half mile away. If the operator is not by a radio, the ship is required to signal the bridge with several blasts from its horn.

Ms. Glover said: *You have to be real careful, because when the lights go on and the bells start ringing, some people go crazy trying to see how fast they can get across the bridge. A clanking thud announces that the wedges balancing the bridge in place have been removed. A whining hum begins as the bridge starts its 90 degree turn. Once the bridge stops, a trawler moves through the opening.* Lottie takes note of its name and waits for the trawler to clear the bridge before reversing the process that ends with traffic streaming across the bridge. The whole process takes eight minutes.

She said: *There is a lot more to bridge tending than most people think. You have a lot of lives in your hands when you control both water and road traffic. What*

Pirate's Den - 1990

most motorists do not realize is that in all but emergency cases, water traffic has the right of way over road traffic, according to the Coast Guard's regulations. It is much easier to stop a car than it is to stop a tug pulling a string of barges.

October is the busiest month for bridge tenders. She said: *It seems like I'm opening the bridge every five or ten minutes when the yachts and sailboats start to move south to Florida. But things quiet down in winter when water traffic is minimal.*

PIRATE'S DEN

Margaret Paliotti said: *Joe was in the marines at Camp Lajeune when I came here to live and we were married when I was 19. We lived in the area from 1954 to 1958, then spent some years in Brussels in the Diplomatic Service.*

In 1963-64, they ran the Topsail Marina at Topsail Beach. It was a busy marina with five charter boats operating. Joe worked at the marine base and started to take an interest in "Island politics" becoming mayor of Surf City in 1971-72. He served again as mayor from 1982 to 1987, and from 1991 to 1993.

The Pirate's Den was formerly an army building. It was a garage, then living quarters, until it became a bar in 1968-69 called The Windjammer. Later, Joe and Margie changed it to the Pirate's Den.

During the Hurricane Diane evacuation, Joe was busy saving the town while Margie checked to see that their stuff was safe, putting everything in the freezer. She told me: *I was alone for about five minutes inside and when I tried to go back outside to evacuate, the door was stuck and I couldn't get out. On doing a quick check all around, I found all the doors had been boarded up. I called the town hall and Joe and the chief came to my rescue pulling the plywood off the door, and let me out.*

Being delayed so long while others were leaving, Norma Hall wondered where Margie had been. They had been looking all over for her. Margie said: *I was locked in and thought I would have to ride out the hurricane in the Pirate's Den.* The newspaper carried an article:

> Wife in Stormy Situation. The mayor of Surf City locked his wife in their restaurant, Pirate's Den. She was rescued by the rescue squad who opened the door which was boarded and nailed shut.

The Pirate's Den was a favorite meeting and eating place in Surf City. It had a rustic charm that was just right for a casual evening. Joe Paliotti would "hold court" there and often locals would gather there at the big center table to snack and talk. The talk was most probably giving someone a hard time about something, all in great friendship. The waitresses completed the bill with their blunt efficiency. You never failed to have a tasty Italian dish that brought you back time and time again. Clams and linguini, yum. And I still have my T-shirt that says, "I survived the waitresses at the Pirate's Den."

I once brought friends from New York to the Pirate's Den for dinner. After their eyes adjusted to the dark and they saw the duct tape peeling off furnace pipes and ceiling insulation, their first reaction was: *Why did you bring us here?* Their warm comments about the food and homey warmth soon answered their own question.

Sadly, on March 13, 1993, the Pirate's Den burned. The "Storm of the

Century" whipped up a frenzy of winds and ocean. Wires were torn and frayed by the winds killing electric power. This also shut down the water system. As the electricity turned back on, the surge caused a flash at the Pirate's Den that started a fire. Since there was no water system to fight it, and the nearby fire truck was empty, another fire truck was called. It arrived too late to save it.

The whole island mourned the loss of this piece of history. Everyone wanted the Paliottis to rebuild and try to recreate the Pirate's Den. But this was an undertaking they weren't ready to take on. Instead, the Paliottis moved their business to the Villa Capriani in North Topsail. The cuisine can still be enjoyed, but the ambiance of the Pirate's Den is gone forever.

NORTH TOPSAIL BEACH

OCEAN CITY

Mrs. Caronell C. Chestnut welcomed me this evening at her beach cottage and put me at ease with her warm, easy way. She loves to talk about Ocean City, and belies her 80 years with an infectious enthusiasm. She and her husband Wade were primary founders of Ocean City and she continued to be involved in its development long after Mr. Chestnut's death. Wade Chestnut died in 1961 but got to see what he had envisioned 12 years before come into fruition.

For years, blacks had no place at the beach in North Carolina except for a small place called Seabreeze which was about 15 miles from Wilmington. They would go to the Carolina Beach sound then motorboat to the ocean beach where they were allowed. Caronell said: *A favorite taste delight was a clam fritter for five cents and we would save our pennies to buy them.*

Edgar Yow owned the one mile stretch of property three miles north of Surf City, which was to become Ocean City, from beach to sound. It was Edgar's intention to provide the opportunity for blacks to own beach property. This was not a popular position at that time because of racial segregation, but he had the confidence and drive to see it through. He shared his idea with Dr. Samuel J. Gray, a black physician in Wilmington, who then involved the Chestnut brothers, Bertram, Wade, and Robert who were in the automobile repair business. Dr. Gray and the Chestnut brothers and their sister Louise, bought the first tracts of land.

An interracial corporation named Ocean City Developers was formed and headed by Robert Chestnut, Sr. to sell property to blacks. Wade conceived the idea of naming this section of the island Ocean City and served as secretary of the corporation. Wade became most passionate about creating a beach for black ownership. He took over the development, sold his share in the auto repair business, and sank all he had in the development. He bought and remodeled the tower to be a restaurant and tackle shop. During those early start-up days he slept in a small room in the tower. There was nothing here but beach, sky, and the firing range. It wasn't long until he built a house and moved his wife and two young sons to the beach.

Three houses were built concurrently in 1949-50. The first to be moved into was Mr./Mrs. Wade H. Chestnut's house, followed by Mr./Mrs. Stephen Rodgers, of Fayetteville, and Mr./Mrs. Henry Mallette, Sr., of Wilmington. Wade and a partner, William Eaton of Fayetteville, built what was then a 10 room motel in 1952. The intent was to build up the area to further encourage development of a carefully planned town with

Wade Chestnut II   Caronell Chestnut

Ocean City Pier

residential and separate commercial areas and a family-type of beach. Restrictions were such that loud frivolity and rowdiness were forbidden at the beach in order to provide a quiet, restful vacation. No trailers were allowed and there was a requirement that homes be built from the ground up.

Caronell said: *Many blacks were skeptical of this opportunity to buy property and it was slow to develop. They wondered if this was a gimmick. People were invited to come to Topsail, stay in private homes, and I would cook for them before the motel was built.*

At first there was no electricity and no good road to the north of Surf City. Jones-Onslow Electric Membership Corporation brought in electric. Some years later, streetlights were financed and installed by beach residents.

The crabbing at the New River Inlet was excellent and as the tide went out everyone would head for it. One year they caught so many crabs that their containers would not hold them all. Caronell recalled: *They took trousers off the boys, tied the cuffs, (which some weren't happy about) and filled them with crabs. Crab gumbo was a favorite soup that everyone tasted happily.*

Hurricane Hazel took our cottage along with about a dozen more into the sound. This meant that Ocean City had to start over. We rebuilt in 1955 and in 1960 Hurricane Donna took out the basement but the cottage was built on pilings so

Chestnut Episcopal Church

it stayed intact. At the same time, the pier which had been built in 1959 was damaged.

Camp Oceanside was established here in 1955 and was the first Episcopal camp for blacks in the Diocese of East Carolina. They would close 10 rooms of the motel for campers from 1955 to 1957. A dormitory and dining hall were then built.

The Wade H. Chestnut Memorial Chapel was built in June 1957. The dream of this chapel began in 1952 when the Rev. Edwin E. Kirton, who was then Rector of St. Mark''s Episcopal Church in Wilmington, N.C., held cottage services on Sunday mornings in the home of the Chestnuts during his vacations. *People would carry chairs down the beach to our cottage for services,* Caronell recalled. *These services were so well attended by the beach residents that the Rt. Rev. Thomas H. Wright, Bishop of the Diocese of East Carolina, welcomed the opportunity to erect a chapel to serve the spiritual needs of the residents and campers.* One week after the land was given, the frame was up and services were held in the framework. Every beach resident is considered a member of the chapel regardless of their "home" denomination.

About 25 years later, after integration, a diocese ad-hoc committee was formed to decide the fate of Camp Leach, a white camp and Camp Oceanside, a black camp. It was merged in 1985 to become Trinity Center at Emerald Isle and Camp Oceanside and Camp Leach were dissolved. At Trinity Center a building was dedicated to Wade H. Chestnut and Rev. Edwin E. Kirton in recognition of the continuation of what was started here in Ocean City, and is called the Chestnut-Kirton Centrum.

In 1976, Ocean City Developers, Inc. was dissolved because it had served its purpose, and the Ocean City Beach Council was formed to manage town affairs. A second organization, the Ocean City Fishing Pier, Inc. still exists and Mrs. Chestnut is its president. A restaurant and tackle shop on the fishing pier and the motel are still in business in Ocean City Beach today.

Topsail Island has a history of people gathering to celebrate. Ocean City had such a gathering July 9, 1989, celebrating its 40th birthday. It began with a Eucharist Thanksgiving Service. The celebration weekend was July 15-16 which included contests and a community picnic. A reminiscent program was conducted with presentations and historical plaques. Sunday at the church service, Judge Henry E. Frye, Associate Justice of the North Carolina Supreme Court, was guest speaker. A birthday reception concluded official activities at the community building.

Caronell concluded: *In earlier days the community was a very close-knit one. If you had company, everyone met your house guest. Families would come down to stay from June until Labor Day. The men would commute on weekends from their work. Today, with many working husbands and wives, the residents come and go on weekends and stay for a two or three week vacation. Today, there are four permanent residents and about 100 families who stay during the summer.*

A MEMORIAL

Caronell Carter Chestnut

Caronell Chestnut passed away on September 26, 2002 and she is missed by a legion of friends, associates, and me. Her obituary expressed high praise and recognition of her devotion as an active parishioner at St. Mark's Episcopal Church over the years. A highly educated woman, she served as a chairperson on many committees and worked tirelessly with civic groups in Wilmington, receiving many official awards and recognitions.

But I knew her best for her groundbreaking work here at Topsail Island. Caronell and her husband Wade succeeded in the founding and development of Ocean City as a vibrant Black community. Caronell was an inspiration to me and I enjoyed a long friendship with her.

A year after Hurricane Floyd wreaked terrible destruction to the Ocean City community I visited Caronell at her home in Wilmington. She reflected: *This has been a vital community starting from sand and beach to a thriving community. We built and rebuilt as the storms took their toll, always bringing the community back to fullness. There has always been so much vitality here that it saddens me to see us in this lull, but I believe in the people and in our ability to overcome adversity. It is my sincere hope that we can rebuild our businesses and see our community thrive again.*

I, too, am hopeful that Caronell and Wade Chestnut's legacy can thrive as it has in the past, and that their vision will continue to guide the next generation of residents.

PERMUDA

Permuda Island, just north of Surf City, comprises about 50 acres of land. The North Carolina Division of Archives and History verified Indian tools, bones, and ceramics dating back to 2,000 BC unearthed on Permuda. It has an old farmer's bridge access, and I'm told that a "rough woman" raised crops among snakes for years. In the last 10 years a controversy raged about building condominiums on the island. Fishermen and environmentalists feared that development of Permuda would destroy the sound's lush clamming grounds, fishing, and archeological sites. Lena Ritter led the charge to save it and succeeded. The North Carolina Conservancy purchased Permuda in 1986, conserving it as part of the state's *estuarine sanctuary system.*

Permuda Island Bridge—circa 1994

At Chadwick Bay near the north end of Topsail Island, an "ossuary" or a burial pit 10 to 12 feet in diameter was unearthed. A ceremonial burial pit containing thousands of human bones were discovered. An archaeologist from the state Division of Archives and History confirmed

Permuda Island Bridge—2004

their dating of the year 1300. The bones represented about 150 different individuals.

The bones revealed that the Indians were most likely Algonkian. They were normally considered nomadic tribes that moved seasonally to the coast in spring and fall when fishing and oysters were most plentiful. But the presence of the "ossuary" indicates it may have been more important than a temporary site.

The North Carolina Algonkians had narrower heads and larger cheekbones than their northern neighbors, which helps distinguish them, according to a University of North Carolina anthropologist. The last remaining Indians abandoned their land in North Carolina in 1803 to join their kinsmen on reservations in New York and Canada. Archaeologists believe that Algonkian people used dugout canoes such as the "Batson Canoe" displayed in the Topsail Island Missiles and More Museum.

Reference:

Coastwatch Magazine. UNC Sea Grant, September/October 1992.

ASHE ISLAND

Ashe Island lies north of Permuda adjacent to the Rogers Bay Family Campway. Nautical maps still carry the Ashe Island name today. Dr. Hunter Heath acquired Ashe Island in 1950.

Marshall Dotson, a Jacksonville, NC Attorney, has been instrumental in carrying out legal matters for Dr. Hunter Heath

Ashe Island Estates—2004

for many years. He offered his recollections of Ashe Island History.

In 1726, John Baptista Ashe received a land grant for 1,000 acres located between New River Inlet and Stumpy Point Inlet that included portions of what is now known as Ashe Island.

In 1792, John Spicer received a land grant from the State of North Carolina for 200 acres that appears to be a portion of land known by the name of Ashe Island. (Grant Book 1, Page 106, Onslow County registry).

By reason of various conveyances, marriages, and inheritance, the lands covered by the Ashe Grant and the John Spicer Grant became owned by the Yopp Families, the Everett Families, the Spicer Families, and the Hobbs Families - all prominent names in the Stump Sound/Sneads Ferry area.

For more than 100 years, Ashe Island was farmed by the Spicer and the Everett families and by T. R. Murphy. Farm animals and farm implements were ferried to the island from Turkey Point Landing. The late Dr. Hunter Heath continued to farm Ashe Island from the date he acquired the island in 1950 until his death in 1989. He established a Trust under which the proceeds of sales from Ashe Island and other properties owned by him would be given to the University of North Carolina Medical Foundation for the purpose of funding research for in vitro fertilization and methods to combat world over-population.

The Trustees of the Hunter Heath Trust, preserving the natural marshes and wetlands as well as the Maritime Forest on the Intracoastal Waterway side, thereafter divided Ashe Island into ten-acre tracts of land. Appropriate restrictive covenants were recorded and designed to protect the island from over-development, preserving the natural areas and waterways to promote quality residential homes. There are currently four homes in this development.

The gated entrance to Ashe Island is located adjacent to the Rogers Bay

Campground. Dr. Hunter Heath formerly owned the campground land and it was purchased from the Trustees about 1992.

DOUGLAS GRAY

Douglas Gray was born on Holland Point Farm in 1922. Holland Point is on the mainland near Tar Landing. His father, Gib Scott Gray was a farmer who grazed 600-700 head of cattle behind Holly Ridge on about 3,000 acres. He and a friend Bill Hardison, who was like a brother, took care of the cattle. Douglas could remember them herding them over to just below Permuda at Dixon Point to the beach to graze in the late 20s. They would dig holes down four to five feet into the sand for their fresh water supply. They had done this for many years.

Douglas' father would go out west to get a carload of cows and bring them home. There would be a clip in their ear to identify them. The hogs had ear clips, too.

Permuda Island was incorporated very early. Gray said: *My father had a lease for 25 years. He would put hogs there for fattening up. The sound would freeze over because it was largely fresh water from creeks. D.V. Justice, my granddaddy, would walk across the ice at Permuda Island to bring feed to the hogs and cattle. At times, cows would wander off into the marsh and be eaten by 15-18 foot alligators.*

They would build wire cages out in the front of the boat for flounder fishing. They would light pine knots on fire in the cage so they could have their own light.

Oysters were in abundance. Too much salt made oysters poor so they would take oysters up the creek to sink the boat in fresh water to fatten them. Then the men would gather the oysters and the women would crack them with an ax blade. They would then pick the largest for the lid of the pail and pack them to keep them from spoiling. He and his dad would go to Burgaw and Wallace and walk up and down peddling fresh oysters.

After the Intracoastal Waterway, environmental people looked into shore damage and they blamed landowners and farmers. The waterway had changed the whole marsh system because of yachts, cargo ships, and barges causing disturbances. The straight sides eroded into shallow shores and sloped sides of the canal. The changes allowed more salt into oyster beds, ruining them. The Camp Davis laundry also caused oyster kill. Oystermen filed claims against the government and got paid. Later there was oyster kill again but nobody to blame. They had to wait for recovery—beds had to rest.

Campbell ran an oyster roast in Fayetteville and would come every week for 100-200 bushels of oysters in winter. Dewey Justice had oyster roasts here at Thomas Landing. They would steam oysters in a wet sack on a metal plate over hot coals. Justice would have cars waiting for roasted oysters. Across the road, L.M. Davis had oyster roasts, too. You could get a gallon of oysters from a bushel, but today you are lucky to get a pint.

Mosquitoes were bad but the army sprayed the swamps, which helped. But we still have them. After Camp Davis, people tried to use the trees cut off by guns. The sawmill couldn't use the timber because of shrapnel. When the land was sold to a paper company, they had a process for getting shrapnel out of trees.

Bob Powers from Wallace would come to the farm each Friday and pick cows to butcher. They would cut them open and string them up in oak trees. After butchering they would load the meat on white sheets and take them to Wallace to the meat market. Often, no money would change hands, they would barter or trade meat for goods and supplies. Behind Holly Ridge they had dip baths to run cows through to kill ticks. Ticks were a real problem to them. One way to control them was to burn the pine needles and undergrowth in the woods. If it was burnt every three years it would keep the undergrowth down and the ticks were kept under control. They also had a tick bath on the island just south of where the Scotch Bonnet Pier is now.

Near the Scotch Bonnet Pier, was Gray's Fishery in the late 1920s. There were small camps behind the dunes. They had a pitcher pump for water from a shallow dug well. Fishermen would come out to the island and stay for a week at a time. They would use a surf boat, a dory which is pointed at each end, to fish in the ocean. They would bring in their catch and load them on a sled to take them to sound-side and into boats for the trip to Holland Point Landing. At the farm, they would split and salt the fish and pack them in wooden barrels, take them to Wilmington Depot and train ship them north. Fish caught for shipment were mostly popeyed mullet.

They would also haul ice from Wilmington as blocks packed in sawdust. The ice would be half melted by the time they got it to Holland Point Farm so they had to rely on salting to preserve the fish.

When the Intracoastal Waterway was dug, in 1929-30, the dredges were to meet here but the one coming from the south met difficulty and they met at Wrightsville. Gray says: *It was difficult to herd cows across the water now and they had to be retrained to swim across to Topsail. Later, my father died and I was assigned a guardian who proceeded to sell off property. When Camp Davis came, they sold all their livestock. Holland Point Farm is bordered by Beasley Creek which also forms the Pender Co. and Onslow Co. line.* He has an original survey in English writing.

He recalled: *Where Rogers Campground is today, there was a 70-80 foot dune which is near Ocean City Pier. They would go up to the top of the dune to see where the cows were. They could free-range graze all over the island. There was an artesian well near the Scotch Bonnet location that flowed fresh water. There was also one in the lower end of the island near where tower #1 is today. A third artesian well is located at Morris Landing, which still flows into the sound.*

SCENIC FLIGHTS

Gene Gunter said: *The nearest thing to legal stealing we've found. I love to fly, love people, and love Topsail Island. Topsail Scenic Flights gives me a way to enjoy them for myself and to show others this wonderful island from another viewpoint.* Scenic Flights is based at the Topsail Island/Surf City Airport, at North Topsail Beach, North Carolina.

Gunter, a retired USAF Lt. Colonel, owns and operates Topsail Scenic Flights. He is an FAA Certified Commercial Pilot and shares the duties from flying to cutting the grass.

The Topsail Island/Surf City Airport was located between Wilmington and Jacksonville, NC, some 500 yards from the ocean. A 2,700 ft. x 100 ft. turf runway was opened in June of 1982 by Les Garrison, Gene Gunter and Wilbur Jackson. Formerly a soybean field donated by a local developer, it was converted to a landing strip using a borrowed road grader. The first landing was by a local aviation legend Jeff Jeffords.

The scenic flights are 10-35 minutes long and tour either the northern or southern two thirds of the island, or the whole island by customer choice. He said: *Often the customers want to see their homes or land recently purchased. Many realtors fly their customers, taking advantage of the first class tour and time savings. We fly 15-20 "real estate flights" each month.*

According to Gunter: *In 10 years we have not had one dissatisfied customer, in fact many have made the tour a part of their vacation every year since 1982. My special gratification is having a youngster return and proudly state he is taking flying lessons after his first flight with us. We spend extra time with the "future pilots."*

Scenic Flights employs one full-time pilot, five part-time pilots, and an airplane mechanic. They are certified instructors and have soloed twenty-five students there. They are rightfully proud of their spotless safety record.

In addition to scenic flights Gene has assisted the law in enforcement efforts and search and rescue missions.

Visitors are encouraged to "fly in." Many visit for the day, a weekend, or longer. A nominal landing fee is charged. "Fly-in's" camp free. They can walk to the beach, sun, fish, swim, eat great seafood, or just hang around. The airport has a beach shower and picnic area. Golf courses are nearby. They had a fly-in from Germany a few years ago, and he camped there for several days.

Gunter believes the Topsail Island/Surf City Airport can offer economic benefits for the Island. Few coastal communities like Topsail Island have airport access and it could attract business and the ability to fly-in for vacations here. He has worked with local businesses to form vacation and entertainment packages.

The years of flying tours have been very rewarding for Gunter. He said: *I haven't made a lot of money at this, but the payoff has come in the smiles of people who have flown the tour. Many have sent cards and letters of appreciation from home.* A grandmother wrote asking him to replace two certificates for her grandchildren who were sad about losing theirs. She told of how they talk about that flight over the island and it was important to be able to give them new ones for their birthday. Gunter said: *Letters like that are the best rewards.*

Unfortunately, the "Scenic Flights" ended about 2001 after 20 years' service to island sightseers.

ROGERS BAY FAMILY CAMPWAY

Topsail's one-of-a-kind campground is a haven for many interests. Rogers Bay is about 25 years old. The seasons bring fishing enthusiasts in the fall, some hardy campers in winter, a rush of families in early spring, then summer family camping, often for the entire season. It has a unique availability of ocean and sound beaches and has many campsites located under historic island oaks.

TOPSAIL BEACH

BEGINNINGS

By the 1960s, there was a cluster of year-round residents in the area and many building lots had been sold for vacation homes. Several businesses had taken root: Bill Warren's Soda Shop, Herbert William's Topsail Motel, Godwin's Grocery Store, Lewis Orr's Real Estate and General Contracting, Tom Humphrey Grading Contractor, Dewey Justice's Breezeway Motel, and Forest McCullen, Builder. It was time to provide services for this growing community and it was thought to be time to incorporate. Mike Boryk lead the movement, calling together the "characters" and the first Board of Commissioners were Tom Humphrey, Forest McCullen, Herbert Williams, Dewey Justice, and William Godwin, with Lewis Orr presiding as mayor. He also served again as mayor in 1973 to 1975.

The proposed plan to incorporate was brought to property owners at a town meeting. They filled Emma Anderson Memorial Chapel to capacity. Mayor Orr presided and heard loud outcries of opposition. He heard equally vocal support in favor of the proposition.

In 1963, the bill was passed in Raleigh that created the Town of Topsail Beach. With no municipal building yet constructed, the first of many board meetings was held in Lewis Orr's business office. With great foresight, the first order of business was to establish a Zoning Ordinance and a Building Code. Next was a ban on mobile homes. At this time there were only four soundfront lots between the Sound Pier and New Topsail Inlet.

Slim Rackley was hired as police officer. He was headquartered in his own home. Prior to incorporation, garbage and trash were collected by

Topsail Beach Officials - The Characters

"Fats," a well-known local person. Early on, residents paid for his services on an individual basis. In the new municipal structure, he signed a contract with the town and stayed on in the same position. Police protection had been available on the same basis.

Another early action was to assess a Privilege License tax, which taxed themselves as businessmen. They passed the law anyway. On the occasions when there were no funds to meet fiscal emergencies, the commissioners simply dipped into their own pockets and each loaned the town $100.

The following are excerpts from a letter dated November 9, 1966 and signed by Burke Bridgers, who has a long history with Topsail.

> ...Topsail has meant a great deal to me since I first fished there in 1907, and all the years that followed up to 1963...Undoubtedly I would have died many years ago except for my wonderful vaca-

tions there each summer camping in a tent up to 1912, when Theo Empie and I purchased the southern end of the island and erected a fishing camp near the inlet. At that time, the north side of Topsail Inlet was about where the white church stands today.

Up until 1941, or thereabouts, there was no way to get to Topsail except by boat. The army took over the island, built a small pontoon bridge across the Inland Waterway, and a clay road almost down to the inlet. After the army vacated, the navy took over and we did not get the property back until 1947-48.

Sometime after 1951, Louis T. Moore wrote a colorful account of the origins of Topsail Beach which I excerpt:

At the southern end of Topsail Island, there is a most entrancing and alluring seaside area. Since 1947 there have been developed adjoining delightful residential sections, New Topsail Beach, and Topsail Inlet Terrace. The first from an initial investment of $40,000, within four years is now a thriving modern settlement of three hundred or more fine homes. This village has been developed by the Anderson interests, formerly of Wauchula, Florida. The second development is still owned by the original investors. They are the Bridgers-Empie interests of Wilmington...It is not beyond the realm of reasonable conjecture to estimate the valuation of the two developments in the neighborhood of three million dollars. Additional increment is yet to come.

Topsail Beach - Looking South circa 1952

Topsail Beach looking North from Inlet circa 1952

What has happened in the foregoing statements is the actual result of a fish story—possibly the most amazing and fruitful piscatorial yarn ever conceived in the mind of mortal man. One can well content himself with the forceful declaration that what now is being told is simple and unvarnished truth...Our story deals with a simple, forceful, and factual outline. "Believe it or not" as the celebrated late Robert L. Ripley would ejaculate, it has been quickly followed with a modern miracle of commercial development and expansion...

Now for the fish story. Let us go back to the halcyon days of 1911. During that year, Messrs. Burke H. Bridgers, Theodore G. Empie, of Wilmington, a brother of the first mentioned Robert Bridgers, and two friends, R. E. Calder and H. Sidney Williams, decided to visit the island for a fishing day. That they were surprisingly and amazingly successful is attested by a photograph...This picture displays, side by side, no less than twenty-two splendid specimens of channel bass or drum, ranging in weight from 20 to 45 pounds.

The following year, in 1912, Messrs. Bridgers and Empie made a personal survey of potential fishing grounds from Georgetown, SC, to Ocracoke, NC. They finally concluded that the most prolific and satisfactory fishing was here at Topsail Island. They lost no time in acquiring for the modest sum of $3,000, an extensive area of several hundred acres on the southern end of the island. This included, as well, ocean beach frontage in excess of twelve thousand feet.

Mr. Empie was known far and wide among his friends as a wit of the Will Rogers type. In agreeing with Mr. Bridgers to make the purchase, he observed, casually, "Well, we can buy this terri-

Topsail Beach looking South circa 1952

tory for a mere song. We can fish here to our heart's content for years to come. When we get so aged and feeble that we are unable to assault members of the finny tribe, please know we can then dispose of our holdings in a way both satisfactory and profitably." That Mr. Empie proved to be a prophet of no mean talent and vision is confirmed today by the several millions in value which modern business methods have evolved, and displayed at New Topsail Beach... This

Topsail Island circa 1952

wonderful development has taken place on their acquisition of forty years ago that was merely a windswept, barren area.

The State magazine reported May 26, 1951:

NEW TOPSAIL BEACH - Driving northeast from Wilmington on US 17, you will come to the village of Holly Ridge. Be on the lookout for a sign which directs you to a paved road on the right to New Topsail Beach, one of North Carolina's newest beach resort developments.

This development was started just two years ago by J.G. Anderson and his son, J.G. Jr. New Topsail Beach today, with more than 10

Breez–way Inn Buildings circa 1949

beautiful homes, ranging in value up to $30,000, and numerous commercial, owned by prominent people of North Carolina.

..New Topsail Beach is a friendly resort with every natural advantage and its fishing waters are "out of this world," as one fisherman expressed it. There are stores, school buses, daily mail service, telephone service, fine drinking water, community church, and many other facilities which makes for completeness of the modern town.

The waters around this resort won the "Grand Area Award" for prize-wining fish caught during a fishing rodeo in 1950. Four hundred feet of pier has just been completed protruding into the clear blue waters. For the convenience and pleasure of New Topsail Beach visitors and town folks, modern bath houses and picnic grounds will soon be ready. In addition to its fine fishing waters, the surrounding areas abound in all kind of game. The area is famous for its deer hunting and duck shooting. In rounding out the completeness of New Topsail Beach, Anderson has provided the modern Breezway Inn and Cafe for the convenience of visitors.

Anderson expresses satisfaction in being "back home," after his many years of successful development in Florida. Mr. Anderson realized the importance of carefully thought out restrictions. These are quite detailed.

The following restrictions were required by purchasers of Topsail Beach property:

FIRST SECTION RESTRICTIONS, Pender County

THIS CONTRACT AND AGREEMENT, made and executed this the 25th day of February, 1949, by between and among J.G. Anderson and wife, Maidie W. Anderson; J.G. Anderson, Jr., and wife, Lillian M. Anderson; Jeff Flake, widower; and J.W. Crews and wife, Olga Crews, all of Wauchula, Florida, and E.N. Davis and wife, Gladys T. Davis of Frostproof, Florida:

WITNESSETH, That whereas the parties to this contract and agreement have acquired a certain tract of land in Pender County, North Carolina, to J.G. Anderson and others dated November 6, 1948 and recorded Book 277, Page 171, Registry of Pender County...whereas it is the purpose of the parties to this contract and agreement to subdivide said tract of land and to designate the same as "New Topsail Beach"...

"...the subdivision aforesaid, known as "New Topsail Beach" shall be conveyed and owned at all times hereafter subject to the following restrictions, limitations and provisions:

FIRST: That no lots in said subdivision shall be sold to or owned by any Negro, Mulatto, Japanese or Chinese or person of such extraction.

SECOND: That on the lots in Block 1, 6, and 13 ...known as "New Topsail Beach," no buildings shall be built closer than 50 feet to the ocean front line..."

THIRD: No buildings in any area of said subdivision shall be built closer to side lines than 5 feet, but where more than one contiguous lot is under one ownership..."

FOURTH: That there shall be no outside toilets in any section of this subdivision.

EIGHTH: All construction within said subdivision shall be carried out according to the following rules;

a. No home or business place in an optional area or residential area shall be smaller than 720 sq. ft. of floor space on the ground floor..."

b. No temporary "shacks" to be built in this subdivision.

c. In any trailer park or motor court area, all buildings must be neatly built and of substantial size to be attractive.

d. All garages, servant's quarters, boat houses, piers and docks which are built on any lots...are to be built in corresponding order with homes and business houses in that area..."

ASSEMBLY BUILDING - Now Topsail Island Community Center

Looking toward the sound, from the corner of Flake and Anderson Blvd., you will see a large structure. This is the Assembly Building. During the 1946-48 missile program, it was used as a missile assembly and storage facility.

The Assembly Building has had a number of owners including the original developers. J.G. Anderson and M. Boryk were said to have "horse-traded" the building over the poker table a number of times. In fact, many properties were horsetraded. This building has had a number of

Assembly Building circa 1992

Assembly Building circa 1985 (top)
Assembly Building Roof Timber Structure

incarnations including: Caison Building Supply, Red Barn Steakhouse, The Bald Pelican, and Roy Hill's Arsenal Centre, a mini-mall with a Soundview Restaurant (1984). They all seem to fall on hard times, owing to the short tourist season and other factors.

In the 1970s, the Red Barn Steakhouse was in business. During its time as a steakhouse, the cinder block wall paintings were done and it was carpeted.

Assembly Building - South Side View

Then, for a period of five years the building housed the Bald Pelican. It was managed by Jeff James who employed Tim and Mitch Barnes as bartender and all-round worker. Mitch painted the Bald Pelican sign. When they first opened, the task of pulling up the carpeting fell on Tim and Mitch. They slaved and worked to get it up but it was stuck fast, keeping some small pieces attached to the floor. They needed to be ready for dancing so they brought in beach sand to "smooth" the floor. After

Assembly Building - 1992

Inside of Assembly Building

a couple nights of dancing, the floor was sanded smooth and they took out the sand. Everyone howled and they brought back the popular sand as their dance floor.

It was a popular place and packed in people over the weekends, often 400-500 people. They had well-known dance bands like The Band of Oz, Maurice William & the Zodiacs, who made the song "Stay" popular. They also had The Sidewinder - Rock & Roll Band, Polar Bear, Embers, and Doug Clark & The Hot Nuts. Of course beach music was the most popular, but they brought in contemporary music, too. People came from towns like Wallace and Rose Hill.

They could only sell beer and wine. It was the only place at the south end of the island where you could buy beer. Brant Polzer worked there in 1981-82 as bartender. He said: *We were creative and advertised topless bartenders. The male bartenders would be without shirts and wear tuxedo ties. There were the inevitable barroom fights on Saturday nights, but they managed to contain them pretty well inside. The town people objected somewhat, but to those inside it was a lot of good, clean fun without serious problems.*

BREEZ-WAY INN AND CAFE -
Now Breezeway Restaurant and Motel

At the corner of Davis Ave. and Channel Blvd. was a group of buildings of which only the smallest building remains. The "Bumblebee" Army barracks and mess hall were originally connected as the Breez-way Inn and Cafe which accommodated about 65 people. It was named Breez-way because it was said that there was always a breeze rocking the chairs on the porch. Mr. and Mrs. Waitus Bordeaux ran the Breez-way for J.G. Anderson, the island developer from 1949 to 1950. This was the first motel on the island. Eunice Justice ran the Breez-way for Mr. Anderson in 1951. One year later, Mr. & Mrs. Dewey Justice traded their Thomas Landing oyster business and home for the Breez-way.

Dewey and Eunice Justice had married in 1938 after he convinced her to come from Raleigh to Thomas Landing to live. On an earlier visit, she had seen what life there would be like. No lights, no telephones, no indoor plumbing, and the nearest post office was at Folkstone, five miles away. She said: *It seemed like the end of the world.*

Breez-way Inn circa 1952

They built a two-story building that housed an oyster packing business downstairs and living quarters upstairs. *I put the first nail in it in April of 1939,* Mrs. Justice said. The store featured gas, groceries, and oysters. It was located by a simple sign that said: "D.D. Justice." He owned 50 acres

Dewey and Eunice Justice

of oyster beds in Stump Sound and he ran oyster roasts for seven years. The packing business went on for 15 more years.

When Camp Davis was opened, just down the road at Holly Ridge in 1941, they served oysters to people who had never eaten oysters before. Mrs. Justice said: *I didn't know that you weren't supposed to seat commissioned officers with non-commissioned officers, but they all got along fine.*

Maybe being hungry for oysters, hushpuppies, and coleslaw made the breach in military etiquette acceptable. Servicemen would stand in line for up to two hours waiting to feast on roasted oysters. Once they tasted an oyster, I never had anybody who wouldn't keep on eating them, she said.

Justice lived in the area all his life. When he was a boy, his family made a living harvesting oysters. Dewey said they would fill 30 to 40 gallon sized buckets with oysters and haul them to Wilmington to sell. Because the trip was made by mule and cart, anyone traveling that far had to spend the night along the way. He said they were sometimes able to sleep while the mule kept going because it wouldn't venture off the path cut by cart wheels.

J.G. Anderson, the developer of Topsail Beach in 1949, was responsible for the Justice's move across the sound. During the island's postwar development boom, Anderson hired Dewey Justice and his nephew Douglas Gray to run a party fishing boat for Topsail's visiting fishermen. Then, in preparation for the summer of 1951, Anderson asked Eunice Justice to come to Topsail Island to run the small motel he had established there.

Eunice Justice's initial summer as manager of the Breez-way and chief cook at the restaurant stretched through the next winter. By the summer of 1952, Dewey and Eunice Justice owned the motel and restaurant. It would be another 13 years before the family would build their home adjacent to the motel complex.

Work was steady at the Breez-way, especially during the summer. *We were the first motel on the island,* Eunice said. *One building had seven rooms with private baths and the other had 16 rooms with hall baths. We were always full on the weekends. In the restaurant, we served seafood platters, clam chowder, and homemade pies.*

Through the years, the Justices became synonymous with the Breez-way and with the life of Topsail Island. Dewey Justice was a member of the incorporating council for the Town of Topsail Beach. He served as councilman for four years and was mayor for two.

Dewey established the first official post office in 1953. He served as postmaster for the town for 10 years, a job he remembers as a mess and an aggravation. His duties were close at hand, with the post office window and boxes located just inside the Breez-way Cafe. *I would put the mail up,*

Dewey Justice at Tar Landing

225

sell stamps, money orders, and envelopes, and handle box rents, he said. He
was paid $48 a month for the chore.

There was another job for which Justice never minded volunteering. He
worked with the Weather Bureau as their Topsail Beach contact for 21
years, checking on local weather every two hours whenever hurricane or
storm conditions arose until 1976. In 1954, Hurricane Hazel was under
his watchful eye and they knew it was time to leave. Having to drive
across the only bridge at this time, the going was slow. The water was
choppy and rough. Eunice said: *We were sure we would get rocked off the
pontoon bridge before we could cross it.*

When they returned, what awaited them was a lot of changes. They were
transported by the marines in amphibian "ducks," a vehicle that can
travel on either water or land, because the pontoon bridge washed away.
Some homes washed into the sound, others moved into the streets, and
cement homes were blown apart. Only about 10 houses of 300 still were
standing. The Justice's house stood with comparatively little damage.
Before she entered the house, Eunice looked around: *There were no sand
dunes. You could stand on our front steps and see straight to the ocean.* Debris
was scattered everywhere. Inside the house, water had been 34 inches
deep. The cleanup would last for months. Water and the use of toilets

Tar Landing - Oyster Shells

Breezeway Motel circa 1992

were almost non-existent and the marines brought in drinking water.

The next summer following Hazel, Diane hit. She caused a lot of wind damage, taking off many roofs. The cabin cruiser docked in the back of the house sank. She had ridden out the wrath of Hazel, only to have a stake pierce her hull during Diane. The Justices have stayed through some bad hurricanes, in the earlier years, staying in the Assembly Building for safety at times, but in recent years they said, "never again."

The Justices sold the Breez-way Inn and Cafe in 1972 to Dr. M.L. Cherry and the old buildings were torn down. A new two story building was constructed by Forest McCullen, builder, and the Cherrys renamed the business Breezeway Motel and Restaurant. Mrs. Justice has left a legacy in her famous hushpuppy recipe which is still served today. The Justice home stayed in its place next door and commands a beautiful view of the sound with its spectacular sunsets.

J.G. ANDERSON'S OFFICE -
Now Gift Basket

At the corner of Davis Ave. and Anderson Blvd. the Gift Basket is a revised building that used to be flat-topped and served as Mr. Anderson's

J. G. Anderson, Developer - Office (top)
J.G. Anderson

original office. J.G. Anderson, et al, purchased the lower end of Topsail
Island which consisted of about one and one-half miles of property, basically ending at the current Soundside Market Restaurant. He purchased
it from Helen Bridgers and Evelyn Empie for $40,000. (Note streets bear-
ing the Bridgers and Empie names near here.) Anderson built this building for his office. It was his first permanent structure here. He undertook
serious marketing of the New Topsail Beach development. Anderson
mounted a tremendous neon sign on top of this building that would spit
and sputter all night. Eventually, it had to be taken down because of a
sagging roof.

J.G. Anderson

Rachel Magnabosco said: *J.G. Anderson was a dynamic and enterprising man who could sell refrigerators to Eskimos.*

Esther Godwin recalled: *Anderson was a man everyone respected. He sometimes commanded it. He had asked one of the builders to pick up the extra pieces of wood and saw horses a couple of times. When that didn't work, he soaked it all with kerosene and sent it into flames.*

Esther went on: *Mr. Anderson built his office, and all the furniture was painted bright orange. He said it was his lucky color and his desk, files, and all were that gaudy bright orange. He got people to come out here to provide services and help build Topsail Beach. He had a barber from Fayetteville set up a weekend barbershop at his office building.*

This building too, went through a number of uses. Then, in 1973, Louis and Mary Lou Muery established the Gift Basket, which was to become a solid island business that operates from March through December.

Mary moved her craft school and handmade gift business to Topsail Beach. Louis developed something of a specialty in mounting sharks' teeth. He found a tooth five inches in diameter and says that Topsail Island has more sharks' teeth than other islands. People find the fossilized teeth by simply concentrating on black objects in the sand at the edge of the water. The sharks' teeth are then easily mounted as a necklace or pin.

The Muerys believe the town must start planning for a proper sewer system that will protect health and environment. Islands have to plan ahead for this inevitable need. Louis believes the direction taken by any community depends more on the vigilance and determination of those governing to maintain the kind of community most of its residents desire.

Gift Basket circa 1992

NEW TOPSAIL ENTRANCE PILLARS

Looking up-island a block from the corner of Davis and Anderson, you will see white brick remains of pillars on each side of Anderson Blvd. Mounted atop these pillars were tall fluorescent lights which beckoned visitors and residents at night. They were controlled from Mr. Anderson's office. New Topsail Beach started at these pillars. Surf City ended at the "S" curve. In 1963, as they put together the Topsail Beach incorporation details, the story goes that the Topsail Beach limit was set to Davis Street, then to Ward's Warehouse (Surf City.) A meeting was held at the Emma Anderson Chapel and lawyer Cliff Moore set an arbitrary line halfway between the pillars and Ward's Warehouse. This then became the Topsail Beach/Surf City demarcation line.

GODWIN'S, FIRST GENERAL STORE

The corner of Flake and Anderson Blvd. is a familiar sight to longtime residents and visitors. The first general store, another Topsail Island institution, is still owned by the Godwin family. (You will note that there is a Godwin Street at the lower end of Topsail Beach). Esther Godwin said: *Mr. Bland and my husband James Averon Godwin were in business together in Fayetteville. Mr. Anderson invited them to come to a meeting and offered a free lot if they would come and build a business here. Averon didn't accept the offer but Mr. Bland did. He built the New Topsail Market in 1949-50. After a couple of years, Averon came here alone to run the store and Mr. Bland went back to Fayetteville. After several years, Averon bought the store. I wouldn't come at first, having three small children but we came to live here to be with him. It was a safe place for a family. I mostly objected to being out here away from people we knew, and alone. I was not very secure when storms came, because we didn't know what we do today about storm warnings. Oddly, we would go out in the storms and actually play in them.*

Esther Godwin was a smiling, likable woman, I would guess in her late

Godwin's Store circa 1992

70s. She said she has an open house and welcomes anyone who wants to come and visit. I enjoyed her generous hospitality, complete with delicious deep-dish chocolate pie and coffee.

She said: *I was scared of the pontoon bridge. It was so unstable, up and down with the tides, making it a shaky thing to cross. It would regularly wash out during storms and leave us stranded. We would have to go to the landing and bring across groceries and supplies by boat, trying to meet the bread and supply trucks when they were to be there.*

Averon built some boxes for the mail giving Topsail Beach its first post office. Later when the Post Office was to be a paying job, he decided not to continue with it. Dewey Justice became the first official postmaster. Esther said: *Our son Bill was in the Navy and on the aircraft carrier that picked up the first astronaut. He went to college at Fayetteville. When his father died in November 1976, he came home to run the store. I thought the children would want to go out in the world, but they preferred to stay right here in the area. My daughters also live nearby.*

J. Averon Godwin

Bill maintains the Godwin tradition with his store. It is still basically the same as the original building. It survived Hurricane Hazel with little damage. However, on the opposite side of the street, Godwin's Sport Shop & Grill survived Hazel, then was carried away two weeks later by a tornado. Esther said: *Averon was having an argument with the insurance adjuster about Hazel's damage to the store when the tornado hit. It lifted the roof off the* sport shop and wrecked all but the wall where I was standing. It happened so fast without warning I said: "Lord have mercy!" Broken lumber was dropped all over the insurance man's car and the roof blew out to sea never to be found. Averon asked: "Well young man, I suppose you see this as flood damage too?"

Esther recalled: *Forest McCullen was a good guy through thick and thin. He was jolly and worked hard. When we came he was busy tearing down military buildings and doing building projects. Storms came and washed away some and he would just start over. He is happy farming and riding his tractor today. My son Bill worked for Forest during winters.*

J. Averon Godwin and Sports Shop

Ms. Catherine King was one of the best teachers you ever saw. She taught several generations. She was a little rough with her discipline, pulling hair at times, but the kids learned. And there were other characters. Hum and Mable Vestal were a cute odd couple in their 50s who were apparently well-off. They had a nice cottage here on the sound. They also had a beautiful home in Wilson. His handlebar mustache and neckties worn as belts matched his eccentric character. Mable always wore long earrings and a gay, loud scarf around her neck. Hum would come to Averon when he needed anything. Once he came to the door and I invited him in. He seemed depressed and I asked him to breakfast. He said: "Esther honey, you don't know any more about a drunk than a man in the moon." He would sign a check so Averon could get him what he wanted until he dried out—a fairly regular occurrence. Everyone knew them and enjoyed their peculiar ways.

Hurricane Hazel was a devastation that everyone points to as a landmark. The whole island was a mess. She said: *We had comparatively little damage, but the boats at the sport shop washed away, some as far as Surf City.*

We gave up the boat business after that. With all the rebuilding after Hazel, we kept the store open and had crackers, sausage, and cheese lunches for workers. They had auctions for lots and if one had strong conviction, you could have bought lots for $500 and done well. I didn't want to invest and stay. It has been a good life here for us though.

Sun `n Fun Recreation circa 1960

James Averon Godwin was always involved in community, school, and church affairs. He was one of the original Town Board "Characters," when the town was formed. Slim Anderson called from Florida and asked Averon if he could name a street after him. He agreed and it still carries his name.

Jenkins' Roller Skating Rink - 1992

SKATING RINK

There is another Topsail Island institution, the Jenkins' Skating Rink which was originally built by Anderson at the Jolly Roger site, as the "Fun In The Sun" pavilion. Sonny Jenkins was running it for Slim Anderson, son of J.G. Anderson. Sonny built the current skating rink and post office in 1966 when the original rink building was converted to the Jolly Roger Motel by Lewis Orr. The skating rink is still a favorite of vacationers because of its unique recreation, including vintage 45RPM record music. Doris Jenkins has been the postmaster since Dewey Justice turned it over in 1963 at the Breez-way.

Jolly Roger Motel Patio and Pier - 1992

LAUNCHING PAD - Now Jolly Roger Patio

Behind the older "rounded roof" Jolly Roger Motel is the launching pad location. It is now part of the Jolly Roger Motel patio. It is 14 inches of concrete with an underground concrete bunker used by scientists and technicians who were involved in the missile launchings. This bunker is bombproof and is now used for motel storage.

The Jolly Roger Pier nearby is yet another longtime institution. Lewis Orr, one of the "founding fathers" and still an involved citizen was instrumental in the incorporation of Topsail Beach. He was mayor for a time and has quite a stake in Topsail Beach development. In 1954, he

Anderson House - 1992

built the Jolly Roger Pier to see Hurricane Hazel take it out three months later. He bounced back and rebuilt the pier and continued to rebuild over the years when storms whacked off 100-200 feet. Nine years later in 1963, he built the original Jolly Roger Motel and expanded it twice in 1977-78 and it is still in the Orr family. Mr. Orr is a builder and believes in Topsail Beach. He said: *I felt it was important to rebuild immediately for the health of Topsail Beach and help instill confidence in people that we could build a community.*

ANDERSON HOUSE - Now Phil Stevens' home

The two-story red brick house with white pillars at the corner of Scott Ave. and Anderson Blvd. is the Anderson House. Mr. Anderson built the house in 1952, intending it to be the model of more to come. He wanted Mrs. Anderson to move here from Florida but she would not move until he built a house like her home in Wauchula. His development momentum slowed, in part because of the setbacks due to Hurricane Hazel. The house did survive Hazel without significant damage. There was originally a wall around the property similar to the chapel wall. It was removed in 1961 because storms would leave trapped sand behind it.

EMMA ANDERSON MEMORIAL CHAPEL

This Chapel was funded in a unique way. In 1949, Mr. J.G. Anderson, developer of the beach, offered his lots to prospective buyers with the proviso that they make 10% of the purchase price a check to the "Church Fund." He stated: *"You will get credit three ways: first, on your lot; second, you get credit for helping to build the church; and third, you can deduct this amount from your income tax.* (In 1953, the IRS ruled that this policy would not be allowed.)

The first lot was sold in June 1949 and the chapel was sufficiently completed to hold services in 1951. The chapel was originally intended as a non-denominational church and remains so to this day. It is unique in that it serves a vacation and resort ministry which is committed to be "... fundamentally flexible to involve children, youth, and adults in constructive activities which enhance the opportunities for personal growth and realization for Christian freedom."

Emma Anderson Memorial Chapel - 1992

Emma Anderson Chapel—2004

There is a story of intrigue that took place in 1953. When Reverend Barney Davidson of Fayetteville, who was the minister for the week, was missing for a day, lights were on late at night in the chapel. He surprised the congregation by having painted a large picture of Christ which remains on the back wall. Hurricane Hazel took the roof but the painting was left untouched.

An interdenominational church, the policy of the church is to have a property owner sponsor a visiting minister each week, who saw to cleaning of the church and made provisions for fresh flowers. The visiting minister had the use of a cottage and each considers it a rare privilege to come for the week to Topsail Island, bringing their best sermons to churchgoers.

A student of the ministry is engaged for the three month summer season as a coordinator of the youth program. The activities are announced and a program distributed for vacationing youth. It provides a source of entertainment, Christian experience, and involvement with other youth.

On November 7, 1976 two faithful and dedicated workers for the church died. Edward Warren and James Averon Godwin served together on the board, died on the same day and were buried at the same hour. This must have been a deep impact on this small community.

The chapel suffered some damage from several prior hurricanes, but Floyd caused serious roof destruction. The roof was raised and two wings added that significantly increased its size and assured a stronger roof. I am told that you can see by some of the old hymnals that they are

Tower #1 - 1992

faded because of exposure to sunlight and water when Floyd took the roof.

PHOTOGRAPHY TOWER - TOWER #1

On Hines Ave. at the sound, you will find a tower home. These towers sit on 20 foot pilings and, as owners find out, are virtually indestructible in that they are made of reinforced concrete. They are placed precisely at scientifically derived distances between towers and their latitude and longitude documented. A brass plate on the patio reads: "US Coast and Geodetic Survey TOWER ONE - 1947." The tower was first converted into a home about 1949. It was owned by Mr. and Mrs. Wiatus Bordeaux and they lived in it from 1949 to 1954. It has been rumored that Miss Thaddis (as she was known) rode out Hurricane Hazel in October 1954 in the top of the tower.

STREET LIGHTS

The people of Topsail Beach helped each other over the hurdles of the early days, "making do" for themselves while putting together a community. A good example of this comes from the late 50s when it was decided that street lights were needed. Several folks recalled with a shudder, "It was dark here." William Warren and Dewey Justice collected $100 from a number of businesses and residents and Jones-Onslow

Warren's Soda Shop - 1953

Electric Membership Corporation installed street lights. Each business and resident who had a light paid their own street light bill until the town was incorporated and took it over.

WARREN'S SODA SHOP

Warren's Soda Shop was a long-standing business in Topsail Beach. It was at the corner of Crews Ave. and Anderson Blvd. (across from Town Hall). William Warren and Rachel Warren Magnabosco opened the first soda fountain on the island in the early 50s. It was located across from the current town hall. They also sold patent drugs. In 1954 Hurricane Hazel buried the soda shop inside and out under 28 inches of sand. But they were back in business the next summer. They built Warren's Soda Shop at the corner of Davis Ave. and Anderson Blvd. (currently The Beach Shop) in 1959.

Teenagers vacationing, and permanently living there found the soda shop important as first employment and used it as a means of learning about working with others. It also brought people together who stayed together. Being a family business and a center of activities, it started managing rental properties. When Paul Magnabosco was 16 years old he was a key member of the cleaning crew. He said: *In those days, especially in a family business, you did what you had to do. A girl from "down the street"*

240

was hired to help. Susan turned out to be excellent help. At Paul's mother's encouragement, they began dating and were married during their senior year at N.C. State University. The youth minister from Emma Anderson Chapel assisted with the service. In January 1995, they celebrated their 20th wedding anniversary.

William Warren and Rachel Magnabosco supported the Rescue Squad in a special way from the soda shop. If there was a manpower shortage to respond to a call, and one of the soda shop employees would be allowed to go. That often put the store shorthanded, but William and Rachel believed that responding to the call was essential. Eventually, enough recruits were trained to cover the emergency duties without borrowing from the soda shop shifts.

Paul said: *Topsail was a place where families could relax and enjoy being there. No doors were locked—it was safe. We were all like one large family. People would borrow each other's cars—you could just leave your keys in it and not worry. We frequently had house guests, especially employees whose parents were away from the beach house for a few days.*

The soda shop featured a large hand-sized hamburger steak patty with grilled onions. It was a Dagwood-like sandwich with all the trimmings. This sandwich

Warren's Soda Shop - Fountain Dept. 1960s

was called "Unkburger" since it was William Warren's creation. William was Paul's uncle and he called him "Unk" since he couldn't say Uncle William when he was only a few years old. The name stuck and everyone on the island affectionately called him "Unk."

The soda shop was a local hangout for kids. This was one of the few occupations for kids and everyone wanted to work there. Saturday and Sunday were the big days. They were busy enough that they worked three shifts. Schedules were alternated between 9A.M. to 1P.M., 1P.M. to 7P.M., and 7P.M. to 11P.M. Even with many kids wanting to work, it was tough to keep them on task when the surf was up.

Warren's Soda Shop circa 1960's

Maria Faison Mann, nicknamed "Ri Ri", tells a soda shop story. Her face crinkled into a smile as she recalled how she worked at the soda shop at Topsail Beach and a lady would come in every night for her ice cream. She knew where her ice cream was kept, but would slide open every refrigerator cover and look on the way to where her flavor was. John King, `, and Jim Hundley thought it would be a blast to help "lay Ri Ri out" as dead in the freezers holding a lily at her chest. When the lady did her search through the freezers, she was shocked by the spector and Ri Ri was looking for other employment. (It is unsure whose idea it was, but I guess we could ask the guys who were involved. John still lives on Topsail Island, Emery is a college professor, and Jim a physician in

Wilmington.)

In the 1960s Paul recalled that an Akron, Ohio family came to Topsail Island. Everyone knew everybody and the folks from Ohio were greeted by name each time they came to the soda shop. They enjoyed feeling at home on the island and spread it back to Ohio. Within a few years, more than a dozen Ohio families were vacationing at Topsail.

Topsail had a notable visit when John Kennedy, President of the United States, came to North Topsail to view a military naval and air assault exercise at Onslow Beach. He was aboard the USS Enterprise Aircraft Carrier offshore.

In 1974, with a northeaster blowing, Paul and his cousin Bo Warren went fishing. Their grandfather warned them not to go because it would be a terrible fishing day. They caught over 300 pounds of jumbo bluefish, spanish, and king mackerel. They had them piled into a 16 foot boat and the transom was dipping below water level. A photo was published in the *Raleigh News* and *Observer* and Paul got calls from all over North Carolina wanting to hear about the trip.

Technology has improved especially over the last 25-30 years: From driven pipes in the ground for an iffy water supply to a city water system; cable television; telephone service from rotary party lines to private touch-tone phones; recent introduction of cellular phone coverage; broadcast TV and FM radio with more stations and stronger signals, with the recent addition of a local FM station.

They closed Warren's Soda Shop for the evening to watch the Apollo moon landing. About 20-30 people gathered in their living room to watch live TV coverage. They had one of the few color TV sets on the island.
Paul said: *Fishing seemed better in the early 1970s. I recall catching 30 kings in one morning in my 16 foot boat and that was before I started using live bait. (menhaden) By the mid-1970s, using live bait, my brother-in-law Paul Shelton and I caught a 112 pound, 10 ounce tarpon-six feet eight and a half inches long, the third largest tarpon caught in North Carolina that year.*

During the early 1960s (7-10 years) my spending money came from selling sharks' teeth to jewelry manufacturers in Virginia. Sharks' teeth were much more

Ground Breaking for Rescue Squad Building

plentiful then and I still have two perfect teeth four inches long.

Rachel Magnabosco was elected to the town council in the 1960s. So far as we can recall, she was the second woman to be elected to the council. The first was Mrs. Wilbert "Lettie" Lee.

TOPSAIL BEACH VOLUNTEER RESCUE SQUAD

A community "first" that was supported by soda shop kids, was a Volunteer Rescue Squad. Marrow Smith was the first person in charge. He was able to get a used ambulance and arranged training from the Red Cross and Ogden Rescue Squad. Norman Chambliss let them use his old International Scout to get started. Each year they had a fund-raising effort. Later, as they got more organized, a duty roster was made up and they gave the community support that was not available before. The bulk of their calls were for heart attack and drowning. They also assisted Surf City from time to time.

The Rescue Squad became a vital support group for Topsail Beach. Marrow Smith was the first chief and was instrumental in getting the squad organized. Ogden Rescue Squad assisted with Red Cross training and sold us a 1957 Cadillac ambulance. They also consulted on what equipment would be needed. Summer residents—high school and college students—provided most of the manpower during the peak vacation season. Permanent residents took care of the sparse off-season calls during the 1960s and 1970s. The rescue squad was an instant comfort for vacationers, especially the elderly who were concerned about being 35 miles from the nearest hospital.

The Articles of Incorporation of TOPSAIL BEACH VOLUNTEER RESCUE SQUAD, INC.-A Non-Profit Corporation-dated November 29, 1969 names the directors. Directors are James C. Bethune, M.A. Boryk, Marrow Smith, and C.A. Peterson.

The Charter dated June 28, 1971, shows Charles Peterson, Christine McCullen, and Helen V. Stewart as officers, and renamed the Corporation, TOPSAIL BEACH VOLUNTEER RESCUE SQUAD AND FIRE DEPARTMENT, INCORPORATED.

The Rescue Squad was in the process of officially forming for two years culminating in the dedication September 6, 1971, of a $25,000 headquarters building complete with a community room. It was also equipped with a three bay garage for the fully equipped 1968 ambulance, a boat, and a fire truck which they hoped to purchase soon. Over twenty residents completed first aid courses and received Red Cross certificates.

The dedication address was given by Congressman David Henderson, and Howard Holly, auditor of Pender County, served as master of ceremonies. Floyd H. Stewart, Jr. was chief of the Topsail Beach Volunteer Rescue Squad and Fire Department. The membership is principally college students during the summer season.

Paul Magnabosco recalls taking care of the radio equipment until he graduated from N.C. State in 1975 with a degree in electrical engineering. *I held various positions in the squad and was captain in 1974-75. My rescue squad uniform is displayed frequently at the Assembly Building on special occa-*

sions. *From the late 1960s through 1975 I do not recall a single loss of life while a patient was in the care of the Topsail Beach Volunteer Rescue Squad.*

The early days were not so organized. Norman Chambliss recalled: *I went down to Godwin's store, when we first got here. Bill Godwin's father sat right where Bill does today. I went in there to pick up something, Mr. Godwin and Slim Rackley asked me to come to Detroit with them. I asked, "Why are you going to Detroit?" They said they were going to get a fire truck—going to start a fire department. Mr. Godwin would be the captain, and Slim, a lieutenant.*

Slim Rackley

Norman asked: *How about that fire truck I see at Surf City? If I had a fire, who would I call?* They looked at each other, and told him to call Bessie Mae Batts. Then Slim was reminded that the last time they called Bessie Mae, she sent a fellow down here who was drunk and he hit three cars on the way down. *Luckily, I never had to call Bessie Mae.*

EARLY POLICE DEPT.

Mr. Slim Rackley was the local policeman for years. He was a colorful character. Norman Chambliss recalls being told: *since you have that place at Topsail Beach there is something you have to do. There is a fine fellow down there, Slim Rackley. He has a protective agency called the Topsail Protective Agency, and his job is to look after your house in the wintertime. I don't know if Slim will even look at your house in the wintertime, but when he asks you to join, be sure to join. If you get on his list, for $15.00 a year, and you are down at my house at a little party, and you have a little too much to drink, Slim would run you right home. But if you are not, you will be in the Burgaw jail in 30 minutes.*

Sure enough, not long after that, Norman was taking out the garbage and saw brake lights. Slim backed up and he joined his group. Norm said: *Slim put a sign on the back of my house and gave me a card that had a private eye on it. He was a fine guy who did a splendid job at the beach. But this was an interesting side that I recall.*

Lee Hunt Mims adds that she would always remember Slim because when she was a teenager and the kids got rowdy he would haul them out and take them home before they got into trouble.

Humphrey's Original Cracker Box

TOM HUMPHREY

Tom Humphrey was one of the appointed founding fathers when the town of New Topsail Beach was founded. He resigned after two and one half terms in about 1974. At that point the water was in, and Tom said there wasn't any other big issue he was interested in at that time.
Back in early days, 1920s and 30s, prisoners were kept in cages on docks. They fished for Mullet and Spot, processed them, and shipped them to the state prison to feed prisoners.

Bob Humphrey said: *My Grandfather, J. Thomas Bland, was an attorney who obtained property in exchange for legal fees. The Atkinson family formerly owned the property. This property was on about one half mile of land from the former Seafood World toward Topsail Beach, including hordes of mosquitoes. On this land was the Bland Cabin which Dad helped build in the 1920s. He was about 13 years of age. They tied bundles of lumber behind a boat and pulled it over from the mainland.*

Dad had been to the Bland Cabin a number of times in the 30s, by boat. When we first came to the island in 1948 in a car, we couldn't find the cabin. Someone came over later and found it for us marking the place off the gravel road the government had put in. Then we came and stayed a week.

Humphrey's After-Hazel Cracker Box - 1992

In those early days, we often had frightening storms with lightning and fire balls from light sockets. Of course, the storms nearly always killed the lights until repairs were made.

In 1942, the US Government had taken over the island for military use, so little activity was allowed until 1947 when they got word that the property was to be turned over to the owners.

The Bland family drew lots in 1948 for shares of the property and Tom Humphrey built a house south of Surf City. He put in running water, a gas stove, refrigerator, and kerosene lamps. Shortly after, Ed Yow built his house at the ocean side. Happy Lewis also built around the same time. A year later, he wired the house for electricity and got electric lines brought in. They were on the island only for the summer months until 1952.

Bob said: *My dad worked at Wilmington, then moved here in 1952 opening a convenience store and tackle shop just south of the Topsail Beach town line. He named the store the Cracker Box, I guess because it was kind of shaped like a cracker box. It was located in a spot where there was great surf fishing. There were always a lot of kids around in the summer and people in and out of the Cracker Box for food and supplies. Business went well with lunches, gasoline, and rental boats. In 1953 he added on to the Cracker Box. They even got a TV and were able to get channel six—that was it.*

In October 1954, Hurricane Hazel took the whole thing, all but the gas pumps. Hazel cleaned off Topsail Island and put it back to its beginning. At least 30 frame homes washed across into the marsh, near King's Creek. Cinder block cottages just broke up and some were left with entire walls missing. Humphrey's house survived. Our family had gone to Burgaw during the storm.

A lot of cottages were intact with everything in them in its place. There was no practical way to get equipment over there to bring them back. Fishermen and others living over on the mainland in shacks, found them a source of building materials. A lot of scavenging took place and cottages were taken apart piece by piece to became homes for many. Inside plumbing and all became part of their homes. If the owner didn't get there first, they owned it.

Some recollections of the aftermath of Hazel tell of how island folks helped support one another. The hurricane was devastating to many. It washed out some of the new drawbridge abutment almost washing out some of the causeway. The water was about seven feet above high tide and took the pontoon bridge right out to its channel. A surge went up the waterway then came back—a mad rush of water.

During Hugo, the Isle of Palms took a 17 foot surge. It can supposedly take a 12 foot surge but a 17 foot would really

Forest McCullen circa 1956

Humphrey's Cracker Box Pumps after Hazel

wash over a lot of the island. Fortunately, Hugo went another way south of Topsail.

Bob said: *We were brought over to the island on a Marine "DUKW" to look at damage. My father found a display freezer part way up the beach and knew the Cracker Box had to be gone. Also found cases of motor oil and other stock strewn up the beach. Later they pulled the freezer out of the sand, cleaned it up, got it working and used it for ten years. It looked bad but I guess it worked. Our Jeep had been left on the island and we used it to carry people around to check their properties and cottages. The reason the Jeep was left here was because I had lost the key.*

Lib Mallard from Wallace had a cottage next to the Gift Basket since the early 50s. They brought her by Jeep to see it and it was completely gone. She was sobbing and as they looked around, found it way over by the Breezeway Restaurant trapped between other buildings. All was intact—the bed was made and all things were still in the cottage. She had it moved back to its original spot.

Bob recalled: *Hurricane Hazel's damaging of homes was bad enough but even worse, the island economy was wrecked for some time. It really hurt the Cracker Box business and it took over six years to recover.*

In 1955, they rebuilt the store but the business was gone. Even though piers and some businesses rebuilt up and down the beach, people did not come like they did before Hazel. There was a period of time before people risked rebuilding their homes so it took years for businesses like the Cracker Box to recover.

That same year Sonny Jenkins built the roller skating rink. He installed a 45 RPM record changer and amplifier for skating music. It is still in use to this day.

Tom Humphrey was having a hard time making ends meet and sold off five lots. With this he bought a dump truck to do business. He would fish for flounder all night to buy gas for the truck. He started a grading business which his son Bob has carried to a grading and foundation business today.

Forest McCullen was one of the appointed members of the incorporation of the town. He was a contractor who owned the lumber building at the current Hedgecock Lumber location. He and Lewis Orr, Sr. built most of the original houses here.

Bob remembers: *Forest was quite a wild young fellow. He originally hailed from Clinton, NC. He always drove a Jeep. He had it in the ocean many times and the ocean salt must have rusted the brake line. Once when he swerved in to the Cracker Box, the brakes failed and he crashed right through the side of the building.*

He was always busy, running around like a chicken with its head cut off. Always had to have his way. He was a nice guy but he would get upset if someone didn't agree. He was always falling out with someone. When the town formed, it was over politics. He would come to the meetings and yell to make his points. When they had the first election, he convinced two people to file along with him. One of them got on the board but Forest didn't.

He couldn't get along with anyone after that. He and his fiery temper always seemed to cross swords with the town. Once he got mad at everyone because the board fired a building inspector he had managed to get appointed while he was on the board. They fired the inspector for bad performance. He just went wild about it. (Interestingly, in recent years he seems a changed person who you wouldn't believe could have been so short tempered).

Just thought of another person I knew for years around the beach. Captain Kenneth Andrews was quite a nice guy—kind of a friend of a friend. He was captain of party boats and took many people out to good fishing. He was an adventurer too.

I remember once, we had a Nor'easter that caused our school bus to get hung up on the bridge. The pontoon bridge would rise and fall with the tide and the bus couldn't go over the hump. We had to wait until the tide went out. The frame of the bus just hung up on the ramp.

In 1957 Bob discovered girls. Now he was able to drive around anywhere. Those days, kids were able to do so since the island was remote and there were no police to enforce driving laws. By 1959, Bob was 16 years old and found lots of entertainment on the island. There were bars, night clubs, a skating rink, miniature golf courses, and Barnacle Bill's.

Topsail Beach - Jolly Roger Pier circa 1956

Humphrey Street was so-named because the town needed to name it something. It wasn't necessary to petition the town to do so back then.

Bob wrapped up with: *The New Topsail Inlet is moving as you know. The inlet was just below the chapel and as the land builds southward, it has a kind of bulge on the end. Years ago, the Sea Vista Motel had a lot of space between it and the ocean. They had two major grassy dunes and they kept building up. They built a gazebo and used the area for games. Later, as the Inlet moved southward, the beach started eroding some 40-50 feet a year until the Sea Vista was threatened. Re-nourishment by the Corp. of Engineering put the beach in shape so it is OK for awhile.*

LEWIS ORR

Lewis has a ruddy complexion, carries a broad-faced grin and has a business-like demeanor. He is retired but stays involved in his family businesses. He was one of the "characters" who were the original founding fathers for New Topsail Beach. In this role he was appointed the first mayor.

Lewis was born beside the Pamlico River, in Washington, NC, and has always loved the water. After he earned a degree in engineering from NCSU, Lewis spent a four year tour of duty during WWII in the Naval Civil Engineering Corps at Panama where he met his first wife. Lewis left the navy a full Lieutenant.

In Panama, there are a number of Chinese and Hindu shops. Lewis said: *My wife found an ornate Chinese carved chest made of camphor wood and teak which became her "hope chest." She*

Mayor Lewis Orr, Sr. - 1963

stored Irish linens, silver pieces etc. in it and it moved with us wherever we lived.

After WWII, Lewis first worked for a contractor in Durham who built a school in Trenton. Longing to get back to the ocean and wanting to go into business for himself, Lewis saw a chance to go to Topsail Island.

Lewis jokes that he arrived on Topsail Island a year after Columbus. *When I came there was plenty of fresh air, good water, and good fishing, and the people had done a good job of preserving these things.*

Topsail Beach Town Line

He found few cottages, sand and clay streets, no water system, one store, no piers, and one restaurant when he drove over the old pontoon swing bridge and onto the island. *The military roads were full of potholes, making a four-wheel drive a necessity,* he said.

On a cold February day in 1951 he bought a lot. J.G. Anderson and three other partners from Florida were developing New Topsail Beach. About the only businesses here were Shorty's Grill and Tackle Shop at the end of the street, the old Breez-way Inn and Bland's Grocery and Filling Station.

Slim Anderson built the Sun and Fun Recreation Hall in 1953 which was to become the first Jolly Roger Motel. This building had a skating rink, movies, and on the first floor, a bathhouse. Lewis ran the skating rink until Hurricane Hazel struck.

He built the first Jolly Roger Pier as New Topsail Ocean Pier Inc., in 1954. Hazel took it out four months later. The Orrs also lost their home and car in the storm. He rebuilt the pier right away because he thought the beach needed a shot in the arm. By doing this he felt that people would have more confidence and would also rebuild.

Topsail Island fell on hard times for several years after Hazel. Banks wouldn't lend money for building because insurance coverage was difficult to obtain. Many people were scared and didn't want to live here because of fearing another storm would come in. It took years before Topsail was showing much progress. Looking out at the ocean, Lewis said: *These storms are a part of the price we pay for this beauty. I have always believed the uncertainty for us living here is well worth our life style. One of our ongoing jobs is preserving the beaches, an investment we must make.*

When the "characters," a small group of outspoken businessmen independents felt the town needed organization, Lewis was conned into being the first mayor in 1963. He also served again as mayor in 1973-75.

Lewis' next venture was the Blackbeard's Restaurant. In 1966, he bought the Topsail Beach Skating Rink and converted the building into the original Jolly Roger Motel, with 19 units. It was later expanded in 1977 and 1978 to the largest motel in Pender County. The Jolly Roger and Blackbeard names were chosen because of their historical significance on the island.

Lewis Orr, Sr. - 1994

Lewis built the Ocean Pier Motel for Clarence Smith and operated it for several years for him. Rooms rented for $6.00 per night. He said: *At one time, I was in real estate, renting cottages, operating a pier, a motel, and a restaurant. I was working day and night, seven days a week. And all the while, I was—no my wife was raising a family.*

He converted the Sun and Fun Recreation Hall into the first Jolly

Roger Motel in 1966. The first expansion into today's Jolly Roger was in 1977 and the last building in 1978, making it Pender County's largest motel. I asked him if he accumulated property by being prepared to buy as they became available. Lewis said: *It's not quite that simple. You have to create a market to get growth. Just sitting on property won't generate capital growth. You have to move property to have it grow in value.*

Lewis had a North Carolina State University ring with a charmed life. He repeatedly lost it and would find it later. One incident that stands out is when he was casting a net for bait. Later he noticed his class ring was missing. He had flung it into the sound while casting the bait net. The next morning he looked for it at low tide and there it was, perched high and dry on the mud.

When Hurricane Hazel hit, their house was blown into the sound except for about a 10 foot section of wall. His class ring was on the bureau because there was a stone missing and he had intended to take it to the jeweler for repair. Hazel took the ring. The Chinese chest disappeared. Also many other possessions that had meaning were missing.

They stayed at Jacksonville during the hurricane. Afterward, they came to what is now called Olde Point and got a fisherman to bring them over to Topsail Island to survey the damage.

Two years later, he found his class ring half buried in the sand near his house after a storm. From time to time, they would find pieces of their Royal Dalton China, silver, spoons, etc. in the sound. Another important find was his favorite shirt which he found a couple of years after Hazel, underwater in the

Lewis and Verna Orr—2004

marsh. He fished it out, washed it, and wore it for several years after that. Amazingly, he also found the lid from his wife's Chinese chest in the marshland after a storm about two years after Hazel. He brought it home and put it in the attic of his office.

Lewis' wife, Anne, died in 1972. On November 23, 1974, Lewis and his present wife, Verna, were married in the first big wedding held in Emma Anderson Memorial Chapel. They had both lost their spouses by death before they met.

Verna saw the ornate carved lid and asked Lewis to have it made into a coffee table, which he did. Incredibly, about four years later, 24 years after Hazel, they had a carpenter in to look at some work to be done in their bathroom. He admired their coffee table and casually said that he thought his uncle had a chest that was carved just like it. But he didn't think the chest had a top.

Lewis got the particulars of where the carpenter's Uncle lived and started on his way. He finally found the little house by the RR track near Wilmington, feeling much excitement. Lewis thought: *Will it really be possible for this chest to be the matching one for the lid? The unshaven man came out on the porch in bare feet and demanded, "What do you want?"*

Jolly Roger Pier - 1992

I said, "I understand that you have a Chinese chest." The man replied, "I do have one but don't want to sell it." "I don't know that I want to buy it," I said. He then replied, "It's in the little house out back—look out for snakes in the weeds."

The chest was under a lot of other stuff. "Right pretty," I said, "Where is the top?" "No top — thought I'd make one someday." "A lot of work," I said, "Can you carve that well?" "Hmm, I don't know." "Why don't you sell it to me?" "I'll see if I can do something with it." "What is it worth?" he asked me. "Getting a top made will be expensive. How about $20?" I asked. "No, not enough—How about $25?" I gave him a 20 and a 10 and he returned a five dollar bill.

I loaded the chest into the car trunk and locked the lid. As I pulled away, I said, "That was my chest from years ago that was lost in Hurricane Hazel and I have the top." "Well I'll be damned. I bet I could have got a lot more out of it," he said to me. "You sure could have," I said, and punched the accelerator to dig out of there fast.

Lewis recalled two airplane accidents where a small plane that was stunt flying crashed into the ocean near the Jolly Roger Pier. Mrs. Donahue from Winston Salem was a passenger on board. Surfers got her out OK but the pilot was killed. The other accident was between two jets that collided at approximately 30,000 ft. Pieces of the wreckage fell at the southern tip of the island and two pilots parachuted down. Mullens got one pilot out of the water with his small outboard motor boat. Lewis impulsively jumped in his charter boat, which he didn't know how to operate, and got down to the crash site. The other plane, a photo reconnaissance, plane had a valuable camera aboard and crashed out further in the ocean. The marine helicopter tried to find it to salvage the camera. We are not sure if they ever found it.

Lewis admits that he has an impulsive side. He grew up in Washington, NC, and would drive his family up there to visit on holidays and such. They were coming back across the bridge at Washington and he pulled into the marina to buy cigarettes. As they left, he backed around the building which made his family curious. He had bought a boat, while buying the cigarettes, and was hitching it to the car to take home.

Lewis points out something a lot of us don't realize in our travels around Topsail Island. The maritime forest is unique and beautiful on our island. The old oak and cedar trees appear stunted and shaped by the sea air. As you look at them and hike through some of the wooded areas, there is a new insight about the island that does not show itself at first glance. They also provide over 200 different species of birds with a sanctuary.

A news story in the mid 50s captioned "Lassoed at sea," told of Lewis Orr, who has seen such strange animals as sea lions near his fishing pier, spotting an even stranger sight. Lewis and several companions spent about three hours chasing an alligator before he was able to lasso it and bring it to shore. He said the capture was the first.

Lewis said that one of his disappointments is that the sewer project did not go through as a collaboration with Surf City. He said: *This will hurt us in the long run as I fear that some of our decisions are too self-centered and short range. Eventually we will be polluting the sound and something will have to be done. Both Kenny Andrews and Dallas Ritter were in the charter fishing boat business "captaining" for me around 1954-56. I helped Dallas get started here.*

An observation about the mentality of the people here is that they love the sea and they hold out for their first love of fishing. Sometimes an "islander" will work on some wage earning, but soon they want to stop and go fishing. This view of life is one that entrepreneurs are often jealous of, yet they can't really understand. The islander's demeanor is one of a genuine love of the sea and all else has to wait. They are well-liked but not necessarily to be emulated in today's drive for financial success.

Lewis Orr's commitment to Topsail Beach is total. His example has been incorporated by his two sons who are well thought of businessmen. Lewis Jr. is managing the Maritime Way development, and Robin is managing the Jolly Roger Pier/Motel. His daughter, Tessie, went to Spain as a college Spanish major. She met and married a native businessman CPA and settled in Spain to raise a family.

Lewis' aim is to maintain quality businesses, a community he is proud of and a good place for families to live. He works hard to achieve it. Lewis and Verna have traveled the world and say, without hesitation, that their most favorite place is Topsail Island.

MORE RECOLLECTIONS

Herbert Williams

Herbert was a cordial, soft-spoken yet sure man of action. His quiet, relaxed demeanor hides an inner driven desire to produce with excellence. You can see evidence of this in his carvings and woodworking projects of recent years. He was an early influence in the development of Topsail Beach as one of the original founding fathers. He built and operated the Topsail Motel and started the Century 21 Action Real Estate business.

Herbert saw action in WWII with the submarine service on the *USS Sea Leopard*. He and Myrtise were married in 1941 and raised three sons who remain here at the beach and involved in the Century 21 Action Real Estate & Construction business. He worked for a period at the North Carolina Shipyard at Wilmington, then owned an auto dealership business in North Carolina and in Florida.

Herbert said: *We moved to Topsail Beach in 1953 and built the Topsail Motel having purchased the land from Harvey Jones. Lumber and supplies were bought from Caison Building Supply and we started building November 1953. We were in our house six months and Hurricane Hazel took it away in October 1954. We rebuilt it right away and were able to reopen in July 1955. While we were building, the crew stayed at the Breezeway and enjoyed Mrs. Justice's great food.*

When we were allowed back on the island after Hazel, Beaver Barwick and I walked from the Surf City Pier to our Topsail Motel. As we walked, we speculated, "Is it there, I wonder what is left?" We just kept walking and wondering. All the oceanfront buildings including our house were gone. Two weeks of motel receipts were lost. We were able to gather our personal belongings in one pillowcase. It is hard to express just how it is to lose everything.

One thing that sticks out is how dark it was after the storm. (This comment has been made by several reflecting on the stark loneliness of the darkness with no electricity.)

We had a Banks pony and kept it in a corral on the sound side. This pony was wild. It would throw Sidney in a minute. Myrtise was determined to show the kids how to ride it, but she was thrown, too. When Hazel came through, the pony had water up to his belly and swam with the hurricane. Talmadge Batson found him after the storm, near US17 highway.

Herbert Williams circa 1991

I used to have a Model A pickup truck with big tires. Our three boys, Sidney, Hiram, and Mark, the Orr boys, and Ralph Justice had great times with it.

It seemed there were many more fish years ago. We caught many drumfish on Lee Island.

The old original settlers held thousands of acres of land. Among them were James W. Sidbury and Verlinza Sidbury. They would drive cattle across Permuda to Topsail for winter grazing and back to the woods for the summer. One of them had a country store on the sound. They would grow produce and load it on wagons to go to Wilmington.

There was a story about Empie Sidbury's farm on Becky's Creek, that a paraffin sealed chest was unearthed. A sharecropper working for Sidbury found it. No one seems to know if there was anything in it. If so, the recoverers kept it secret.

Mr. Redd was one of the first sheriffs in Onslow County. The Redd house is located near Pulpwood Landing. This is located within a mile of Tar Landing where Dewey Justice had an oyster house business. Story goes that in the 1890 hurricane a large sailboat was blown from the sound up into the front yard. That is somewhat inland for such a "beaching."

The Williams family owned and operated the Surf City Pier for four or five years. The pier was originally built by Beaver Barwick and Jim Hubbard.

Herbert recalled: *Harvey Jones was quite an island character. He used to invite people down for shrimp. He would net the shrimp in the sound, start a big iron pot of sound water boiling, throw in a handful of salt with the shrimp complete with heads. These parties were a feature of island living and friends and neighbors were called in to partake. They would just pop off the heads and eat.*

Sidney, our son, loves such parties and has become a celebrated chef. He cooks many fish delights such as shark or whatever is available at the time. Southern Living magazine featured one of his bashes several years ago. This kind of party—some of them impromptu—has been a hallmark of Topsail Island living where we share these delightful get-togethers.

JANE (BLAND) WATSON

Grandfather John Thomas Bland was a judge at Burgaw. When Grandad bought the land, Grandmother asked "Why did you buy such property?" He said, "It will help hold our family together." Which it did. Land was from the former Seafood World fish house to Ms. Mayrand's property. They had a black worker Lewie, who would row them over in the 1920s.

Judge Bland's daughter, Lorena Bland, was first married to Tom Humphrey's father. Her second husband was Henry Williams. She said: *Aunt Lorena leased land to Walker who was the leader of the Gold Hole dig, in the late 1930s. They used the fishing shack that J.T. Bland and sons had built in*

Bland Cabin

the early 1930s as a base of operations and brought everything over by boat. A beach was built on the sound from the Gold Hole diggings at Bland's Landing. The sand dunes were much higher then, but they of course looked like mountains to a child. The shack was rustic, rough hewn wood. There was a diary on the wall of who came over the years, and how many fish they caught. It was one big room with bunk beds. The pump outside took forever to prime but gave cold, sweet water. They used lamps at first. Mosquitoes were so bad they went to bed by the edge of dark so lights wouldn't attract mosquitoes.

Lewie would cook for them. He would row the boat to the mainland for groceries—would promise candy when he returned. Kids couldn't wait for their BB Bats candy—what a treat.

Just after the beginning of World War II, Dorothy Bland Stern and some kids rowed over to the island to stay at the shack. They didn't come back and some feared they had drowned. The Coast Guard had picked them up and kept them on the boat overnight. Nobody was allowed on the island at that time.

In 1948, the surviving children of John Thomas Bland had a family meeting to draw lots and divide the property among the nine children. Jane's mother, Norma Bland, widow of Joseph Wharton Bland, drew the lot containing the fishing shack. The shack was used as a cottage for her and her children, Joe, Dorothy, Jane, and Jack until the 1960s when it burned.

Benjamin and Mae drew the tower and they turned it into a home in 1950. They also built a building across the road. They had decided to ride out Hurricane Hazel and when the water started coming over the dunes, she got scared and they got off the island. As she reached the mainland, she got out of the car and kissed the ground. Hazel did not damage the tower but Mae was so frightened that she didn't want to live there. The shack was also still in place, with nothing disturbed. An icebox and bathtub washed up near there and they put the tub by the pump. Benjamin sold the tower. They lived out their lives at Burgaw. They never came back to live on the island.

EVELYN OTTAWAY

Evelyn and her husband, the late Kenyon Ottaway, heard in Knoxville, Tennessee that Topsail Island was a good place to vacation. They agreed and bought two building lots. When they came to see about building on them in 1965, they traded them toward the tower home. They had no idea that was what they were going to do, but liked what they saw and found a way to buy it. The Bland family owned the tower originally and

Bland Tower Home - now Ottaway, 1992

had converted it to a unique home.

The tower home offered an unusual home for two special people: Evelyn, with a passion for music no doubt affected by her father who played with John Philip Souza; and Kenyon, who retired in 1975 from a long experience in the printing business.

The Topsail Island Historical Society has recognized Tower # 3 as a historic building. This was the third of eight photographic towers that housed cameras and tracking equipment for Operation Bumblebee rocket firings in 1946-48. Surveyors use the tower as a benchmark for them because of the precise and recorded placement.

Their tower is a hardened structure that made repairs difficult. They renovated the bathrooms because water pipes were outside, subject to freezing. It was some back breaker to bring the pipes inside because of having to drill through 12 inches of solid concrete to do so. The only remaining problem had been water leaks, but after some years, they resolved them. Their tower home is located right on the beach.
The Ottaways came to Topsail after Hurricane Hazel. Kenyon is not new to hurricanes, because he lived through a worse hurricane on Long Island in 1938. He was superintendent of a printing company and his presses were underwater—he got home five days later. They were never concerned about hurricanes because they would get the warning and just leave.

Ken had been on the Surf City Planning Board. He was very concerned about the quality of life on Topsail Island. They have to keep a watch-ful eye on developers who would bring ill-advised plans. He reflected on his disappointment over Topsail Beach's unwillingness to go in with Surf City on extending the sewage system and the deep wells on the mainland. They both will be needed someday.

Evelyn recalled: *Losing items in the sand and having them reappear months and years later was always an amazement. Island people have many stories about recoveries. Some years ago, after a northeaster, someone found a lot of 1940 vintage coins near the Surf City Pier with a metal detector. They lost 20 feet of sand with that storm.*

HAPPY LEWIS COTTAGE

Robert and Anne Richards have lived at Topsail Island for many years. Anne goes back even further because her father, Harry "Happy" Lewis used to come from Wilmington to the island to fish.

Harvey Jones and Harry were in World War I together. Harvey had a house on the sound in the early 40s that burned. The "Gold Hole" folks dug a shaft in the late 1930s, about 150 feet north of the Happy Lewis cottage on Harvey's property. They were afraid that kids might fall into it. Hurricane Hazel filled it.

Happy Lewis Cottage circa 1950

Harvey Jones lived on the sound side prior to WWII. He had the first house build on the south side of Surf City. He owned the land on Topsail Island that is now Queen's Grant.

The Happy Lewis Cottage, built in 1949, is said to be the first house on the ocean front south of Surf City.

Anne recalled: *We have lived many places but always came back for the summer. We could walk out the front door anytime, throw in a line and always catch something. Even with all the beach erosion up and down the island, the beach is 60-80 ft. wider than it was in 1949.*

Two weeks after Hazel, Bob Richards' mother and father were driving toward Godwin's Store and a tornado tore the roof off the building right in front of them. Another Hazel story is told about C.W. Twiford, church historian, who had lost his whole house, including a set of glasses with sayings on them. Incredibly, some time later one of the glasses reappeared in the sand bearing the saying "How Dry I Am."

CAPTAIN KENNETH ANDREWS

Captain Andrews was tall and slim with gaunt, angular face and intent eyes. It seemed right to call him "Captain" because he embodied such a rich history of Topsail Island and the sea. Andrews' life traversed 81 years of Topsail history.

Kenneth Andrews and his spouse lived on their land near Sloop Point. After working at the Gold Hole for four years until 1941, he worked at the Wilmington Shipyard. He then was a commercial fisherman at Hampstead. For a brief five weeks he and his wife tried living in Utah after World War II but desperately homesick for the sea, he hustled back to Topsail, never to leave again. The trip was so expensive he had to give up his land to pay off debts. He took work on a shrimp boat, then became captain of several party boats, taking groups deep sea fishing. During off season, he would set crab and blackfish pots. Oysters and clams were plentiful for harvesting.

Captain Kenneth Andrews

Captain Andrews, and others making their living by the sea, seem to have a different outlook on life from most of us. They live with the uncertainties of weather and ocean, yet find a way to survive.

Andrews said: *When things were slack or off-season, we would go out*

268

for oysters and crab or do other kinds of work, but as soon as we were able, we'd get back to fishing. I reckon you have to love it to get along with it.

He ran charter boats from 1948 to 1974, operating out of various docks such as the Breezeway, *Virginia Ann*; the Dolphin Pier for Harvey Jones, *Captain Vick*; Sound Pier for Lewis Orr, *Davis Brothers*. He then worked with Ivey Lewis, as co-captain, for five years on the *Buccaneer*, Topsail Marina.

He said: *I was always proud of my boats. My business was always good and I had good clientele because I kept a good boat. It was always clean, painted, and I knew where to fish.*

September and October are the best fishing months going right through November. Some people just wanted to go out for a ride. They did not always want to fish. We had a charter of six people and their wives one day. They were preachers. When they were out to sea, they opened up a big chest of beer and chicken.

I have taken divers out for salvaging from wrecks. One marine diving team got 10-15 lead bars from the Phantom, a sunk blockade runner near the New Topsail Inlet. The state stopped such salvaging so the marines didn't go out any more. In the 60s, a light airplane was stunt flying and dipped a wing in the water cartwheeling it into the ocean near the Jolly Roger pier. It killed the pilot but his lady passenger was rescued. We tried to hook the wreckage with a line but there was a hard SW wind and rough seas. I hooked it and broke the line, then gave it up for the day. The next day we could not find the wreckage anywhere.

One day when I was chartering for Harvey Jones, I was late getting to the Dolphin Pier. Harvey said, "It's too bad you are late. You missed a charter. Two people here from Winston-Salem wanted you to take them out to sea because they had a small lead box of cremated body ashes to throw overboard. When you didn't get here as expected, they got impatient and asked to cast them here, so they threw the box from the end of the pier."

Maria Faison Mann is a petite, bright, and engaging woman who flashes an impish grin as she tells of her recollections as Captain Andrew's First Mate. Maria was known by her friends as "Ri Ri." She had fished all her young life and was sure she could do it. After she persuaded Andrews to try her as First Mate, John King went with her to show her the ropes. Handling the lines was tricky. There were wire lines for big fish and they were expensive and would break if tangled. She was mate on a 50 foot boat named *Pal*.

She said: *There were two compasses on board and they often varied as much as 15 degrees from each other. She would head out at the lower steering station keeping all headings in mind so she would know how to get back. They had a two-way radio and Andrews was on it a lot with his cronies. Buddy Mizelle, another captain, had a unique voice on the radio. His high-tider accent (from north of Morehead-Outerbanks) was different enough that only a few people could communicate. We had no markings, buoys, depth-finders, or fish-finders. Kenneth somehow knew where fish liked to go.*

Maria Faison Mann

We would head out New Topsail Inlet at 6 A.M. Kenneth would have his eyes glued to the water, and like it was a superstition, he would always say, "That inlet is a mess." High tide or low tide, it didn't matter. They had to know how to think like a fish. Kenneth never came back without fish. His philosophy was we do not charge customers for the ride. I do not believe he would have taken peoples' money if they didn't get a fish. Maria said: *I am just sorry you never got to fish with him. You would have enjoyed it.*

There was such competition among captains, yet they called each other to help find fish. They teased each other about their success, or lack of, but would all stick together. All wanted others to make it. They were their own safety net, helping one another if in trouble.

Kenneth was a real gentleman. He made smoking an art, and he used it to help navigate. The cigarette would always hang from his lip just so and the burn line of smoke would tell the apparent wind direction. This was important in navigation and turning without snarling the lines.

We had a runaway engine incident on the *Pal*. Mechanical problems were a way of life. The diesel engine runs on air, fuel, and compression. One of the things that sometimes can happen is a runaway engine,

Captain Andrews at the Wheel

Lee Hunt Mims

which could self-destruct if not stopped. Nothing could stop it except shutting off the air. We had just warmed up the engine and closed the hatches to get underway when the engine started to runaway. Captain Andrews yelled for a rag. Maria said: *I told him there were none here, then I pulled off my T-shirt that he stuffed into the air intake, saving the engine. He gave me one of his Pal shirts and after that I always wore it. The runaway was a scary affair but Kenneth had taught me to respect possibility of problems and how to deal with fear.*

But when he was dying, there was fear in his eyes. He couldn't breathe. He talked endlessly about fishing. His many friends sat with him, in their turn, John King and Ivey Lewis were with him to his end.

Captain Kenneth Andrews would have an impressive "family tree" of captains that he helped to put on the ocean. He signed, verifying Maria's experience and ability as a qualification for her captain's license. (She has, in turn, signed for 10 captain's licenses.) She worked as a boat delivery captain for three years. When she delivered a boat to Walter Cronkite, she agreed to be his captain. This meant many trips to interesting places in 1979 and 1980.

Maria wrapped up with: *My year with Kenneth was full of adventures with engines breaking down almost every day. We were baked in the sun, salted, rocked, rolled, and rained on. When you live with that for a time it puts a different perspective on what matters. When you caught a lot of fish and got back OK, it was a fine day.*

In 1965 the Goldsboro *Daily News* told of another unusual first mate. Titled "First Mate Makes Em Reel," it told of Kenneth's First Mate.

> A good-looking, female, blond, teen-ager is the last thing you would expect to see working as first mate on a sport fishing boat. Most any morning early risers at Topsail Beach can watch 17-year-old Lee Hunt of Raleigh swabbing down the *Captain Vick*. She is preparing the 43 foot charter boat for a day's trip to the Gulf Stream.
>
> She got a trial run one spring weekend when Captain Andrews had a charter and no help. Lee promised to try real hard if he would give her a chance. He did and today the captain claims he has never had a better helper than Lee.
>
> The boat averages about four days a week, which means Lee is on board by 6 A.M. and back at dock around 5 P.M. It's a long day but she loves every minute of it. Not only is Lee handy with the mop and pail, but she can pilot the boat, rig the lines, bait the hooks, gaff the large fish, and reel them in. Occasionally, too, she takes a turn at baby-sitting if there are youngsters on board who get restless.

Does she have any trouble with the men who go out on the *Captain Vick*? *Oh, no, they're real nice. When you pay that kind of money to go fishing, you want to fish.*

Lee, now a youthful mother of two, is lanky and tall with magnetic brown eyes. She recalled her experience with Captain Andrews. Her voice choked as she said: *He was the most caring, gentle, and sincere man I have ever known. He was like a father figure and I will never forget him.*

There weren't many jobs for a young girl on Topsail Island. If you were lucky, you might land a secretarial job, soda jerk at the soda shop, or waitress at the Breezeway. It was rare that a girl would consider working as first mate on a fishing boat.

Captain Andrews had told her he could not consider her first mate without experience. She kept after him for days to give her the chance. He finally agreed and she worked for him for three years. Her work was primarily in the summer vacation months but she also worked spring and fall fishing charters.

She recalled: *The Captain Vick docked at the Dolphin Pier in the sound so we had to go out New Topsail Inlet. I would get up early and walk down to the boat, load it with ice, and check everything. Captain Andrews would do his check and we were ready to go. We would head for the inlet and he would always fix his eyes hard on the channel with both hands gripping the wheel. The inlet was treacherous and he respected it. Often times, his cigarette would burn down to his lips and I would take it away for him. He was so sincere about his respon-*

Lee Hunt Mims

sibilities and would not risk hurting anyone. The party was everything and his major concern was safety.

At the same time, Kenneth was fearless at sea and once in a storm a headboat Buddy's Pirate with 50 people on board was in trouble. They had broken steerage, which is a disaster in heavy seas. They had lit a trash fire in a barrel to get attention and the fire went out of control. We stood by, along with other captains, to help rescue the people.

He had all the characteristics of being gentle, tough, conscientious, and bold. His starched uniform was always perfect, and he wore black laced tennis shoes. Kenneth would order shrimp and we would eat together. He would always ask about breakfast, since I would often skip it. He would have a can of sardines for me in case I had not eaten.

Kenneth always impressed me to be special, to make something of myself. One bit of advice he gave was don't get yourself into something you cannot get out of. When we were in storms we would talk for hours. He was always protective and once when a date came to the boat to meet me, he let me know what he thought of him. He was not impressed. One day, I was dangling my feet in the water. From up on the bridge, Captain Andrews was yelling and shaking his fist to get my attention. I could not understand what he was yelling, then saw the shark at the side of the boat.

King and dolphin were the most prized fish. But I remember once when we were pulling in Spanish and it was raining. Nobody wanted to come in, so we fished in the rain. These are times the captains like to talk about.

Captain Kenneth Andrews had no regrets about his life on the ocean. He had many experiences to recount and with good friends he maintained contact through to his last days. All those who knew him remembered the captain as the "genuine article."

J.B. BRAME

J.B. and Caroline Brame consented to my coming to their home to talk about their recollections of Topsail Island and generously allowed my perusal of their personal files. In addition, they entrusted me with irreplaceable photos so I could have copies made. I want to express my appreciation for the hospitality and generous giving of their time and interest in my search for historical information.

Caroline is a lovely woman of quiet distinction who keeps a tastefully managed home and is very much a partner to JB's endeavors. J.B. has retired and will be counting on his family to carry on the family business. He is soft-spoken and very open about sharing his personal information yet is apparently a tough businessman of integrity. J.B. was past president and now chairman of the Brame Company in Durham. He is a warm, family-oriented man, right-

J.B. and Caroline Brame—2004

fully proud of his accomplishments and very sensitive to what really matters.

He said: *There was an older gentleman in the Rotary Club who was in the insurance business and he and some of his cohorts developed an interest in the Surf City area. I was a young kid in the Rotary Club at the time and, long story short, I picked him up at his home one day about 5 A.M. and drove to Surf City and met Mr. Ward. I bought six lots from Al Ward for $5,000. New Topsail Beach hardly existed at that time as I remember. I returned home a young man with a note on buying those six lots. That was about 1948. I sold them off in the next three or four years.*

Mr. Anderson, Sr. was developing New Topsail Beach in the 50s. Caroline and I went down there in 1953 and bought a spec built house. In October 15, 1954 Hurricane Hazel took the house and the boardwalk leading to a gazebo at ocean's edge.

Something that I thought was rather amazing was the reappearance of pieces from a captain's chair after a storm in 1984. One year and six months later a piece of a broken rung was found. Six months later, the matching piece of rung was found. I still have the pieces, and the broken chair which I will repair someday.

I think it is interesting to note that Hurricane Carol preceded Hurricane Hazel by several weeks in 1954. Prior to and during Carol we weren't aware that it was a hurricane and were told to get off the island when it was nearly over. I saw the power of the ocean with my own eyes and saw the precarious position we were in on Topsail Island.

When we were warned that the bridge was about to go, we went with our family in two cars. We had to wait for the bridge to come down to drive on and then float the other way to drive off of it, one car at a time.

At that time, he wrote to Senator Lennon, from Wilmington, to see what he could do to help save Topsail. It was certainly bigger than we could handle ourselves.

J.B. continued: *We purchased three lots at auction sale from Anderson on May 11, 1957. We bought the tower about 1958 to replace the beach house but didn't find it suitable for the family. I've heard that Sonny Jenkins stayed in our tower during Hurricane Hazel. Several people have broken into the tower during storms to get shelter. I really don't object to that because I probably would want to do so myself.*

Lewis Orr built the house we now have in February-June 1961 and we moved in July. Sonny Jenkins was working for Lewis at the time. The house was made of materials from a military building. Camp Butner near Oxford, NC was built as an emergency camp for training during the second world war. I saw an advertisement in the paper of an auction sale for buildings. I was the high bidder of $3,600 for a building 37x150 feet long, with no support columns, oak flooring and strong timbers, built the way the government builds them. It was some kind of recreation building. As I walked through it I said it would be the building I can replace my beach house with. Lewis Orr looked at it and said: "Yes, I think we can do it." The roof trusses were built like you wouldn't believe of heavy timbers and bolted together with lumber rings. We dismantled the building board by board, bolt by bolt, flooring piece by flooring piece, and hauled enough *of the materials to the beach site. The rest was disposed of.*

In the years after Hazel, a sand fence was put out about 50 feet in front of the house that caught sand and built in a good beach front. Then with the Camp Butner building available, it all came together to rebuild at the beach. It turned out to be one of the best built houses on Topsail Beach.

People ask us why we built so close to the ocean. They don't realize that when we built the house it was about 200 feet from the ocean. In fact, we had a 60 foot board walk from the house to the beach, at high tide. Later we added another 100 feet to cross sand dunes that had built up. While property and beachhouses are important, as I get older I find that things have no meaning per se. A thanks or acknowledgment that you are loved means more than anything.

Excerpts from a newspaper article - 1961

A drowning occurred that involved J.B. and his son: Tuesday afternoon August 15, 1961 at Topsail Beach, a tragedy that didn't need to happen occurred. A young military couple, newlyweds of two weeks, Marine Private Alvin Pruett and his wife Rita were swimming near New Topsail Inlet.

They swam to a sand bar in the mouth of the inlet and stayed there until around 4:45. As both were swimming back to shore, Mrs. Pruett ran into some strong undercurrent and an incoming tide. Her husband tried to help her and in the effort was overcome by the strong waves. Mrs. Pruett told rescuers she held her husband's unconscious body afloat for almost 45 minutes in chin-deep water until beach residents heard her calls for help. Because of rough waters there were no other swimmers around.

Deane Hundley, III of Wallace, who was employed during the summer months at Warren's Soda Shop at Topsail, heard of the swimmers in distress and rushed to the shore. Seeing the situation, he immediately ran to get his family's boat, some distance up the beach. He tried to make his way to the sand bar where the young woman was calling for help. At first his efforts were futile because of the high waves, but he finally worked his boat in close enough to throw a life preserver to her. The woman was unable to move. Anchoring the boat, Hundley jumped into the water, swam to the sand bar, and after some time managed to get the woman and her unconscious husband into his craft.

In the meantime, J.B. Brame of Durham, was trying to assist with his larger boat. The sea was heavy and swamped the smaller boat leaving Hundley and the couple in a half-submerged craft compounded with a fouled propeller. Brame and his twelve year old son managed to get a line to them and took them into his boat. By this time it was certain that the man was drowned.

The smaller boat had to be abandoned to the waves, and the four in Brame's boat feared they may be lost to the waves, too. J.B. told Hundley to skipper the boat, as he was skillful with the waves. J.B. kneeled over the man and gave him artificial respiration, continuously and desperately until reaching shore and the rescue squad, to no avail. The rescue squad applied artificial respiration, twice detecting some signs of life, on the way to the hospital. But he was pronounced dead on arrival at the hospital. Mrs. Pruett was treated for shock and exposure and released.

J.B. Brame and Deane Hundley were both commended for their daring rescue. Beyond the grief of the families, Topsail Island people were stunned and learned another lesson of profound respect for the power of the sea.

WE RODE OUT HURRICANE HAZEL IN A CAR!

Reaction to a hurricane experience is curious. A few people gratefully abandoned the island, never to return. Not so, for the Smyres. They rode out Hurricane Hazel in an Oldsmobile on Topsail Island. Undaunted, they built a house two years later right across the road from the dune that had protected them.

Estalene Smyre is a full of life, 78 year old lady who re-lived her night of terror. Time had not dimmed the raw fear of that night of screaming winds and pounding surf washing houses into the sound.

Estalene Smyres

She and her husband Clyde were visiting Bill and May Moon. The Moons had retired here and knew the ways of the island. As Hurricane Hazel approached, everyone was urged to leave the island. Estalene kept saying, "We'd better leave. The man told us to get off." Clyde said, "We will do what the Moons decide." Bill Moon declared, "My home is here and I'm staying. Besides, I've been through these things before and we will be OK." So they stayed. Estalene told me her story.

She recalled: *That night as we played cards at Moon's house, the winds howled and got fierce. In addition to us four, there was a woman from Charlotte and a third couple with children ages three and five. The storm pounded against the house and when the front porch ripped loose, we all got scared. Bill said, "Let's get into two cars and get off the island. I'm afraid that block wall might cave in on us."*

It was about two o'clock in the morning. We brought Sylvia Lyles with us in our Oldsmobile. The Moons took the other couple and kids with them in their Buick. We picked the heavy cars and left Sylvia's Ford behind. We struggled out in blinding rain and the cars nearly bogged down in the unpaved road. About 100 feet from the house we saw half a duplex crash into the ocean. The other half was left blocking the road.

There was no use going further. We wedged the cars bumper to bumper against the dune and cedars at ocean-side across the road. The waves were already coming across and foam was covering Bill's car so we couldn't see it. As the storm tore at us, the cars rocked with the wind and waves. We weren't sure what might happen. I told Clyde: "If this car turns over I'm going to hang on to that cedar." He said: "You could never hold on out there." Sylvia chimed in: "I'll be right out there hanging on with you."

Even with all this, we felt somewhat in a good position with our protected place in heavy cars. Bill just kept feeding the kids chewing gum and candy. The wind went ominously quiet as the "eye" went by. We knew then we could make it through the other half of the storm.

After about 12 hours, the wind and rain slacked. We had decided to stay in the cars until the water was calm so we could see where to walk. We were fearful because we had seen electric lines down and sizzling in the water. As we stepped into knee-deep water we saw the house in the middle of the road toward Surf City. The ocean had broken through just above us and also just below. After we saw all the destruction, we said: "What crazy idiots we were." We were just lucky to be alive.

When we got out I told everyone: "The next time the man tells us to get off this island, I'm going." I looked at Bill and said: "And you can stay if you want to." He said: "I'll go with you." The rest chimed in: "We'll all go."

We waded up to our knees in water back over to Moon's house. You couldn't tell where the road had been since it was all covered with sand. As we went to the front door, there was the prettiest snake you ever saw. It was bright orange, brown and other colors, curled around on the screen door. The water was clear so we waded around to the back door watching our step.

We found furniture all over the back of our property. Ceiling boards and other pieces of houses were all over the place. We pulled stuff out of the sound and set them up in Moon's front yard so people could see what was found. We walked around on the island setting up chairs like it would help to put things upright.

We got up to Warren's Soda Shop and just beyond it was a big brick grocery store that was totally destroyed. Just cans of food all over the place. You couldn't know what anything was because all the labels were off. It was a fairly new store beside where Hedgecock Lumber is today. We hadn't dealt with the new store much because Tom Humphrey's Cracker Box was close to us. The hurricane moved the Cracker Box across the road where it was later rebuilt. Nothing but gas pumps were left there.

The day after the Hurricane, Slim Rackley and a black man were singing and hitting each other as they swung a bucket between them. They rode out the hurricane in the building at the Dolphin Pier. Slim ran the Dolphin Pier, and said when the hurricane hit they had decided to get drunk and die happy.

I don't know how they did it, but two kids age 10 and 14 climbed into Harvey Jones' tower during the storm. I don't know their names but their mother had left them to take a third child to the doctor just before Hazel hit. They were OK but found huddled in the corner of the tower the next day.

We'd find kettles hanging in trees as though someone had put them there. There was a boat that looked OK except with a tree rammed through the other side. Whole sides of houses were gone and yet towels were still hung neatly on racks. In one house plates were on the shelf and cups still hung undisturbed on hooks. Shells were all over the place.

We walked to the Topsail Motel and set up chairs and other furniture that was strewn around. Further up the island we found a house that had a Hammond Organ in it, sitting in sand. We picked it up and put it on blocks so it wouldn't be ruined. The owner said later we saved it. The owner was a Marine Captain who later brought in a helicopter. He loaded the organ and other things they owned and took them off the island.

All the way up beyond Surf City we counted 30 houses in the sound. Some of them were eventually saved. A lot of them were still there for a long time until either salvaged or wrecked. Another marine took a boat and he and his wife went out to their house in the sound. They found every piece of their silver but one fork. Then she felt around and found it, too.

There were a lot of marines on the island to help. They brought big trucks in and made a track for us so we could get out. We still couldn't get off the island because the bridge was gone. We were here about two weeks and there was no way to let our family know that we were OK. A man from Durham came out here and he called our families in Charlotte. It was several days before they knew we were safe.

Harvey Jones had sent word that we could use anything we find up at his little pink motel. We really didn't need anything. People were very helpful of one another.

May had some friends from Wilmington who came over by boat to their little pier bringing water and food for us. We took the grill off the stove and made a place outside for a fire for cooking. It was just like camping out. We actually had a good time.

Finally, we were told we could get our cars out. There were deep tracks in the dirt road. The man told us to follow him out but be sure to keep stepping hard on the gas to keep going through the sand. We had our car and Sylvia's car to get out. I picked our car since I was used to it. He said: "Don't let it stop," and I didn't. Clyde came behind me and the barge came and took us across.

The Moons soon had their house back to normal and we kept coming back. Two years later, we built our house next door to them—right across the road from the cedars where we spent the night with Hazel.

SURVIVED FRAN - THEN JAILED
LIZ BECKINGHAM

A "State of Emergency" is difficult for everyone, especially for the police who are committed to insuring the safety of citizens and property. As such, they must be impartial and strictly enforce the law. But it doesn't help to know this when we feel victimized by the system that is in place to protect us.

Liz Beckingham tells her story: *I suspect that some memories have become fuzzy over the years and that I remember them as I choose to remember them. But I clearly remember how traumatic the situation was for me.*

Liz and Tom Beckingham—2004

Bertha, in 1996, was our first hurricane and it was not much of one. But there was an overall lingering feeling of frustration about the difficulty of getting back into town and to our properties. Town officials had a hostile group on their hands at the roadblock just west of the swing bridge, the day after Bertha. There was little response to the crowd's need for information about when we could go back to our homes. Many of us stayed overnight at the Food Lion parking lot because we had given up our motel rooms and could not get others. There were several policemen at the roadblock with full "riot" gear. It was incredible to see. All we were asking was to get back to our homes, but we were told that we could not do so because it was unsafe. When we were allowed back in, it was with a police escort.

Then came Fran on September 5th and 6th. Both my husband and I had responsibilities at work for the welfare of the staff and office in Wilmington. At home, we had already prepared for days ahead and were packed up to leave, but by the time we got to Topsail Beach we were running late. As we wound up our preparations, the wind started to howl and rain increased with a fury.

The hurricane was predicted to hit further up the coast. Another couple was seriously considering staying on the island based on the difficulties around getting back on the island after Bertha. By the time we finally decided to leave, the wind was so fierce that we couldn't risk it and we had to stay. Our friends Steve and Patty Walter joined us at our house.

I don't remember much about that night that would be different from what one would expect. The worst of the storm was after nightfall. Before it became completely dark, we saw docks and debris floating down the sound. Our dock was completely under water and our neighbor's boat was bouncing up and down on its cradle. We spent most of the night putting buckets all around the house to catch the rain. The wind never seemed extremely bad, but it was constantly moaning hour after hour. We watched the water seep into our bottom floor. We moved as much as we could to our second floor. We tried unsuccessfully to raise our vehicles up to prevent them from flooding, but three feet of water engulfed them.

The wind finally diminished early in the morning. It became a bright sunny day, with still a great deal of wind. There was an eerie feeling in general. We expected our neighbor's boat that had been on our lift, to be gone. But the anchor had caught on the dock so we now had transportation. The water that had covered the island was gone except on low-lying areas and the road was still flooded. Almost all of our shingles were gone, exposing the bare wood roof. Trees were uprooted, the pieces of roofing debris, home wreckage and household items were scattered everywhere. It looked like war zone.

We left by foot about mid-morning to go to our friends' home to evaluate the damage. We went by way of the beach. We passed the town commissioners, town manager, and police in a Hummer. They waved and asked if we were ok and gave us a general update. Returning to our home, we all worked to clear over a mile of Anderson Blvd. so that emergency vehicles could get through. We met another town official later in the day that told us about the services available to us. I mention this because no one ever said we were in violation of any curfew orders.

The next day, a man came by with a Topsail Beach Volunteer Fireman hat on. He was coming to check on our neighbor's house. He said he was opening his business in Topsail Beach to feed the reserve troops and that he had a phone and hot coffee. Shortly after he left we got on our bikes and headed into town. Our main purpose was for coffee and to see if I could use the phone for a business need. We were there about 15 minutes talking to one of the police officers. Town commissioners and military reserves were nearby.

Suddenly, we were arrested for leaving our property during an emergency. The Topsail Beach officer even tried to handcuff me. I was particularly emotional. I asked if we could go back to our home to get identification and money and take care of our 14-year-old dog Max, left outside. Our house was completely open. My husband had no shirt or shoes and was only in a bathing suit. We were taken to the magistrate in Surf City. We were questioned and treated as if we were criminals. Our intentions were obviously legitimate and we were on our very best behavior. But we were transported to the Burgaw Jail.

The jail keepers were not pleased to see us. They had no power and did not have the staff to "deal with this type of nonsense". We were put in cells. Because I was extremely distraught, my husband had been assured that we would not be separated. The first thing they did was put my husband in a cell with two other men and I was sent to the women's division. I was placed in a 4X6 cell with one small metal stool. There were no windows or light. The guard let me keep the door cracked so I could see. She did her best to calm me but the other prisoners were screaming for bathroom visits, food and just in general. She could not offer much assistance to me.

We were jailed for about 6 hours. Finally we were able to locate a friend in Wilmington to come and get us. Then we had to post bail. Incredibly, our bail of $500 each was $250 more than the man sharing the cell with my husband who was there for a second offense of selling drugs to minors.

The best thing that happened that day was hearing our friend enter the jail shouting out, "I'm here for the Beckingham Jail Birds." He was laughing, as did many of our friends after hearing what had happened to us. My jailer escorted me out, making me promise that I understood that she had treated me better than most and I was not to tell my friends of this special treatment. This was the second bright moment of my day.

We were able to go back to the Surf City roadblock. The Topsail Beach police allowed me to travel with a vendor delivering port-a-potties to the beach, to pick up our dog and some things. My husband was not allowed to go because he had "an attitude" after conveying his displeasure about our treatment by the police. We did not get to our house until almost dark. This was due in part because the wife of the vendor wanted to take a tour of the island so she could video the damage. The officer helped me try to secure the house. Our dog was nowhere to be found and we could not stay, as it would soon be dark. As it turned out, our friend heard about what happened to us and had traveled along the sound to rescue Max. It was several more days before we knew Max was safe and we could get him.

We were not allowed to move back into our home for almost three weeks. The town continued on a curfew and it was always a worry to be sure to get to the roadblock by the 5:00 deadline. I feared the law and my confidence in the police and those in control as my protector was shaken. Every time I see pictures of an ordinary looking person being officially handcuffed I am reminded of my experience.

Fortunately, we had and continue to have lots of local support that makes this a great place to live. Our situation became a major issue during that year's commissioner race. At the candidate Q & A concerns were raised about hurricane response and homeowners being arrested. I would not stay again for a category

3 hurricane [Fran]. But I would consider staying for category 1 or 2 [Bertha & Floyd]. What happened to us seemed an unnecessary extreme.

As I talk with Topsail Island residents and police, they all feel better prepared for hurricanes and emergencies in recent years, and conflicts, such as the Buckingham's, have been minimized. It does take some acceptance and understanding of the need for strongly enforced rules that have to be followed to assure the safety and protection of people and property.

BILL CHERRY

Bill Cherry, a long-time resident and businessman in Topsail Beach, also tells of his Fran experience. He often rides out hurricanes and Fran was no exception. He, too, found himself at odds with the law. But he remembers it with less angst.

Bill was helping the Oppegaards and others after Fran, and was walking back to his Breezeway Motel when he was arrested for being off-property. He recalls that there were five of them arrested; two were ticketed, and he and two others, the Beckinghams, were jailed at Burgaw. He bailed himself out and looked at the experience rather philosophically. He said: *It's fact and it's life on the island. I hold no grudge with town officials as they have to enforce the law, but it just seemed a little excessive.*

MORE TOPSAIL CHANGES

GROWTH AND EVOLUTION OF TOPSAIL ISLAND 1996 - 2004

Noorth Topsail Beach, Surf City, and Topsail Beach are distinct communities yet they are all family oriented and maintain their individual charm. They each have their own police and fire departments and at least one park. Residents and visitors can enjoy biking Topsail's miles of bike paths that are continually being extended. There is roller-skating and miniature golf in Topsail Beach and other family activities on and just off the island. There are the Missiles and More Museum and the turtle hospital, both favorite places to visit. And, of course, the beaches are playgrounds for swimming, surfing, sunning, and searching for special seashells or for shark's teeth. Tourism and vacations bring many visitors who often decide to purchase a cottage or even to move here.

Hurricanes are critical moments in Topsail Island's history. The major ones were described in an earlier chapter. The one-two punch of Hurricanes Bertha and Fran was especially effective in the destruction they caused. Both residents and police have learned much in terms of public safety. Protection against looting during disasters makes enforcement of strict rules for re-entry a must. Revised building codes and stricter regulations are having a big payoff as evidenced in recent storms. All the new buildings are safer and more storm resistant structures, and they have esthetically improved the island's appearance.

As a Topsail Island observer over the years, when I visit I am always struck by how the island is changing and improving. Yet at the same time it retains some of its older ways. For example, at Topsail Beach, Sonny Jenkins' roller skating rink that my family enjoyed in the 1990s

Roller Skating circa—1994

Topsail Beach Post Office—2004

Roller Skating Rink—2004

is still functioning. Postmaster Doris Jenkins and the Post Office are in their place, and Bill Godwin continues to sit at the cash register by the front door of his vintage grocery store.

But the building boom of the past 4 years has increased each town's size with extraordinary housing construction. Land and home values continue to rise. A local publication *Encore* reported in 2004 that land sales ranged from $175,00 to $895,000. They also reported that there were about 200 homes listed ranging from just under $200,000 going up to $1,500,000. Single-family home building permits for the three towns show a dramatic increase. North Topsail Beach issued a steady 29 permits per year

North Topsail Beach—Some recent additions to the town.

Villa Capriani—2004

St. Regis Resort—2004

Topsail Dunes Condos—2004

North Topsail Beach Town Hall—2004

Surf City—Some recent additions to the town.

Treasure Coast Square—2004

Condominiums—Surf City—2004

Wings—2004

Beach House Marina and Yacht Club—2004

The Fishing Village—2004

The Corner—2004

Docksider Gifts and Shells—2004

Topsail Island Trading Co.—2004

Tiffany Motel—2004

Surf City Park—2004

Surf City Town Hall—2004

Chamber of Commerce—2004

Herring's Bait and Tackle Shop—2004

Sears Landing Grill and Boat Docks—2004

Beach Care
Family Practice &
Urgent Care—2004

Surf City
Pharmacy—2004

Topsail Beach—Some recent additions to the town.

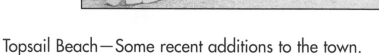

Quarter Moon
Bookstore—2004

Century
21 Action,
Inc.—2004

South Beach Villas and Yacht Club—2004

Maritime Way—2004

Latitude 34—2004

Top Sail Beach Town
Hall—2004

The Blue Gecko—2004

until it tripled to 94 in 2003; Surf City issued about 63 per year and nearly trebled to 171 in 2003; Topsail Beach stayed fairly steady at 25 permits then jumped to 32 in 2003. Interestingly, Topsail Beach, primarily a residential community, has 1,100 homes with 450 of them year round residents, up from 250 year round residents ten years ago. Many new and upgraded businesses provide needed services. Prior pages show a sampling of businesses, town buildings, homes and condominiums that show progress.

PUBLIC SAFETY

With such growth, public safety and property security requires more police and fire protection in each town. In 1996, for example, North Topsail Beach had 8 full time officers and 2 part time officers; in 2004 they were increased to 10 full time officers and 6 part time. Surf City had 7 full time officers and 2 reserves; in 2004 there are 12 full time officers, 8 reserves and 3 auxiliaries. Topsail Beach has increased from 4 full time officers in 1996 to 7 full time officers in 2004. They maintain aggressive patrols of the beach with an ATV and have a police boat that patrols Banks Channel from Surf City to New Topsail Inlet. During events they stay close to the crowds on bicycles and Surf City even has an officer on surfboard...radio and all.

North Topsail Beach police established a relationship with Camp LaJeune and have been able to outfit their department with surplus Humvee's, trucks and motorcycles. This enabled Surf City and Topsail Beach to do the same and all three towns now have military vehicles for use in emergencies. On top of that, Harley Davidson gives each town a motorcycle each year for their use.

All three towns have been fortunate in that the Chief of Police for each town has served long terms providing continuity for years. North Topsail Beach's Daniel Salese has been Chief of Police since August 1998, starting as an officer in 1992; Surf City's Mike Halstead, has been Chief since January 1999; Topsail Beach's Rickey Smith, Chief since 1987, started as an officer in 1983. The towns have valuable police experience in various situations especially unique to a barrier island during hurricanes and emergencies. Procedures have been improved over the years, and they have better prepared residents than in years past. All three towns have hurricane procedures and information on their websites. They work together to notify and instruct in such emergency situations. To protect property and assure safety of the people the police set up roadblocks and Emergency Operation Centers at the Sears Landing Bridge and the high-level bridge to manage re-entry to the island. Residents cannot return until their town administration declares that residents can re-enter. This is always a difficult time for residents anxious to get to their properties.

Another troubling phenomenon that becomes a real policing and traffic nightmare is the crowds that come to photograph and look. Media reports about Topsail Island hurricane damage bring people from everywhere to see it. While property owners are trying to secure their properties "gawkers" try to get everywhere to take pictures and videotape it all. It is a real challenge for police to keep the island secure.

During Hurricanes Bertha and Fran the police had to strictly enforce the procedures. It did cause some struggle with residents who believed they should have immediate and unlimited access to their properties. With more awareness, interchange of ideas and education, everyone understands the need for the rules and is more accepting. There have been fewer conflicts and less looting in recent years.

Fire protection is excellent in all three communites. North Topsail Beach Fire Marshal Thomas Best tells me they have four paid firefighters and 25 volunteers. Surf City has five full time firefighters and 19 volunteers headed up by Ken Bogan, Fire Marshal. Topsail Beach is managed by Kenneth Creech, Fire Marshal, and he has 24 volunteer firefighters, two of them continuously serving for over 30 years since the fire department was formed. The dedication of these volunteers at each fire department assures the protection of homes and businesses. They are also unsung heros and it is important that their work is recognized.

TOWERS OF TOPSAIL

The towers from Operation Bumblebee have changed over the years, finding new uses and a new life. Sturdy structures, sometimes difficult to live with and nearly impossible to modify, a number of determined owners have converted them to structures of beauty. They have geodet-

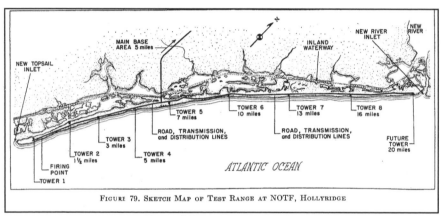

FIGURE 79. SKETCH MAP OF TEST RANGE AT NOTF, HOLLYRIDGE

Map of Towers circa–1946

ic plates that mark them as survey points attesting to their permanence. They were built to be stable in order to reliably track and photograph missile launchings. One characteristic that I notice when visiting the tower homes is the quiet…there is a perceivable hush of any noise when you move from an exterior room into the tower. And the view is spectacular when you are at the top. There are seven photographic towers and a control tower, which is near the Assembly Building. The eighth photographic tower, at North Topsail Beach, known as the "Jefferys Tower," was demolished in 1989 as it had been an unmanageable trouble spot because of trespassers and even a death. There was also considerable erosion that threatened the tower, so the decision was made to tear it down.

Tower 1—2004

Tower 1 Great Room—Tay and Lloyd
Bost—2004

Tower 1 Sound View—2004

Tower # 1.

Lloyd and Tay Bost – owners

Lloyd and Tay Bost purchased this south-most tower and attached concrete block building in 1991 and over the next several years renovated it into the magnificent structure you see today. Their living quarters incorporates the tower yet maintains the tower's identity. They tried to rework the concrete building that had been attached for years, but had to demolish it in 1995. In the early days, their son Geoffrey stayed there during several summers while he worked on the island. Mr. Bost recalled: *The ground floor had an "Indiana Jones" kind of well, a snake pit, but it didn't seem to inhibit Geoff's desire to stay or his partying.* The building was completed in 1996 and completely furnished just a week prior to Fran. Fran tore off some roofing and some inside walls were soaked, but they had relatively little damage.

Lloyd and Tay live in Virginia and come often as they

Tower 1 Bedroom—2004

can. They usually have friends with them and share the enjoyment of their tower.

In May 1998, their daughter Wynne was to be married at their tower home. As the time drew near, a big Northeaster was approaching and they shifted plans. She was married in the Assembly Building and their planned-for reception there followed. They were grateful for the protection of the Assembly Building.

Control Tower.
J. B. Brame – owner

Located between the Assembly Building and the launching pad [at the Jolly Roger Motel], it was the tower that controlled rocket launchings nearby. This tower was purchased by J. B. Brame in 1958 and was converted to be a family beach cottage replacing their beach house that was lost in Hurricane Hazel. Sonny Jenkins found refuge there during Hurricane Hazel.

Control Tower—2004

Tower # 2.
Sterling Bryson – administrator

This tower is located at Queen's Grant and is still in its original form. Because of its unaltered state, it is listed on the National Register of Historic Places along with the Assembly Building. It was acquired by Island Development Corporation from Harvey Jones' heirs in the 1970s. The owners plan to keep the outside appearance as a tower and probably use it for business meetings and such.

Tower 2 Queen's Grant—2004

Tower # 3.
John Gresham – owner

The prior owners Kenyon and Evelyn Ottaway purchased the converted tower from the Bland family in 1965. It is located right at the Surf City/Topsail Beach town line. The concrete block attached tower home was a snug little place and was perfect for the Ottaways. The home part was totally destroyed by Hurricane Fran, but the tower remained intact. John purchased it in 1997 and plans to renovate the tower as a beach cottage.

Tower 3—2004

Tower 3 John Gresham—2004

Tower # 4.
John West – owner

John purchased the property and tower frame in 1998. It was renovated to a home in 1999. This tower is located near the S curve in Surf
City. For years the structure looked like a skeleton of concrete. It has
a geodetic plate marker dated 1947. John built a side deck and sitting
room overlooking the beach. This project is an innovative design from
the ground up primarily within the original tower framework. A spiral
staircase takes you from the ground to the top floor. The decks that
grace each level also add to the charm of this beach home. The exterior
is tan stucco with the concrete frame painted cream, similar in appearance to the original block walls on these towers. At the top, a loft bedroom was built as a cupola on the
roof. West preserved the integrity
of the tower as a delightful creation and livable home.

Tower 4 Kitchen—2004

Tower 4 Sitting Room—2004

Tower 4 circa—1998

Tower 4—2004

Some early history was discovered in my query about Tower 4. Esther Atkinson Stubbs and her husband Alfred Stubbs owned and lived in the tower in the mid-1950s. According to a nephew Michael Meares, he lived with them in the upper two levels. They devoted the first floor to selling hot dogs in 1953 and 1954. He recalls: *The tower leaked badly when it rained since the concrete seemed porous. It was painted green and had HOT DOGS in script red letters on its wall. The venture was not very successful and only lasted about two summers. I don't believe it reopened after Hurricane Hazel.*

Tower # 5.
Ken Richardson - owner

This tower is located several blocks north of the Surf City Pier. Ken purchased it in 1994 and undertook a number of renovations over a period of six years. It is one of the tallest buildings on the island because of a penthouse on top of the structure.

Tower 5—2004

Tower 5 From Beach—2004

Tower # 6.
Lenny Denatis – owner

The original Ocean City tower renovation was the first building project for Wade Chestnut in 1950. It grew to be a restaurant, tackle shop and pier complex that served the many fishermen/women who dipped a line there. It is located just north of the Surf City town line in North Topsail Beach. Hurricane Fran destroyed the pier and tackle shop and damaged the restaurant so severely that it still remains to be resurrected. This was a severe loss to the Ocean City community as it was the epicenter of activity there. The tower itself looks sturdy and will, no doubt, be repaired. Future plans for Tower # 6 are not definite.

Tower # 7.

Edward and Cathy Byman – owners

Tower 6 Ocean City—2004

Tower 7 Front View—2004

Tower 7 Ed Byman From Beach—2004

Tower 7 Ed and Kathy Byman Family—2004

Tower 7 Looking into Kitchen—2004

The tower home renovation was built by Tom Curren about 1992. This 4000 sq. ft. home was built around the tower such that the tower cannot be recognized from the street. But the tower is visible

Tower 7 Bertha Bench—2004

from the beach side. Edward and Cathy purchased the home in 1994. They had water damage when Fran blew shingles off the roof. And they have a unique "Bertha Bench" that Bertha brought them. It has been labeled and built into their lower deck. The home is quiet as a tower and has the comfort of large interior rooms. The tower's center level is basically their living room with a panoramic view of ocean and beach. They come to stay in their tower home as often as the sports activities of their sons Logan and Michael permit.

Tower # 8.
Known as the Jeffreys Tower – Marlo Bostic - last owner

This was the northern most photographic tower at North Topsail Beach. According to a Star-News account in 1986, George Jeffreys had renovated it to be a house, but gave up after numerous storms and vandalisms discouraged him and he sold it to Mr. Bostic. Over time it was a continuing aggravation to police and the owner. Mr. Bostic said: *It's really dangerous for decent people to ride by at night...a hang-*

Tower 8 Jeffreys
Tower circa—1996

out for dope fiends and drunks. I've even seen them standing buck-naked on the tower. It was in badly washed out condition for years and reputed to be the site of a number of accidents and suicides. Unable to keep trespassers off the tower, Mr. Bostic had the tower torn down, a massive undertaking, in 1989.

MARITIME FOREST PRESERVATION

The stampede of growth and development is changing the face of Topsail Island. But this success brings with it concerns about the maritime forests that are treasured. The live oaks and other native trees are essential to hold sand in place, provide shade, and they give the island a special beauty we all want to preserve. One of the most sensible environmental programs I have seen has been developed by a group of people determined to save Topsail Island trees. The Maritime Coalition was formed to preserve the island oaks and other native vegetation.

Rebecca Bruton and Pennie Gettinger, of the coalition, discovered that a developer had moved some trees to save them and to enhance his new development at Topsail Cove. This crystallized the idea that a tree exchange could solve problems for those wanting trees and those needing to move them because of building projects. At the same time the tree population would be preserved. A tree mover verified that these trees could be moved at less cost than bringing in a new tree. And the hardy Topsail Island trees are more likely to survive than a new tree from the mainland. Thus the interests of environmentalists and developers are both realized.

The coalition succeeded in convincing Surf City to adopt a new ordinance that will insure that building projects consider this plan. There are already a number of people on the list waiting for trees to become available. The coalition

Maritime Forest—2004

is also working with Topsail Beach and North Topsail Beach to broaden the program, which could serve as an example that other barrier islands will surely want to emulate.

COMMUNITY CENTER

ASSEMBLY BUILDING RECOGNITION

Betty Polzer was recognized at the 50th anniversary dedication of the Assembly Building, November 18, 1995, in Topsail Beach. A plaque was presented from the North Carolina Department of Cultural Resources, which stated "MISSILE TESTS: US Navy successfully tested ramjet engines in rocket flights, 1946-48. Observation towers line Topsail Island: Assembly Building 2 blocks west." This recognition sums up a long, arduous journey, starting in 1989, of the Historical Society of Topsail Island to have the Assembly Building designated on

Betty Polzer and the Plaque presented by
North Carolina Department of Cultural Resources

311

Assembly Building as Community Center and Museum 1993

the National Register as a historic site. That recognition was accomplished June 1993.

The Topsail Island Historical & Cultural Arts Council (formerly Topsail Beach Economic Development Council - TBEDC) initiated "Autumn with Topsail" a cultural entertainment and culinary exhibition that takes place in September each year. Their aim, to purchase the Assembly Building for a Community Center, meant years of effort. Revenue from events, plus funding provided by a state matching grant and residents of Topsail Island, enabled the TBEDC to buy the Assembly Building in June 1995.

QUEST TO PRESERVE ISLAND HISTORY

In researching Operation Bumblebee history, I found that others had been there before. Here is an example of an early attempt to find information in National Archives. This is rather typical, and I encountered similar results in my early search for information.

The letter dated 16 January 1974, is to Honorable David N. Henderson, House of Representatives, Washington, DC; signed by James L. Collins, Jr., Brigadier General, USA, Chief of Military History.

Dear Mr. Henderson:

This is in reply to your 20 December 1973 inquiry, made on behalf of Mrs. Louise Lamica concerning an experimental missile site on Topsail Beach, North Carolina.

The historical source materials on file in this office do not indicate that any Army installation was located on Topsail Beach, North Carolina. Our sources list Camp Davis as being in the vicinity of Holly Ridge, NC and document that it was used by the Army, the Army Air Corps, and the Navy during World War II and for some time thereafter....

In our search for information on Army activities at the Camp, we were unable to locate any material that indicates that the Army used the facility for testing Ram Jets or rockets. But this testing may have been done by the Army Air Corps..... If the experiments took place after WW II, the information would be in the records of the Navy Department.... END

My first attempts to get confirmation of the missile history utterly failed. All we had were some newspaper accounts, rumor, and the actual buildings to go on. All attempts to find information in various military and national archives came up empty. A long-time archivist suggested I contact Navy Archives of Yards and Docks at Port Heuneme, California. A researcher there found some microfilm files labeled Camp Davis, NC. I ordered a copy and happily discovered engineering drawings for the Assembly Building and Towers.

With that information, my contact to Phil Albert at Johns Hopkins University Applied Physics Lab, yielded a "Camp Davis" file from which our pictures and artifacts were gleaned. Breakthrough! They were formerly locked up in "secret" files for some 30 years.

This information proved crucial for justification of the National Register designation, and provided historic information and artifacts for the museum. JHU/APL has been a most cooperative and helpful organization. They have donated the missile displays and all the missile pictures and videos.

There are so many people involved in this sequence of events that it is impossible to mention them all. Compiled from Pender Sounds, Topsail Voice, and personal file sources, I believe the following represents the major influences on the path to preserve island history.

Steve Unger, Editor said: *On behalf of the Topsail Island Historical Society of Topsail Island, summer resident and historian author David Stallman has become a one-person lobby dedicated to saving the Assembly Building (Arsenal Centre) in Topsail Beach. His tasks have focused upon gaining support from individual organizations and local government to purchase and renovate the historic structure.*

He and others would like to see it turned into a community building while preserving it as a site of historical significance. In this essay, David Stallman relates his progress, frustrations, rewards and failures thus far.

Topsail Island caught me in 1986 when I came down from New York to visit my long lime friend Roy Hill. Roy was in the throes of renovating the Assembly Building into a mini-mall with restaurant overlooking the sound, and a recreation place for kids. After putting heart, soul, sweat and a lot of money into it, Roy had to give up his dream when the money ran out three years later.

My initial visit to the island set off an instant love affair. I saw a cottage, bought it later that year, and renovated it to potential year-round use. I immediately started to research island history and decided I must write the book that would portray the island's heritage.

By late 1989, the Arsenal Centre (Roy Hill's name for the structure) was officially for sale. The Topsail Island Historical Society began efforts to have the building recognized on The National Register of Historic Places in early 1990 along with supporting efforts to purchase the building to secure its preservation.

Also in 1989, the Topsail Beach Economic Development Council (TBEDC) was organized by local business leaders Brenda Sellers,

Jane Hedgecock, Kathy Cherry, and Randy Leesburg. Their purpose was to help promote the town's business climate and extend the tourist season. One of their stated goals was to eventually build or acquire a structure for a community recreation center. The TBEDC initiated "Autumn with Topsail," a cultural entertainment and culinary exhibition yearly in September, as fund-raiser.

Conditions seemed right for a proposal to get all interests together and pursue this worthwhile goal, focusing upon preservation of the Arsenal Center. A compelling influence was the support of island resident and writer, Betty Polzer who was already frustrated in her efforts to get the right people on the project. I provided "Operation Bumblebee" archive discoveries.

The first concrete step for preservation came with a meeting of the Historical Society where members pledged to work toward having the Arsenal Centre added to the National Register of Historic Places. The Historical Society soon engaged Ed Turberg, a professional restoration consultant from Wilmington to come and advise them on how to get the building recorded on the National Historic Register.

After some research, Turberg was enthused. His review of the historical documents, and further inquiries, revealed that the Assembly Building was the most *intact installation of its kind on the East Coast. What happened here with rocketry experimentation is comparable to Kitty Hawk's role in the beginning of aviation. This goaded me to push on.*

My first efforts were to put together an initial proposal in March of 1990. A management system could be organized comprising the Historical Society, the Economic Development Council, and the Town of Topsail Beach. We should also promote a total historic theme for Topsail Island that could have its own civic and economic benefits.

Jesse Borchers, president of the Historical Society, carried the proposal to all parties, and helped to gain their support. One of our major concerns was to put a "hold" on the sale of the building until we could get our act together. The real estate company listing the property had already shown it to several potential buyers.

August 1990, we were still adrift without a definite and focused plan beyond our initial proposal. I contacted the IBM Credit Union in Raleigh (owner of the property) and personally relayed our intent. About that same time I engaged J. Phillip Horne of North Carolina State University to work with us on grants and fund-raising. He introduced us to Angschuman De, architect & developer, of Raleigh who envisioned a collaboration of public/private enterprise for this project he defined as a "quiet jewel" for Topsail Beach.

By now, it is 1991 and after presentations to the Town of Topsail Beach, fiscal problems at Town and State levels made it apparent that we had to seek other funding means.

The TBEDC accepted the challenge and organized a steering committee with Betty Polzer to study feasibility and start efforts toward acquiring the building. Past presidents Kathy Cherry and

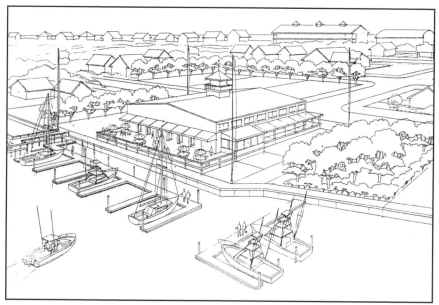

Topsail Beach Community Center - Possible Dream

Sandra Ledbetter kept focus on the importance of this acquisition to Topsail Island. Topsail Voice and Pender Sounds also played significant roles in publicizing these important efforts.

Gary Sunderland designed a proposed "Topsail Beach Community Center" (overnight) complete with waterfront that was invaluable for showing a "possible dream" in pictorial form. He presented his drawing in September 1991 for display at "Autumn with Topsail." It helped us to see a realistic picture of what the Assembly Building could become.

The focus on history and the potential for extending the economic season for Topsail Island seemed promising. Increasingly, Topsail Island people are becoming excited about the prospect of having a culture center for our children, historic displays, a fine restaurant and theater. We could have Art Council events, the Miss Topsail Pageant, educational seminars, retreats, and small convention activities here. University courses of study or ongoing degree programs can also bring greater educational opportunities.

A grant from the National Trust for Historic Preservation was awarded, in June 1992, to the TBEDC for $1,151. It was to help fund an architectural feasibility study for the Assembly Building. State Department of Archives and History helped us by having their restoration specialist visit the site and do an evaluation.

The purchase contract between IBM Credit Union and TBEDC was agreed upon and the signatures in place by July 1992. The Assembly Building has been saved for posterity and now there is a Community Center in its future. TBEDC was to have two years to raise the funds that will complete the terms of the agreement. It is the first priority of those involved in the Preservation Project to ready the structure so that it can fulfill, as soon as possible, its primary goal, a center for island activities.

Then, at last, the Assembly Building was designated a Historical Site on the National Register of Historic Places in June 1993. That recognition is generally reserved for older structures, but the

Assembly Building was unique as the only remaining intact structure of its kind. The Historical Society of Topsail Island received recognition for the Assembly Building, Control Tower, and Tower Number 2 (at Queen's Grant) as a group, in the National Register of Historic Places. Tower Number 2 was included as it most accurately represents a tower in its original state. The Ed Turberg and Historical Society effort began in 1989, to gain this recognition. How about that for perseverance.

Johns Hopkins University Applied Physics Laboratory agreed to populate the Historical Society Museum with Bumblebee artifacts, including missile mock-ups and films showing Camp Davis activities and rocket test flights. Plans called for a small-scale display during the island's annual "Autumn With Topsail" event September 17-18, 1994. The displays brought realism to what happened here. We are now the "East Coast On-site Archive" for JHU/APL. Videos of rocket firings and the actual rocket displays brought many positive comments from visitors. These successes keep spirits up when it seems we are engaged in the impossible.

Then Ed Bowan, State Representative, successfully pushed through a bill for $200,000 matching grant state funds, on behalf of the Assembly Building project. The TBEDC was still in on-going negotiations with the Credit Union, in July 1994, because of a two year agreement to purchase that was to expire that month. The IBM Credit Union has been permitting use of the building, in the meantime. The TBEDC's annual "Autumn with Topsail" hosts over 25,000 visitors to the island, and has become a successful fund raiser as one of North Carolina's premier festivals. The welcome $200,000 matching grant state funds pushed it over the edge.

The TBEDC finalized the ownership papers in June, 1995. Topsail Island now owns a Community Center that offers a gathering place for community events. Recently, the former Topsail Beach Economic Development Council was renamed "Topsail Island Historical & Cultural Arts Council," to better name its purpose.

TOPSAIL ISLAND COMMUNITY CENTER

The Community Center grows in popularity every year. Wedding receptions, meetings of all types, the Historical Society meetings, BINGO every week, celebrations and fund-raising functions make good use of the facilities. It is fully air-conditioned and equipped with kitchen and food serving facilities.

Bost-Hopkins Wedding—
Assembly Bldg—1998

Every October the yearly fund-raiser "Autumn With Topsail" brings ever-increasing crowds to Topsail for the beautiful fall weather, food, drink and music. It is always a first class event and draws over 18,000 people each year. The Topsail Island Historical & Cultural Arts Council sponsors it, and the proceeds are used to

Bost-Hopkins Wedding—
Assembly Bldg—1998

Assembly Building and TALOS—2004

pay for and maintain the Assembly Building.

MISSILES AND MORE MUSEUM

The late Betty Polzer put her full energy into promoting the history of Topsail Island. Her dream to see the Assembly Building as a Community Center housing a museum preserving Topsail's history was being realized. She wrote about Topsail's towers and other stories that distinguish the island. The fledgling Historical Society was becoming recognized as a small force in this effort, but they had difficulty in raising sufficient awareness to finance or build a repository for the island's history.

Discovery of information at Johns Hopkins University Applied Physics Laboratory supported the fact that a significant military program took place here. That information came to light as a result of my research for this book. It was a major influence in justifying why Topsail Island should buy the Assembly Building. Thus the Historical Society of Topsail Island served as the historic cornerstone for the Assembly Building purchase and preservation efforts.

Soon after the building was purchased, the Historical Society had a per-

Missiles and More Rocket Display—2004

Evelyn Bradshaw—Museum Expansion—2004

fect place to establish the Missiles and More Museum. Johns Hopkins University Applied Physics Laboratory donated three missile displays and other artifacts for the beginnings of a museum. It soon became home for other local historical material.

In the early days when the Museum was first being formed, the Historical Society was struggling and they could hardly get 14 to 18 in attendance at meetings. With diligence and determination they have grown significantly in membership and interest in preserving Topsail's history. The Historical Society now draws at least 90 people to their monthly luncheon meetings. They currently have 278 members.

Now well established, in the past eight years the museum has attracted as many as 7338 visitors and school students a year to see displays about Topsail Island's unique history. Its focus is on "Operation Bumblebee," a Navy rocket program begun right after WWII and guided by the Johns Hopkins University Applied Physics Laboratory from 1946 to 1948. Since the early 1990s they have been donating rocket displays, pictures and video about the program to the museum. In 1997, they donated the TALOS missile that greets visitors at the front of the museum. The museum houses many displays and pictures about WWII featuring Camp Davis' antiaircraft training and the role of WASPS, Women's Air Service Pilots, who flew targets over Topsail Island. An old Algonkian dugout canoe found in the salt marshes near Topsail Island, is a particularly special artifact. The museum has continued to add to its collection until it is now bursting at the seams.

Last year President Sue Newsome and the Historical Society's trustees, with the Missiles and More Museum Director Evelyn Bradshaw leading the charge, embarked on a museum expansion program. Evelyn had worked up preliminary plans. They started a fundraising endeavor in 2003 to raise $165,000. Incredibly, one year later they are within $20,000 of their goal. Mayor A.D. [Zander] Guy conducted an exemplary campaign to raise the funds. Construction has already begun and they expect to move into the new wing by this fall. The Historical Society President Sue Newsome and Missiles and More Museum Director Evelyn Bradshaw, along with incoming Historical Society President Jaxie Thornton, have focused the people and resources necessary to make the Historical Society's dream a reality. Jaxie persuaded local contractors to head up the construction phase and they are endeavoring to do the work with local subcontractors and volunteers. Both Historical Society and local business will benefit.

The new Missiles and More Museum wing will expand into the north end of the Assembly Building. This expansion will more than double the museum's size and provide the Historical Society with more usable space in which to store historical artifacts and to display Topsail's history. It will also provide researchers and interested visitors a place for historical research. The new wing is expected to be open by October 1, 2004.

ROCKET IN AN AQUARIUM

The museum was given a remarkable find in July 1994. A booster rocket, used as a first-stage rocket to boost

Rocket washed up at Topsail Beach - Eric Peterson

ramjets up to speed, now resides on display in a big aquarium. It is a four foot tube found with broken fins on one end and corroded. It weighs about 100 pounds. The Frank Sherron family discovered the rocket at ocean side on Norman Chambliss' property.

The Underwater Archeological Lab at Fort Fisher advised that it must be kept submerged or it would deteriorate quickly. Eric Peterson, Town Manager, rounded up a first-class aquarium and the spent rocket is now a permanent display.

ALGONKIAN DUGOUT CANOE

The Missiles and More Museum is also the home of an Indian-made dugout canoe of early 1700 vintage. It was found 17 years ago in the marsh back of Topsail Island by local resident Travis James Batson, then 12 years old, who discovered the artifact while gathering oysters.

Travis, realizing that his find was unusual, reported it to the North Carolina Marine Resources Center at Fort Fisher. They were interested in this artifact, and Travis decided to donate his find to the people of North Carolina. In September 1979, in a special ceremony recognizing the discovery and to express gratitude to the young man for his donation

"Batson" Indian Dugout Canoe

of it, the State Department of Natural Cultural Resources accepted the vestiges of an ancient craft and officially named the "Batson Canoe." For years, it was displayed at the Marine Resources Center, until given on loan to East Carolina University following a request from that school to use if for study of the nomadic Indians who once roamed the North Carolina coastal waters.

The Batson Canoe is recognized by the state as an example of various modifications made to dugout canoes by the Indians during their use of this form of transportation. It had apparently been modified for sailing use, it has an opening for a centerboard and evidence of a mast.

State authorities agree that dugouts such as this one, as well as bark canoes and skin boats, were used by early Indians to travel and establish commerce with other groups. Archaeologists believe that Algonkian people used this early craft. The last remaining Indians abandoned their land in North Carolina in 1803 to join their kinsmen on reservations in New York and Canada. (Algonquin and Algonkian are different spellings to represent the Indian phonetic pronunciation. I chose Algonkian as the most authentic because that was chosen by a researcher who had thoroughly studied them.)

Following the opening of the Topsail Museum, Leslie Bright, Undersea Archaeologist for the NC Department of Cultural resources, in line with a policy of this group for displaying artifacts near their discovery site, offered to donate the Batson Canoe on loan to this museum for display here. Evelyn Bradshaw, president of the Historical Society of Topsail Island, which operates the museum, accepted the artifact when it was presented to the island museum in November 1995.

CINDER BLOCK ART

The Assembly Building has cinder block art from the early "Bald Pelican" days. They are wall-sized murals, inspired by the Cutty Sark label. (If you look closely at the figures on the ship you will see a passenger throwing up over the side.) These murals are still striking and it is hoped that they will remain undisturbed for some time.

Painting of Ship

They were painted by Tom Whitfield, and the story goes that they were painted to repay a bar bill. Mr. Whitfield wrote a letter to the editor to correct that impression, entitled "Painter sets record straight on mural." He wrote: *I can't be angry when such flattering things are written about my work. Really I appreciate the nice words about the murals I painted on the walls of the Arsenal Center in Topsail Beach, but I must refute the story that I did it to pay off a debt.*

For the sake of the truth, I was never fully compensated for my effort and settled for much less than I was promised. I worked hard in the kitchen that summer, for which I was compensated, and nights I painted the mural.

Three ex-Marines-turned-restaurant-entrepreneurs narrowed to one, then to none. But they were nice people and we had a casual working relationship. If they hadn't gone out of business, I'm sure I would have gotten the full amount. It was a great summer.

*By the way, I'm still a working artist. For portraits or perhaps another mural commission, I can be contacted in Greensboro...*Thomas H. Whitfield.

THIRD EDITION NOTES

The transition from the First Edition of ECHOES of Topsail (1996) to the Second Edition (2004) reflected phenomenal growth and enhancement of residences and businesses. The changes from 2004 to 2010 are less dramatic, but should be noted as Topsail Island progresses.

TOPSAIL ISLAND CURRENT POPULATION
North Topsail Beach – 955, Surf City – 2057, Topsail Beach - 581, Total permanent population – 3593. It is estimated that summer vacationers raise the population over 15,000. And yet the beaches are not crowded.

TOPSAIL BEACH
The Karen Beasley Sea Turtle Rescue and Rehabilitation Center is engaged in some major changes. After years of successful turtle rescue and care in tight facilities, there is a new building project that is to break ground in mid 2010. It is to be located near the Surf City Community Center on the mainland.

It will provide much needed hospital/rehabilitation space and a small conference room facility. There is a future plan to build education facilities as financing permits. Besides space, a big advantage for the turtle folks is that they will no longer have to wrap turtles in wet blankets and evacuate them to the mainland when hurricanes threaten.

MISSILES AND MORE MUSEUM
The Historical Society museum in Topsail Beach completed its $150,000 expansion and has enhanced its displays in this new space. The museum offers programs for school children and has increased in popularity every year. The people of Topsail generously support Historical Society work. Currently at 450 members, the Historical Society's museum

welcomed over 9900 visitors to their museum in 2009.

SURF CITY COMMUNITY CENTER
This center was completed in 2006 and provides meeting rooms, an equipped exercise room, gymnasium, tennis courts, and summer programs for kids.

The Surf City Park was completed in 2009 and has a public boat ramp, an amphitheater, picnic tables and a walkway with a unique wooden replica of the swing bridge.

NORTH TOPSAIL BEACH
The Ocean City Beach Community held it 60th anniversary in September 2009. It was a thriving, predominantly Black community initiated by Edgar Yow in the early 1950s when segregation was still in force, with the aim of promoting Black ownership of properties. Wade and Caronell Chestnut headed up the community.

In 1990 Ocean City, Del Mar Beach and other areas north of Surf City merged into North Topsail Beach. When Hurricane Fran wreaked its vengeance on Topsail Island in 1996, the Ocean City community was not spared. They never fully recovered from it. But the spirit of the Ocean City Community lives on through its gatherings and celebrations.

The former Ocean City tower and nearby lots have been purchased by a developer who plans to preserve the tower, important to those who value the Island's history.

WOMEN AIRFORCE SERVICE PILOTS
In July 2009 President Obama signed legislation that honored Women Airforce Service Pilots with the Congressional Gold Medal. This is the highest honor that Congress can give to civilians.

On March 10, 2010 WASP were gathered at Capitol Hill and were awarded their Congressional Gold Medal. This medal was designed and struck specifically for them. Of 300 still living, it was estimated that 170 were able to attend the ceremony. The rest were presented to the families of the WASP honored.

ACKNOWLEDGMENTS

This work was possible because I had the help of more people than I could ever properly acknowledge. My research for the original edition took over seven years of digging in the vaults of the National Archives and Johns' Hopkins Applied Physics Laboratory. That lab is where I found a treasure trove of Operation Bumblebee history, rocket artifacts and the TALOS displays, with the help of Connie Finney and Philip K. Albert. Archivists in Raleigh, Wilmington, Washington, DC and South Carolina were very willing to help search and they celebrated with me when important information was found. This edition has been about a year in the making with a lot of information gathering in the eight years since 1996.

Many local Topsail Island folks were generous with their time and often entrusted me with precious pictures to copy. Interviews gave me much insight into earlier life on the island and I am grateful to those who shared their recollections. They give an otherwise dry history a personal touch. Where possible I have noted sources at the end of chapters.

Behind my work is a good woman, and whatever success we have with this endeavor I owe to my partner, friend and wife Carol. She gave me capable support, merciless editing and a lot of encouragement when I needed it.

AUTHOR'S NOTE

My time with Topsail Island and its people has been a real love affair. I learned patience as I often exerted my northern penchant to move things along. A long-time resident reflected: *You northerners come to Topsail because you love the laid-back style and pace—then you try to change things like up north.*

The most satisfying of this whole historic endeavor was my involvement with Betty Polzer and the Historical Society in the preservation of the Assembly Building and Towers as historic sites. The Community purchase of the building for the Community Center and the Missles and More Museum has assured Topsail Island of the use and enjoyment of this facility in the years to come.

Finally, I will always reflect on my time as resident and cottage owner with real affection. Boating experiences for such a landlubber from Ohio, would never have been known otherwise—sailing on the sound next to porpoises, marsh birds, and trying to make way against the tide. And I will carry with me always, sunsets on the sound that stir the soul, watching storms come and go with the loudest thunder I've ever known, and long walks in the star-filled nights that quiet the heart.

BIBLIOGRAPHY

BOOKS and ARTICLES

Angley, W. "An Historical Overview of New Topsail Inlet," 1984. North Carolina Division of Archives and History Research Branch.

Bishop, N. H. *Voyage of the Paper Canoe*. Reprint, Wilmington, NC: Coastal Carolina Press, 2000.

Bloodworth, M. *History of Pender County, North Carolina*. Richmond, VA: Dietz Printing Co., 1947.

Brownriggs, W. *The Art of Making Common Salt*. London, England, 1748.

Dailey, J. *Silver Wings Santiago Blue*. New York, NY: Poseidon Press, 1984.

Hilldrup, R. L. *The North Carolina Historical Review*, Volume XXII, 1945.

Horner, D. *The Blockade-Runners; True Tales of Running the Yankee Blockade of the Confederate Coast*. New York, Dodd, Mead, 1968.

Johnson, G., Jr. *Rose O'Neale Greenow and the Blockade Runners*. Printed in Canada, 1995.

Johnson, L. *Wilmington Star*, Volume 21, Number 47, 1949.

Kaufman, W. & Pilkey, O. H. Jr. *The Beaches are Moving; The Drowning of America's Shoreline*. Durham, NC: Duke University Press, 1983.

Loftfield, T. C. and Littleton, T. R. *An Archaeological and Historical Reconnaissance of US Marine Corps Base, Camp Lajeune; Part 2 The Historical*

Record, Jacksonville, NC, 1981.

Matthis, A. N. "Letter to Matthis, E. J." Courtesy of Historical Society of Topsail Island. Property of Bradshaw, McRay, 1863.

U.S. Navy. "Civil War Naval Chronology, 1861-1865". Naval History Division, Navy Dept.

Reaves, B. "Reaves Collection." Wilmington, NC: New Hanover Public Library.

Reaves, B. *Weekly Star* article. Reaves Collection. Wilmington, NC: New Hanover Public Library.

Roberts, D. "Men Didn't Have to Prove They Could Fly, but Women Did." Washington, DC: *Smithsonian Magazine,* 1994.

Shomette, D. G. *Shipwrecks of the Civil War.* Washington, D. C., Donic Limited, 1973.

Stallman, D. A. "Historical Tour." Topsail Beach, NC, 1989.

Stallman, D. A. *A History of Camp Davis.* Holly Ridge, NC, 1990.

Stallman, D. A. *Operation Bumblebee – 1946-1948.* Topsail Beach, NC, 1992.

Stallman, D. A. *TALOS – Smart Sky Warrior.* Topsail Beach, NC, 2002

Stick, D. *Graveyard of the Atlantic; Shipwrecks of the North Carolina Coast.* Chapel Hill, University of NC Press, 1952.

"Testing Will Begin at Davis – Kellex operates New Facility for Navy Ordnance." *The News.* Laurel, MD: APL/JHU Johns Hopkins University Applied Physics Laboratory, 1947.

"The Year of the Hurricanes." *Coastwatch.* Sea Grant, NC State University, Raleigh, NC, 1991.

Williams, I. M. and McEachern, L. H. *Salt That Necessary Article.* Wilmington, NC, Belk-Beery Co. Inc., 1973.

OTHER REFERENCES

Camp Davis HQ Document. Public Relations Office, Holly Ridge, NC, 1943.

Camp Davis Book. *Officer Candidate School.* Courtesy of Alberti, H. Holly Ridge, NC, 1942.

Camp Davis News. *The AA Barrage – Camp Davis Military News –* Excerpts. Courtesy Ottaway, G.

Civil War. *Civil War Chronology, 1861-1865.* Courtesy of Phil Stevens.

Clifton, Robert. Interview, *1993.*

Coastal Courier, Vol. 4 No. 37, 1943.

Defense Environmental Restoration Project Real Estate Information for Camp Davis Military Reservation, NC, 1989 [includes War Dept. Corp of Engineers drawing, 1943.]

Flore, R. "Letter," Courtesy of Richards, R. V., 1991.

Johnson, L. "Lone Highway Sign Marks Scene Of Old Salt Works." Wilmington, NC, 12-04-1949.

New York Times Magazine, 1995.

Sidbury, R. Interview, 1992.

The State Vol. VIII No. 53, 1941.

US Dept. of Navy Press Release. "Camp Davis Project," Holly Ridge, NC, 1947.

US Dept. of Navy Document. "Military Announcement to All Hands," 1948.

APPENDIX

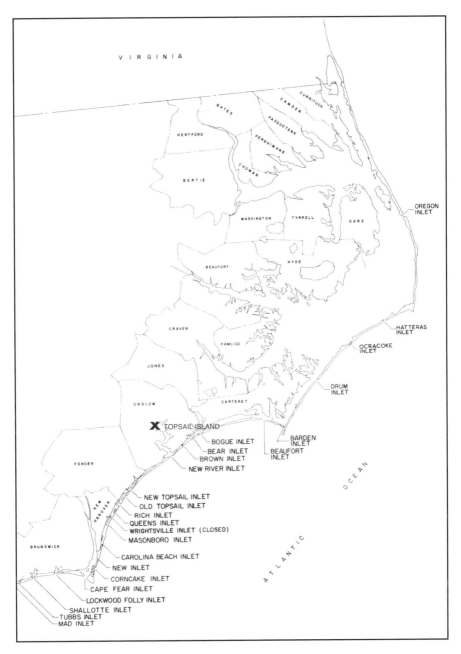

Map of North Carolina Inlets

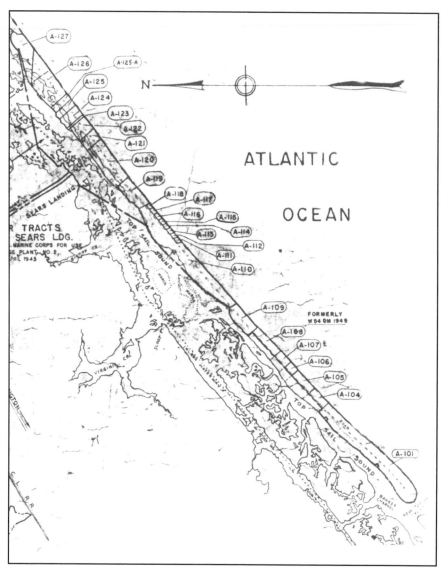

Map of Property Owners by U.S. Military in 1943.

TRACT NO.	LEASE REFERENCE	OWNER	ACREAGE Lease EXCEPT AS Noted
A-101		HELEN S. BRIDGES & T.G. EMPIRE ET AL	363.80
A-104		MRS. DONALD M. PARSLEY	48.80
A-105		R.W. ROBERTS ESTATE	75.50
A-106		NIXON E. JONES	27.40
A-107		HARVEY H. JONES ET AL	42.00
A-108		J.A. NIXON ESTATE	68.20
A-109		J.T. BLAND ESTATE	62.70
A-110		MARY S. WARREN ET AL	273.80
A-111		O.F. SIDBURY	2.80
A-112		E.N. SIDBURY	2.80
A-113		DANIE ATKINSON	2.80
A-114		W.T. SIDBURY ESTATE	2.80
A-115		MAY NEWSOM, MRS.	2.75
A-116		MINNIE HALL	2.80
A-117		ANNIE KING	2.80
A-118		J.F. SIDBURY	2.80
A-119		MILLIE BISHOP ESTATE	69.00
A-120	AX	JAMES H. BATTS, EST. (ROBT. T. BATTS)	144.00
A-121	AY	O.F. SIDBURY	28.00
A-122	AZ	E.E. BELL	40.00
A-123	BA	MRS. JULIA ATKINSON	5.00
A-124	BB	J.D. BATTS EST. (MISS THELMA BATTS)	33.00
A-125	BC	W.T. & HERBERT ATKINSON	22.00
A-126	BE	E.E. BELL	137.00
A-127		V. SIDBURY	82.00
A-128		R.N. SOMMERSILL	356.00
B-201		INTERNATIONAL PAPER CO.	386.50
B-202		MARY E. HOWARD ESTATE	63.50
B-203	P	ELIAS KHEIRALLA	97.40
B-204	O	R.N. SUMMERSILL TRUSTEE	63.00
B-205	L	L.W. EVERETT	6.00
B-206	J	O.H. BISHOP ESTATE (LUCINE BISHOP)	4.00
B-207	K	DELPHIA R. EVERETT	3.00
B-208	I	H.N. BISHOP	5.00
B-209	H	V. SIDBURY	59.00
B-210	G	JAMES T SHEPHERD, HRS. (B.SHEPARD)	10.00
B-211	F	FINLEY McMILLAN	50.00
B-212	E	V. SIDBURY	16.50
B-213	D	O.F. JUSTICE	20.00
B-214	C	D.V. JUSTICE	30.00

B-215	B	LILY H. WALKER	10.00
B-216	A-J	MRS. E.H. WALTON ET VIR	29.00
B-217		(PERMIT TO F.H.A. FOR SEWER 0.095 AC)	
B-219	A-O	MARY JANE HOLDEN	10.00
B-220	A-F	E.F. & VIRGINIA SANDERS	2.00
B-221	M-N	O.H. BISHOP EST. (LUCINE BISHOP)	19.00
B-222	A-P	ANDREW R. EDENS	4.00
B-223	A-R	E.E. & MARY EDENS	3.00
B-224	A-Q	EUGENE BATTS	6.00
B-225	A-H	V. SIDBURY	120.00
B-226		" " (R OF W - SEWER LINE)	.10
B-227	A-M	ELIAS KHEIRALLA	10.00
B-228	A-N	W.M. HARDISON & R.N. SUMMERSTILL, TR	10.00
B-229	A-S	SIMS BATTS	4.00
B-230	A-T	J.E. & MARY CARTER	5.00
B-231	A-U	ROBT. T. BATTS	6.00
B-232	A-V	JAMES H. BATTS ESTATE	6.00
B-233	A	INTERNATIONAL PAPER CO.	1801.10
B-234	No. 1	" " " "	108.80
B-235	No. 3	" " " "	62.05
B-236		" " " "	40.50
B-237		W.M. HARDISON & R.N. SUMMERSILL, TR.	.316
B-238	A-K	ALMON V. BATTS	2.00
B-239	No. 2	INTERNATIONAL PAPER CO.	45.66
B-240	No. 4	" " "	22.25
B-241	No. 5	" " "	33.68
C-301	Q-V Z-Y	STATE BOARD OF EDUCATION OF N.C.	264.00
C-302	T	J.H. BATTS EST. (ROBT. T. BATTS)	200.00
C-303	R	W.J. SIDBURY	5.00
C-304	S	THELMA BATTS	100.00
C-305	U	DESSIE & JOHN ELLIS	5.00
C-306	A-E	T.B. & DAVIE ATKINSON	55.00
C-307	B-G	A.W. KING EST. (MARY E. KING)	30.00
C-308	B-F	W.T. SIDBURY EST. (ADA SIDBURY)	40.00
C-309	X	J.E. SIDBURY	405.00
C-310	A A	MRS. ANNIE KING	214.00
C-311	A B	H&S McCLAMMY	144.00
C-312	W	MARY & J.C. NEWSOM	193.00
C-313	A-C	E.N. & B. SIDBURY	257.00
C-314	A-D	A.S. & HETTIE M. KING	50.00
D-401		W.H. & KATIE SUMMERSILL	700.00
D-402		W.M. HARDISON	329.00
D-403		R.N. SUMMERSILL	50.00
D-404		W.D. COSTON	50.00
D-405		W.M. HARDISON	25.00
D-406		INTERNATIONAL PAPER CO.	187.00

D-407		THEODORE OTTOWAY	4.20
D-408		L.F. EDENS	5.00
D-409		W.M. HARDISON	197.60
D-410		E.F. MIDDLETON	5.00
D-411		R.G. GRANDY ET AL	1004.00
D-412		ALLISON CORPORATION	3340.00
D-413		F.M. SANDERS ESTATE	11.00
D-414		STATE BOARD OF EDUCATION OF N.C.	9769.00
D-414	(1)	" " " " "	12459.00
D-415	(2)	INTERNATIONAL PAPER CO.	3200.00
D-416		E.P. GODWIN ET. AL	196.00
D-417		W.B. KNOWLES	1400.00
D-418		W.B. KNOWLES	513.00
D-420		ALLISON CORPORATION	257.00
D-421		W.B. KNOWLES	43.00
D-422		STATE BOARD OF EDUCATION OF N.C.	32.00
D-423		" " " "	100.00
D-424		J.S. HUMPHREY	133.00
D-425		W.B. KNOWLES	1784.00
D-426		E.P. & MARY J. GODWIN	220.00
D-427		J.R. MARSHBURN ET AL	384.00
D-428		ALLISON CORPORATION	10.00
D-429		CAROLINA LANDS. INCORPORATED	116.00
D-430		INTERNATIONAL PAPER CO.	104.00
D-431		L.F. & DORA EDENS	8.01
1-125-A	BD	A.S. & HETTIE M. KING	22.00
	BH	VALINZA SIDBURY	19.45
	AI	W.H. & LUCILE WEEKS, Lots 1 & 2	3.00
	AI	J.N. & M.E. SANDERS, Lots 3-4-5-6-7-8-9-10	3.00
	AI	J.H. & NETTA LEDES, LOT No. 5	3.00
W2287	ENG 228	MRS. NANCY WALTON	20.00
W 54	QM 1950	STATE BD. OF EDC. STATE OF N.C.	925.00
W 09 026	ENG 3541	ATLANTIC COAST LINE RR	1.94
		ATLANTIC COAST LINE RR LICENSE FOR WYE TRACK 0.53 AC.	

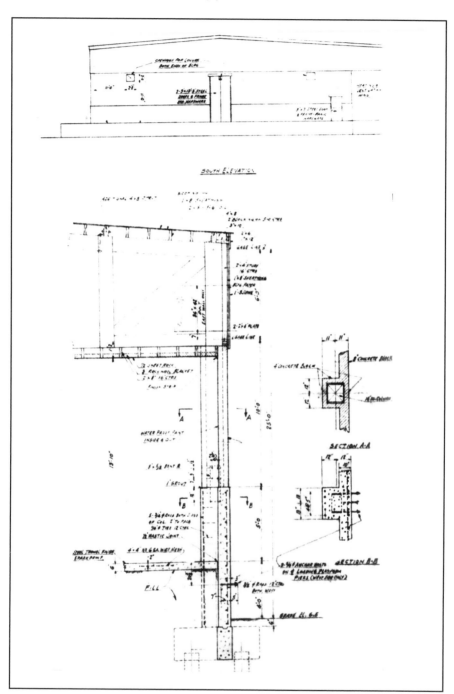

Assembly Building Architectural Drawing

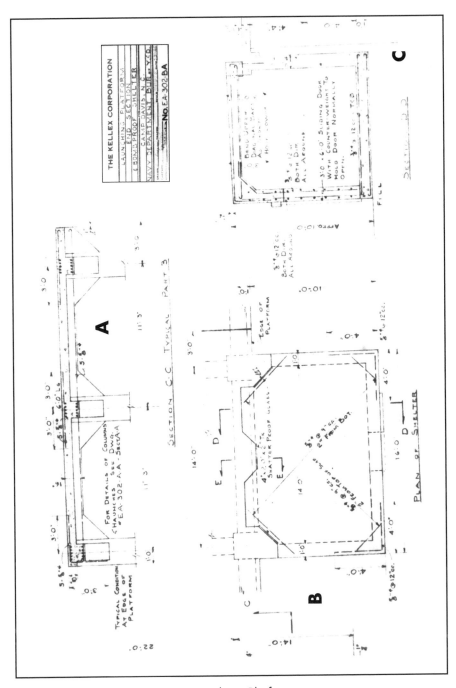

A - Launching Platform
B & C - Bombproof Shelter

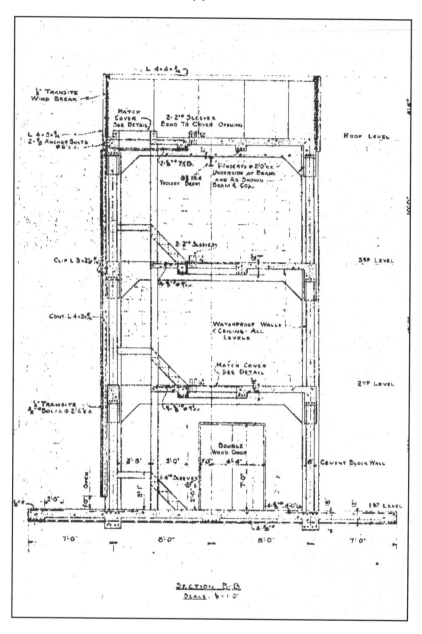

Tower Architectural Drawing

Index

Topsail Island
NORTH CAROLINA